T0380302

NAVIGATING NARCISSISM:

RESILIENCY & RECOVERY

Isabella Imani

THE IMANI MVMT
TRAUMA INFORMED RESILIENCY COACHING

BALBOA.PRESS
A DIVISION OF HAY HOUSE

Balboa Press books may be ordered through booksellers or by contacting:

Balboa Press
A Division of Hay House
1663 Liberty Drive
Bloomington, IN 47403
www.balboapress.com
844-682-1282

Because of the dynamic nature of the Internet, any web addresses or
links contained in this book may have changed since publication and
may no longer be valid. The views expressed in this work are solely those
of the author and do not necessarily reflect the views of the publisher,
and the publisher hereby disclaims any responsibility for them.

The author of this book does not dispense medical advice or
prescribe the use of any technique as a form of treatment for physical,
emotional, or medical problems without the advice of a physician,
either directly or indirectly. The intent of the author is only to offer
information of a general nature to help you in your quest for emotional
and spiritual well-being. In the event you use any of the information
in this book for yourself, which is your constitutional right, the author
and the publisher assume no responsibility for your actions.

Any people depicted in stock imagery provided by Getty Images are
models, and such images are being used for illustrative purposes only.
Certain stock imagery © Getty Images.

ISBN: 979-8-7652-4440-1 (sc)
ISBN: 979-8-7652-4443-2 (hc)
ISBN: 979-8-7652-4441-8 (e)

Print information available on the last page.

Balboa Press rev. date: 11/28/2023

A LETTER OF LOVE
Welcome To My Inner World:

I wanted to take a moment to share something really close to my heart with all of you. You see, I'm incredibly excited about this novel on Navigating Narcissism: Resiliency and Recovery, and I wanted to share why it means so much to me.

You know, life has a way of throwing us unexpected curveballs, and sometimes those curveballs come in the form of toxic relationships. In my late 20's, I found myself on the verge of marrying a highly toxic individual. He conveyed traits closely aligned with Covert Narcissism. It was a rollercoaster ride filled with manipulation, gaslighting, and emotional abuse. And let me tell you, it wasn't easy. It left me feeling shattered, confused, and questioning my own worth.

But you know what? Out of that pain, something amazing happened. I discovered my passion for helping others who have gone through similar experiences. It became my mission to channel that pain into something positive, into creating a space where healing and recovery could be possible for others.

Through my own journey, I realized that there were so many nuances to narcissistic relationships that are not commonly discussed or easily identifiable. It is not just about the grandiose behavior or the obvious signs. It's about the subtle manipulation, the erosion of self-esteem, and the complex dynamics that keep victims trapped in the cycle of abuse. I wanted to shed light on those hidden aspects, to give voice to the pain and struggles that often go unnoticed.

But here's the beautiful part: healing and recovery are possible. In the pages that follow, I want to be a source of support and empowerment for all those who have been through the darkness of narcissistic or highly toxic relationships. Together, we can navigate the complexities, heal our wounds, and reclaim our authentic selves.

In this **evergreen and interactive** novel, we'll go beyond the surface-level understanding. We'll dive deep into the psychology of narcissism, explore the abuse cycle, helping you recognize the patterns, manipulation tactics, and emotional impact that can leave lasting scars and uncover the path to resiliency and recovery. We'll discuss practical strategies, self-care practices, and the importance of setting healthy boundaries. Most importantly, we'll create a safe and compassionate space where you can share your stories, find solace in self discovery, and realize that you're not alone in this journey.

In this empowering novel, we'll be delving into the complex world of narcissism, shining a light on its dynamics, and offering you valuable tools to navigate the challenging terrain of narcissistic relationships. Whether you've personally experienced narcissistic abuse or want to deepen your knowledge to support others, **this novel is designed to empower you with insights and strategies with trauma informed reflection questions to help you process your emotions and experience.**

So, My Loves, if you're ready to embark on a transformational experience, if you're seeking healing, understanding, and a renewed sense of self-worth, then join me on this journey. Let's walk this path together, and remember, even in the darkest moments, there is always hope for a brighter future.

Isabella Imani

Isabella Imani,
Trauma Informed Resiliency Coach,
CEO & Founder of THE IMANI MVMT

Welcome

DEDICATION
& Appreciation...

To my family and best friends - Thank you for reminding me that love doesn't hurt; it heals. You are my greatest protectors and bravest defenders, I love you.

To my former partner - Thank you for not loving me. It taught me how to love myself.

dedication

TABLE OF
CONTENTS

04
Profiling A Narcissist

I|M

This novel has been crafted with care and insight, drawing from the perspective of a Trauma-Informed Coach that understands the cognitive processing of a Neurodivergent.

As you embark on this reading journey, remember that the format is flexible and accommodating to your unique needs.

You can choose to read it cover to cover for a comprehensive understanding, or you can dive into short sections, much like reading concise articles. Every part and piece stands independently while also contributing to a larger narrative.

My aim is to guide you as you Navigate Narcissism, fostering resilience, and nurturing your path to recovery. You're not alone on this journey, and we're here to support you every step of the way.

TABLE OF
CONTENTS

4

TABLE OF CONTENTS

03 Resiliency & Recovery

Disclaimer

Trigger Warning: Sensitive Content

Hey there, before we dive into this discussion, I want to give you a heads-up and provide a trigger warning. We'll be covering some sensitive content that may evoke strong emotions or bring up past experiences for some individuals.

I understand that certain topics can be difficult and may have a profound impact on your well-being. It's important to prioritize your mental and emotional health above all else. If you feel that this content might be triggering or overwhelming for you, I encourage you to take care of yourself and consider skipping this discussion.

Remember, it's okay to set boundaries and protect yourself when it comes to sensitive subjects. Your well-being and comfort matter, and it's important to honor your own needs. If you decide to proceed, please make sure you have support systems in place or reach out to a trusted person if you need someone to talk to.

Take care of yourself, and remember that you are never alone. Your well-being is valuable, and it's okay to prioritize your emotional safety above everything else.

That said, I'd like to highlight what trauma informed care is and why it is so important to understand as it relates to mental health and collective healing. Trauma-informed care is an approach that recognizes the prevalence of trauma and its impact on an individual's well-being. It's all about creating a safe and supportive environment where people feel heard, understood, and respected. Unlike traditional approaches, trauma-informed care goes beyond just treating symptoms—it acknowledges the whole person and their unique experiences.

So, why is it so crucial? Well, trauma can have a profound effect on our mental health, shaping how we navigate the world and our relationships. By integrating trauma-informed care, mental health professionals are better equipped to understand and address the underlying causes of distress, rather than simply treating the surface-level symptoms.

It's about creating a space where people feel empowered and in control of their healing journey. It's about promoting collaboration, trust, and choice, and honoring the individual's strengths and resilience. Trauma-informed care recognizes that everyone's experiences are valid and seeks to create a judgment-free zone where people can feel safe to share their stories.

By adopting this approach, mental health professionals can provide personalized, holistic care that takes into account the unique needs and experiences of each individual. It's all about fostering healing, growth, and recovery while promoting a sense of empowerment and dignity.

Remember, your experiences matter, and you deserve care that acknowledges and respects your journey. If you're seeking mental health support, consider exploring trauma-informed care—it could make all the difference in your healing process. You're not alone, and there are professionals like myself, out there who are ready to support you in a way that feels safe, validating, and empowering. Let's dive in!

The Imani Mvmt

TRAUMA INFORMED RESILIENCY COACHING

04

Healing The Collective One
Individual At A Time

8

Profiling A Narcissist

PART 1 OF 3

3 Key Objectives

1)Psychology & Traits of a Narcissist

2)Narcissists & Empathy

3)Nuances of Narcissism

INTENTIONS

Looking back on your narcissistic or highly toxic relationships, what emotions arise within you? How do these emotions inform your understanding of the impact the relationship had on your well-being and sense of self?

Write your answer in the space below.

_____

_____

_____

_____

_____

_____

_____

_____

_____

_____

_____

_____

_____

_____

_____

_____

_____

_____

Remember, reflection is a powerful tool for gaining insight and promoting growth. Give yourself permission to explore your experiences with compassion and curiosity. By delving into these questions, you can deepen your understanding of the impact of the narcissistic relationship and pave the way for healing, growth, and the creation of healthier relationships in the future.

My Story

RESILIENCY AND RECOVERY

"SOME OF OUR BEST LESSONS WILL BE EXPERIENCED THROUGH LOVE & LOSS."
-ISABELLA IMANI

As we dive in, I wanted to take a moment to share something really close to my heart with all of you. You see, I'm incredibly excited about this novel on Navigating Narcissism: Resiliency and Recovery, and I wanted to share why it means so much to me. You know, life has a way of throwing us unexpected curveballs, and sometimes those curveballs come in the form of toxic relationships. Or in my case, that when time when I confused a life lesson for a soulmate. In my late 20's, I found myself on the verge of marrying a highly toxic individual. For ethical reasons, I am not saying he is a Narcissist. However, he did convey undeniable traits high on the scale of Covert Narcissism. His personality was larger than life but over time deteriorated the longer we stayed together and the closer I got. Our relationship was intoxicating until it became suffocating. It was a rollercoaster ride filled with adventure, passion and hope that slowly turned into manipulation, gaslighting, and emotional abuse.

"Your trauma is a joke. Your work is a joke. You are a joke. The only reason people want to work with you is to get to me. You are a weak, worthless piece of shit. You're pathetic. Loving you sucks. Being loved by you sucks. Eat your feelings. All you do is wallow. Stop crying or I'll give you something to cry about."

These were the "loving" last words spoken to me by the man I almost married. He did everything but hit me. The last three months of our relationship was when the emotional abuse was at its peak. During the most luxurious six weeks away in Italy, there wasn't a single day that he didn't go out of his way to punish me with silence or verbally berate me until he made me cry. Between the facade of happy photos we posted on Instagram and contemplating jumping off of our rooftop our last night Milan, I soon realized that a dream home without peace quickly becomes a very beautiful prison. Losing him was nothing short of unfathomable. But loving him felt like dying a death by a thousand paper cuts.

After going through his phone just weeks before I initiated our separation, I found all the evidence I needed to walk away. And yet, every part of me still wanted nothing more than to stay. You see, for those of us who have experienced abusive relationships, most survivors don't stop loving their abuser - they just stop loving and trusting themselves. During our last fight, I brought up the evidence I found with the screens shots to prove it. Surprisingly, that didn't deter him from denying their existence. Luckily I had called my best friend just three weeks prior to confronting him. During that time she stayed on the phone with me while I secretly packed boxes in preparation for a quick escape should he decide to emotionally abuse me again. And when the time came, I left him and our home in less than 24 hours with just three boxes and never looked back. No person that feels safe chooses to become estranged from a person they are madly in love with. As I made the painful decision to walk away from the man I deeply loved for the first and last time, I thought to myself "Why does this all feel so familiar and what unhealed patterns lead me here?"

And let me tell you, it wasn't easy. It left me feeling absolutely shattered, confused, and questioning my own worth. As I healed from the inflammation the abuse caused in my brain and the psychological pain I experienced I realized I was never going to be the wife he wanted because I wasn't willing to tolerate what the role required: self abandonment, playing small, or enduring his lies, manipulation and abuse. But you know what? Out of that pain, something amazing happened. I discovered my passion for helping others who have gone through similar experiences. It became my mission to channel that pain into something positive, into creating a space where healing and recovery are possible. Through my own journey, I realized that there were so many nuances to narcissistic or other highly toxic relationships that aren't commonly discussed or easily identifiable. It's not just about the grandiose behaviors or the obvious signs. It's about the subtle manipulation, the erosion of self-esteem, and the complex dynamics that keep victims trapped in the cycle of abuse. I wanted to shed light on those hidden aspects, to give voice to the pain and struggles that often go unnoticed.

But here's the beautiful part: healing and recovery are possible. I want to be a source of support and empowerment for all those who have been through the darkness of highly toxic or narcissistic relationships. Together, we can navigate the complexities, heal our wounds, and reclaim our authentic selves. In the pages that follow, we'll go beyond the surface-level understanding. We'll dive deep into the psychology of narcissism, explore the abuse cycle, and uncover the path to resiliency and recovery. We'll discuss practical strategies, self-care practices, and the importance of setting healthy boundaries. Most importantly, we'll create a safe and compassionate space where you can share your stories, find solace in surrendering, and realize that you're not alone in this journey. So, My Loves, if you're ready to embark on a transformational experience, if you're seeking healing, understanding, and a renewed sense of self-worth, then join me on this journey. Let's walk this path together, and remember, even in the darkest moments, there is always hope for a brighter future.

RESILIENT

THE IMANI MVMT

Profiling A Narcissist

NUANCES OF NARCISSISM

UNDERSTANDING THE NARCISSISTIC BRAIN

To begin, let's have a heart-to-heart about emotional awareness and narcissism. So, emotional awareness is all about recognizing and understanding our own emotions and those of the people around us. [1] It's like having a superpower that helps us connect with others on a deeper level and make decisions based on their emotional needs, as well as our own.

Pretty cool, right? But here's the thing, narcissists take a different route. They seem to have skipped the whole empathy part. This enables them to live their lives devoid of compassion, respect, and care for others. It's like their emotional intelligence level is stuck at zero, while they dominate over others and cause significant harm.

As this relates to narcissists and their brain development, there's this fascinating thing called the insular cortex. It's like the compassion and empathy hub. The anterior insula, a part of the insular cortex, plays a big role in recognizing not only our own emotions but also the emotions of others. It's the part that helps us understand and connect with what others are feeling.[2] But for narcissists, this area seems to be relatively dormant. They're so self focused and lack introspection, that they have little to no empathy for others.

Scientists have even done brain scans, using fancy stuff like functional magnetic resonance imaging (fMRI's), to study the brains of narcissists. And guess what? They found abnormalities in the anterior insula, as well as in the gray matter and cerebral cortex (the thinking and reasoning part of the brain). [3]

These are the very structures involved in generating compassion for others. Sadly, due to nature and nurture experiences in their life, their brain's compassion department never fully developed.

Now, I want to make it clear that we're not digging into the under developed brain changes in narcissists to excuse their abusive behavior. Nope, not at all. We're doing it to emphasize the physical and psychological severity of this personality disorder that enables their lack of self awareness, emotional volatility and mental instability.

Because of those reasons, it is important to clarify that the abuse you may have suffered at the hands of these highly toxic individuals is absolutely not your fault. Not in the slightest. Sadly, narcissistic abuse doesn't just affect adults. Children of narcissists also experience brain adaptations from the maltreatment they have endured. Their hippocampus (essential for learning and memory) and amygdala (the emotional control center) become altered as a result. The shrinkage of their hippocampus and amygdala, make it difficult for them to handle their own emotions, especially feelings of shame and guilt. [4] That said, narcissism can be hereditary and is a form of transgenerational trauma within family systems. [5]

As if that's not enough, the damage to the amygdala keeps the victims in a constant state of fear and anxiety. They become hyper-alert to triggers that remind them of the narcissist's abuse, leading to panic attacks, phobias, and other anxiety disorders. It's a never-ending cycle that hinders their ability to live fully fulfilling lives.

In a nutshell, we've taken a deep dive into the technical aspects here, that might be a bit unsettling. But remember, just because narcissists have experienced their own pain, that does not excuse their actions or allow them to cause pain on to others. Narcissistic abuse is never, ever the fault of the survivors, especially when it comes to children. Let's keep that in mind, always. Especially as we continue to learn about the Nuances of Narcissism and understand a bit more about Narcissistic Traits.

Profiling A Narcissist

NUANCES OF NARCISSISM

Moving on! As we continue unravel the fascinating science behind the narcissistic brain I want to highlight their impulsive and dependent relationship with dopamine. You see, narcissists have sensitive dopamine receptors, which means they're genetically wired to be more inclined toward pleasure-seeking experiences. [6] This heightened sensitivity to dopamine can have some interesting effects on their behavior.

Dopamine, often referred to as the "pleasure neurotransmitter," plays a crucial role in the brain's reward system. It's associated with feelings of pleasure, motivation, and seeking out rewards. [7] In the case of narcissists, their dopamine receptors are extra sensitive, which means they may require higher levels of stimulation to experience the same level of satisfaction that others might find in more ordinary activities. Think: center of attention, grandiose, thrill seeking behaviors. This fuels their validation addiction as they attract more narcissistic supply. If this sounds exhausting to be in a relationship with, you guessed right. You can be at an event with a narcissist and feel like your presence alone is never good enough due to their constant need to court attention and validation. Because of this, they become codependent on you shrinking yourself, especially in social situations, so they can feel bigger and better about *themselves*.

This sensitivity to dopamine can lead narcissists to seek out risky and thrill-seeking behaviors, people or careers. They crave the excitement, the rush, and the novelty that comes with these experiences. It's like they're constantly chasing the next high, pushing boundaries, and seeking out intense stimuli to satisfy their cravings. This constant need for excitement can explain why they often engage in chaotic and tumultuous relationships and happen to constantly be a victim of their own self inflicted circumstances.

"In a Mens Health Article, Dr. Ramani, a Narcissistic Abuse Expert, explains that narcissists tend to be reward-sensitive, meaning they live for dopamine rushes fueled by receiving any type of reward; healthier people are able to inhibit their reward responses in favor of their long-term goals (in other words, they can operate on delayed gratification). Due to their reward and novelty-seeking behaviors, Dr. Ramani adds that narcissists not only get bored easily with new things, but also new people. Her theory is that narcissistic reward-sensitivity may explain why narcissists can engage in impulsive, sometimes dangerous behavior—drugs, alcohol, gambling, unsafe sexual practices, or overspending. "They engage in pleasure first," says Dr. Ramani. "And then face consequences later, if ever." [8]

Here's where it gets interesting. Healthy, stable relationships may feel boring to narcissists. The calm and peaceful dynamics that most people find comforting and fulfilling can leave narcissists feeling unsatisfied. The absence of chaos and drama may not activate their dopamine receptors enough, leading them to perceive such relationships as dull and uninteresting. This addiction to chaos can have detrimental effects on their interactions with others. They may create conflicts, provoke arguments, and thrive on stirring up drama in order to satisfy their craving for heightened emotions and stimulation. It's like they're stuck in a cycle of seeking out chaos to feel alive and validated - like they can't get out of their own way and blame others for the consequences of being held accountable to their own destructive actions.

Understanding the link between the narcissist's brain sensitivity to dopamine and their inclination towards risky behaviors and chaos can provide insight into their patterns of behavior. However, it's important to remember that while this genetic predisposition may shed light on their tendencies, it does not excuse or justify their harmful actions. It's crucial to set boundaries and prioritize our own well-being when dealing with narcissistic individuals. My hope, is that by recognizing these patterns and the underlying mechanisms at play, we can better understand the complexities of narcissistic behavior as our best defense against it. This understanding will allow us to navigate these dynamics with greater awareness and take steps towards protecting ourselves and fostering healthier relationships in our own lives.

Profiling A Narcissist

NUANCES OF NARCISSISM

UNDERSTANDING THE NARCISSISTIC TRAITS

Moving on from the brain, I now want us to transition to understanding more of the traits associated with Narcissism. As we know, Narcissism is a complex personality disorder that exists on a spectrum, ranging from healthy self-esteem to pathological Narcissism. [9] While not all individuals with narcissistic traits will exhibit every characteristic listed below, here are some common traits associated with Narcissism:

- **Grandiosity**: A grandiose sense of self-importance and an exaggerated belief in one's own abilities or achievements. Because of this, they often feel the excessive need to high jack situations or interrupt conversations and make it about themselves.

- **Excessive Need for Admiration:** A constant craving for attention, admiration, and validation from others.

- **Lack of Empathy:** Difficulty or inability to empathize with others' emotions or experiences, often disregarding or minimizing their feelings. They are also extremely reactive when they receive feedback in opposition of their perfectly crafted facade.

- **Sense of Entitlement:** A strong belief that one deserves special treatment, privileges, or recognition without necessarily earning it. They are great at "thank you" texts or speeches but struggle with true gratitude or appreciativeness.

- **Exploitative Behavior:** A tendency to exploit or take advantage of others for personal gain, often without remorse or guilt.

- **Preoccupation with Image:** Excessive concern with one's appearance, reputation, or status, and a strong desire to be perceived as superior or perfect.

- **Envy and Jealousy:** Feeling resentful or envious of others' success or happiness and often engaging in comparison or belittling behaviors. They constantly have to put others down to feel better about themselves.

- **Boundary Violations:** Disregarding personal boundaries and invading others' privacy or personal space without permission. They often engage in double standards for personal gain and live by a set of contradictory morals.

- **Manipulative and Controlling Behavior:** Using manipulation, deceit, or coercion to maintain control over others and get what they want.

- **Lack of Accountability:** Avoiding taking responsibility for their actions and shifting blame onto others or external circumstances.

It's important to note that diagnosing narcissistic personality disorder (NPD) requires a comprehensive assessment by a licensed mental health professional. It's crucial to be mindful of as there's a difference between observing one's personality traits without diagnosing it. There is a necessary and ethical responsibility we have as individuals and as a society to reserve placing labels onto others without having the appropriate skillset to do so. That said, these characteristics serve as general indicators and not definitive criteria. It's also worth acknowledging that some individuals may exhibit narcissistic traits without having NPD. Navigating these nuances can be confusing, I know. Hang tight, because we are just getting started.

Profiling A Narcissist

NUANCES OF NARCISSISM

UNDERSTANDING THE NARCISSISTIC TRAITS

The general (and often twisted) psychology of a Narcissist that allows them to justify their behavior include things like:

1. Harboring a great deal of shame but are unable to connect with it and process it in a healthy fashion. As a result, narcissists act without shame. But it's an external act to mask how much shame they knowingly and deeply feel on the inside.
2. An over-inflated sense of greatness and self importance; not because they genuinely feel important but because life experiences made them feel like they weren't. To maintain their self-view of importance, they diminish and degrade others with absolute distain.
3. Narcissists imagine themselves as great people, yet they envy what others have or have accomplished. Nothing outside themselves is ever good enough because deep down, they don't believe they themselves are good enough.
4. Expecting favorable treatment and will practice two-faced standards, even going so far as to break the law or betraying their relationships because they think the rules do not apply to them. We'll talk about this more in the following sections around The Dark Triad. Deep down, they believe that people are expendable and that they deserve to have all their needs, no matter how harmful, met.

Understanding these traits can be helpful for identifying and navigating relationships with individuals who display high narcissistic tendencies. However, it's essential to approach the topic with caution and recognize that individuals with narcissistic traits may also have underlying insecurities or vulnerabilities driving their behavior. This is not meant to justify their behavior but to bring an element of understanding to it. If you find yourself in a situation where you are being neglected or exploited by any individual (narcissistic or not) your best defense will always be to choose distance over disrespect. In most cases, it is not worth wasting your energy trying to get them to understand how they are hurting you. They know they are hurting you. They genuinely just don't care. This was one of the many lessons I had to learn but found so much freedom in once I accepted it. It's because they can't. They have a mental health disorder that blocks their emotional receptors from empathizing with the severity of their harmful impact on others. While they cognitively understand what they are doing is wrong or harmful, their deep internalized shame prevents them from expressing any form of guilt or remorse. This is why getting a genuine apology with changed behavior with strategies to effectively repair is next to impossible. It's a skill they never learned and a part of their brain that was not fully developed.

I want you think of a time when you were dealing with a highly toxic person. How did their destructive traits impact the health of your relationship? How did that shape the way you interacted with them as a result?

The thing about dealing with highly toxic individuals or narcissists is their harmful behavior isn't always overt. In the ways that it is covert, it can often times be more destructive as it slowly deteriorates at a person's self esteem and psychological wellbeing.

Covert narcissistic abuse can be likened to the frog in boiling water analogy. [10] At the beginning of the relationship, the harmful traits may be subtle, making it easy to overlook or dismiss them. However, over time, these traits intensify, much like the water slowly heating up for the frog. As the abuse becomes more apparent, victims may find themselves trapped in a relationship they struggle to escape from. Evert time you deny your intuition about someone, you may end up paying for it down the road. That's why it's so important to build relationships (romantic, plutonic or even professional ones) slowly and with intentionality. That's not an invitation to remain guarded. The reality is, there is no need to be guarded when you remain grounded as this will help you to truly determine who is a safe person to have in your life or who you must keep at a distance. Recognizing these harmful traits early on is crucial to prevent getting entangled in an unhealthy relationship down the road. Being aware of red flags and setting healthy boundaries empowers individuals to protect themselves and avoid falling into a situation that may become increasingly difficult to leave later. From my personal and professional experience, trusting your instincts and prioritizing your well-being can spare you from the long-term emotional toll of covert narcissistic abuse.

Profiling A Narcissist

NUANCES OF NARCISSISM

NARCISSISTIC FAMILY DYNAMICS

Now that you understand a bit about the make up of a narcissist's brain and the traits associated with it, let's learn about the unhealthy family dynamics that enable narcissistic behavior. [11] Narcissistic relationships with enablers can really wreak havoc on the whole family system, especially when there are innocent children involved. It's like a wild storm tearing through the house, leaving chaos in its wake.

You see, when you have a narcissistic parent getting all the attention and their enabler partner nodding along, it creates this toxic dynamic that's hard to escape. The narcissist gets to call all the shots, and the enabler just goes along with it, even if it means sacrificing their kids' well-being as collateral. In a relationship with a narcissistic parent, even the "safe" parent can become unsafe for their children not because of what they do - like yell, use passive aggressive tactics or become physically or emotionally abusive. But because of what they don't do - like stand up to the narcissist or leave the abusive relationship. This isn't an attempt to victim blame as partners are equally enmeshed in a deeply toxic trauma bond with the narcissist. It's to shed light on the impact of children helplessly involved in these dysfuncational family dynamics.

The children can feel neglected emotionally because everything revolves around the narcissist's ego. Their needs and feelings often take a backseat, and that can leave some deep emotional scars.

But, it's not all doom and gloom. Recognizing what's going on is the first step towards breaking free from this mess. Seeking support, whether from friends, family, or trauma informed professionals, can really make a world of difference. Healing and creating healthier family dynamics takes time and effort, but it's totally worth it to give those kids the chance to grow up in a loving and nurturing environment where transgenerational trauma isn't passed on. As individuals who aim to break the cycle of dysfunction in our families, it is our personal responsibility to cultivate and promote healthy family dynamics within our own lives.

That said, the narcissistic family dynamic is like a twisted soap opera playing out in real life. There are some key characters in this drama: the narcissist parent, the enabler parent, the scapegoat, the golden child, and the lost child. Let's break it down:

The narcissist parent is like the star of the show. They're all about themselves, self-absorbed to the max. They crave constant admiration and validation, and they'll do anything to get it. They often put their own needs above their kids' and have little empathy for others. It's like everything revolves around them, and they expect everyone else to play along. They often use anger to control their immediate environment. In this case, their household. In their mind, the person who is the meanest or loudest holds all the power and receives all of the attention with either overt aggression or passive aggression. Woof. Talk about someone who never learned how to emotionally regulate.

Now, enter the enabler parent - the supporting actor to the narcissist's leading role. This parent is basically the coerced cheerleader for the narcissist. They might not be as self-centered themselves, but they too enable the narcissist's behavior. They make excuses for them, defend them, and try to keep the family drama under wraps. It's like they're caught in a codependent dance, and they can't break free. The trauma bonds are deep here as they struggle to stay afloat while the narcissist tries to sink the ship every chance they get.

Next up, the scapegoat - the poor soul who can't catch a break. This is usually one of the kids who becomes the target of the narcissist's blame and criticism. They can do no right in the narcissist's eyes and often end up taking the fall for everything that goes wrong. It's like they're the family punching bag, and it's just not fair. They bear the brunt of the narcissist's wrath as they get blamed for everything that goes wrong. The constant criticism and feeling like they're not good enough can really mess with their self-esteem.

On the flip side, we have the golden child - the favored one. This kid can do no wrong, at least in the eyes of the narcissist. They're showered with praise, attention, and special treatment. But here's the twist - this "special treatment" can also create resentment and pressure on the golden child. Sure, it might seem like they're living the dream with all that special treatment, but it's not all rainbows and sunshine. They can feel pressured to maintain that golden image, and it might lead to a whole different set of issues, like difficulty forming genuine relationships or feeling like they always have to be perfect. In dynamics where the abuser is the father and the golden child is male, an enabling mother could project, over protect and over compensate for the behaviors of her spouse onto the golden child. This anxious attention from his mother could enable a sense of entitlement for a young male, where he subconsciously seeks out a mother figure in all of his partners. In heteronormative relationships, as he depletes his partner's emotional energy he will resent her for expecting emotional reciprocity. He's really just here for the participation points. His emotional entitlement will enable him to shut down or explode when conflict arises as he slowly begins to devalue his partners little by little with microaggressions for not being the mother he always wanted but never had. More on this behavior later, but this unhealed mother wound is essentially what happened in my highly toxic relationship. Healthy narcissism is integrated and not destructive towards others. What differentiates healthy behavioral patterns from unhealthy ones is rooted in (1) an individuals intentions, (2) the way an individual goes about getting their needs met and (3) how they manage conflict effectively. In the case of my former relationship, I learned that a man who has yet to heal his mother wound will take it out on every woman that tries to love him. Until he actively works towards making the unconscious, conscious, he will repeat the same patterns with different partners. Resulting in short term and often superficial relationships with an imbalance of power dynamics.

The parent-child dynamic of narcissism is a complex interplay shaped by early experiences that can leave an impactful mark on an individual's psyche. Rooted in two distinct trajectories, this dynamic can stem from parents who either indulged and coddled, or withheld affection and only gave approval based on perfection.

In the first trajectory, a child may have been drenched in constant attention and praise, leading to a sense of entitlement and superiority. Their parents' constant doting rendered them dependent on external validation and triggered a fear of revealing their limitations. This fear keeps them from venturing into unfamiliar territory, as they dread exposing any shortcomings. Here, a paradox emerges: spoiled and entitled, yet feeling incompetent underneath the façade.

The second trajectory paints a contrasting picture - one of deprivation and dependence. Here, conditional love was the currency, and it was only doled out when the child met unrealistically high standards. This created an insatiable need for validation and approval, turning them into emotional dependents. Constantly seeking affirmation, they fear rejection and often struggle to assert themselves without external validation. The child may avoid taking the initiative for fear of showing their limitations or failures when taking on new ventures if they are rewarded for their achievements one minute and criticized and discarded for their natural imperfections the next. A parent's unfair and unpredictable expectations become confusing and internalized as conditional love was weaponized in instances where outcomes were anything short of perfection. This conditioned the child to believe that love was transactional and based solely on how well they can perform versus who they inherently are. Thereby reinforcing the creation of a Narcissist's perfectly constructed facade that they use to mask their sensitive identity behind.

Both paths converge on the central theme of competition. The narcissistic individual has honed competition into a tool to reaffirm their false sense of superiority. But they're strategic; often only engaging in competition when they anticipate a favorable outcome. This selective approach underscores their fragile self-esteem, as they cannot afford to face failure in a public arena. The narcissistic mindset is rooted in a tumultuous childhood where love and approval were capricious. This duality has forged an individual capable of grandiosity and bravado, yet burdened with self-doubt. Their journey is a quest for balance, an attempt to reconcile their conflicting desires for autonomy and validation. Here, they often engage in a subconscious "I don't need anyone" or "I'll show you" mindset. In this case, the easily offended and emotionally dependent narcissist is a manifestation of their early childhood deprivation and indoctrination.

Profiling A Narcissist

NUANCES OF NARCISSISM

NARCISSISTIC FAMILY DYNAMICS

To wrap up this section about narcissistic family dynamics, there's last, but not least, the lost child - the quiet observer on the sidelines. [12] This is the kid who learns to keep their head down, stay out of the drama, and not attract any attention. They might feel invisible, but it's their way of coping with the chaos in the family. And that can make them feel isolated and unheard. It's like they're trying to survive by becoming a ghost. The lost child, too, often gets lost in the shuffle. They learned to stay quiet, not cause any trouble, and just fly under the radar.

Here's the thing, Empaths, individuals with heightened emotional sensitivity and an innate ability to deeply understand and connect with the emotions of others, often find themselves entangled in toxic family dynamics. These dynamics can make them susceptible to tolerating the abuse of a narcissist. This is further exacerbated by the prevalence of interpartner violence (IPV) among those who experienced physical or emotional neglect or abuse during their upbringing. [13] Enabling behavior involves unconsciously or consciously supporting and facilitating destructive actions or behaviors. Empaths, due to their compassionate nature, often feel compelled to help and heal those around them; even those that hurt them. This predisposition can make them vulnerable to being manipulated and exploited by individuals with narcissistic tendencies, who seek to control and dominate others. Due to their:

1. Empathy and Compassion: Empaths are driven by their deep sense of empathy and compassion, making them inclined to believe that they can positively impact and change even the most difficult individuals. This inherent belief can lead them to endure emotional or psychological abuse from narcissists, as they continue to hope for change and healing.
2. Desire for Harmony: Empaths are driven by a strong desire for harmony and peace in their relationships. This desire can lead them to downplay or excuse the toxic behavior of a narcissistic family member, in an attempt to maintain a semblance of stability within the family unit.
3. Personal Worth Tied to Helping: Empaths often tie their sense of self-worth to their ability to help and support others. This can lead them to accept mistreatment from narcissists under the misguided belief that their value is contingent on their ability to "fix" the situation.

Interpartner violence (IPV), also known as domestic violence, is a deeply concerning issue that affects relationships worldwide. Research indicates a strong correlation between experiencing neglect or abuse during childhood and becoming either a victim or perpetrator of IPV in adult relationships. [14] This manifests as:

1. Cycle of Violence: Children who grow up in households marked by physical or emotional neglect or abuse may internalize these behaviors as normal. As a result, they may unwittingly perpetuate the cycle of violence in their own adult relationships, whether as victims or abusers.
2. Attachment Patterns: Early experiences significantly shape attachment patterns in individuals. Those who experienced inconsistent caregiving, neglect, or abuse might develop insecure attachment styles, which can manifest as difficulty in forming healthy, stable relationships. This can make them more susceptible to entering relationships marked by violence.
3. Normalization of Abuse: Growing up in an environment where abuse is normalized can lead individuals to perceive aggressive or controlling behaviors as an acceptable way to communicate or assert dominance. This distorted understanding of relationships increases the likelihood of engaging in IPV.

The intersection of enabling empaths with toxic family dynamics and the prevalence of interpartner violence among those who experienced neglect or abuse during their upbringing highlights the complex ways in which early life experiences influence adult behavior and relationships. Breaking these cycles requires awareness, education, and support systems that empower individuals to recognize unhealthy patterns and foster healthy, respectful connections. Overall, the whole family system becomes a hot mess. The kids and enabling parent might start internalizing the dysfunctional patterns they see, and it can affect their future relationships and self-worth. This might reinforce their way of thinking that this is how things are supposed to be. This perpetuates the cycle of unhealthy relationships. It's like a rollercoaster of emotions and drama, with everyone playing their roles. But remember, this is not a healthy or happy scenario for anyone involved. Recognizing these patterns can be the first step towards healing and breaking free from the toxic cycle. There's always a chance for change and a more positive path ahead. Change begins with you.

Profiling A Narcissist

NUANCES OF NARCISSISM

NARCISSISTIC FAMILY DYNAMICS

CAN YOU DESCRIBE A SPECIFIC INSTANCE WHEN YOU FELT COMPELLED TO SUPPORT OR TOLERATE THE BEHAVIOR OF THE NARCISSISTIC FAMILY MEMBER, FRIEND OR PARTNER? HOW DID YOUR EMPATHIC NATURE INFLUENCE YOUR RESPONSE IN THAT SITUATION?

Profiling A Narcissist

NUANCES OF NARCISSISM

REFLECTING ON YOUR UPBRINGING, ARE THERE ANY PATTERNS OR DYNAMICS WITHIN YOUR FAMILY THAT MIGHT HAVE INFLUENCED YOUR TENDENCY TO TOLERATE ABUSIVE OR NEGLECTFUL BEHAVIOR FROM A HIGHLY VOLATILE INDIVIDUAL? HOW DO YOU THINK THESE DYNAMICS INTERSECT WITH YOUR EMPATHIC QUALITIES?

Profiling A Narcissist

NUANCES OF NARCISSISM

NARCISSISTIC FAMILY DYNAMICS

IN WHAT WAYS DO YOU FEEL YOUR DEEP SENSE OF EMPATHY HAS BOTH HELPED AND HINDERED YOUR ABILITY TO ADDRESS THE ABUSIVE OR NEGLECTFUL BEHAVIORS IN VARIOUS RELATIONSHIP DYNAMICS (PAST OR PRESENT)? CAN YOU IDENTIFY ANY MOMENTS WHEN YOUR EMPATHY LED TO A SHIFT IN THE DYNAMICS?

Profiling A Narcissist

NUANCES OF NARCISSISM

NARCISSISTIC FAMILY DYNAMICS

CONSIDERING YOUR DESIRE FOR HARMONY WITHIN YOUR FAMILY, CAN YOU RECALL A TIME WHEN YOU CHOSE TO OVERLOOK OR DOWNPLAY SOMEONE'S HARMFUL ACTIONS IN ORDER TO MAINTAIN THE PEACE? HOW DO YOU THINK THIS CHOICE REFLECTS YOUR EMPATHIC NATURE AND ITS IMPACT ON FUTURE SITUATIONS?

Profiling A Narcissist

NUANCES OF NARCISSISM

MALE NARCISSISTS

Now that we understand a bit about unhealthy narcissistic family dynamics, let's talk about the correlation between male narcissists and their mothers. This is not to place blame on mothers what so ever, but to explain how relational dynamics with those who may have either under functioned or over functioned influenced a male narcissist's personality. It's essential to approach this topic with compassion and understanding, as it delves into complex family dynamics.

You see, the relationship between a male narcissist and his mother can play a crucial role in shaping his behavior and personality. Let's start with an under functioning mother - someone who may struggle with her own emotional well-being or self-esteem. [15] In this situation, the innocent boy may have been forced to take on a caretaker role for his mother, even at a very young age. This is known as Parentification. [16] Because of his mother's intense need to feel attachment and security, she may have parentified her son or may have crossed boundaries that led to emotional incest that enabled enmeshment within their dynamic and his fear of engulfment. As he grows older, he may feel a constant need for validation and admiration to fill the void left by this emotional imbalance.

On the other hand, an over functioning mother might be overly controlling and demanding, expecting her son to meet her high standards and live up to her expectations. [17] This could create immense pressure on the boy to constantly prove himself and seek her approval due to his fear of rejection and emasculation. As a result, he might develop a sense of entitlement, believing he deserves special treatment and recognition.

In intimate partner relationship dynamics, an unhealed mother wound will enable him to subconsciously take out his unresolved anger and resentment from his mother onto his partner - using them as a scapegoat to process his projected pain. Because he hasn't dealt with his pain and distain in a healthy way, he might start projecting his insecurities onto his partner. This can show up in spiteful and resentful behavior.

For example, he might constantly seek validation and attention from his partner, expecting her to fill the emotional void he experienced in the past. If she can't meet those needs all the time (which, let's be real, no one can 24/7), he might get super resentful and even lash out. It's like he's looking for her to fix what he couldn't heal in his mother.

Or, he might flip things around and become overly controlling, just like his over functioning mother was with him. He might start demanding that his partner meets his unrealistic expectations, and if she doesn't, he'll get all angry and spiteful, projecting his belief that *she's* not good enough. It's crucial to understand that this behavior isn't his partner's fault at all. She's not responsible for healing his wounds. But the thing is, he might not even be aware of the root cause of his actions. He's just repeating the patterns he learned from his past. As we take this trauma-informed perspective, we can understand the male narcissist's struggles while also distancing ourselves from them.

This, of course, doesn't excuse any harmful actions towards his partner. In both cases, the male child may not have had the chance to develop a healthy sense of self-worth and emotional regulation. Instead, he may have learned to rely on external validation to feel significant and worthy. This may have reinforced his belief that instead of learning how to control himself, he must find ways to control others. This learned behavior often leads to narcissistic traits later in life. However, it's important to remember that not every male child with an under functioning or over functioning mother becomes a narcissist. Many other factors come into play, such as genetics, early childhood experiences, and external influences.

Additionally, if male narcissists had a physically present, but emotionally absent father who treated him and his mother with inconsistent connection and contempt, he will re-enact this dysfunctional dynamic later in life. Essentially, what was modeled for him in childhood is what he will mirror in adulthood. [18]

Fathers play a significant role in shaping a male narcissist. Although it's essential to remember that not all fathers contribute to the development of narcissistic traits in their sons. The relationship between a father and son can influence the son's self-esteem, emotional regulation, and interpersonal dynamics.[19] Here are some ways fathers can impact the development of a male narcissist:

- **Lack of Emotional Validation:** Fathers who consistently fail to validate their sons' emotions and feelings may instill a sense of inadequacy or the belief that their emotions are not valid or important. This emotional neglect can lead to a need for external validation and attention later in life, which are characteristics commonly observed in narcissistic individuals.

- **Overemphasis on Achievement:** Fathers who place excessive importance on achievement, success, or status may teach their sons that their worth is determined by accomplishments rather than their inherent value as individuals. This can lead to a relentless pursuit of external validation and a focus on maintaining a grandiose self-image, which are traits commonly associated with narcissism.

- **Lack of Empathy and Emotional Connection:** Fathers who have difficulty expressing empathy or establishing emotional connections with their sons may model similar behaviors. Sons may internalize this emotional disconnect and develop difficulties in empathizing with others, a hallmark trait of narcissism.

- **Authoritarian Parenting:** Fathers who adopt an authoritarian parenting style, characterized by strict rules, lack of emotional support, and a focus on obedience, may raise sons who struggle with autonomy and self-expression. This can lead to an increased need for control and a rigid sense of self, traits often observed in narcissistic individuals.

- **Modeling Narcissistic Behavior:** In some cases, fathers who exhibit narcissistic traits themselves may inadvertently model these behaviors for their sons. Children often learn by observing their parents' actions and may mimic narcissistic traits as a way to cope with their environment.

In the end, fostering empathy and compassion can support both the male narcissist and their parents on their respective journeys toward healing and personal development.

However, if you're in a relationship with someone like this, it's crucial to prioritize your safety and well-being. Empathy without boundaries only reinforces self abandonment and enablement. His wounds are not yours to heal. And his unhealed pain is not an excuse for him to use you as a metaphorical punching bag.

The foundation of healthy relationships is rooted in trust, respect, and mutual support. These fundamental pillars serve as the bedrock upon which individuals can develop meaningful and sustainable connections. However, an essential aspect of cultivating these healthy dynamics is the recognition that past traumas, whether experienced individually or collectively, should not be projected onto one another within the relationship.

Profiling A Narcissist

NUANCES OF NARCISSISM

WENDY & PETER PAN SYNDROME

Now that we've profiled the makings of a male narcissist, let's discuss a little bit more about how this plays out in romantic relationship dynamics with a concept known as Pathological Lovers. A "pathological lover" is a term often used to describe individuals who exhibit patterns of dysfunctional and unhealthy behavior within romantic relationships. [20] These individuals typically engage in manipulative, controlling, and emotionally damaging behaviors that can have a profound impact on their partners' well-being and self-esteem. When describing a narcissist, the term "pathological lover" can indeed be fitting. Narcissists display a range of traits and behaviors that align with the concept of a pathological lover. They do so with the:

- **Emotional Roller Coaster:** The erratic and unpredictable shifts in a narcissist's behavior contribute to an emotional roller coaster for their partner. This can lead to anxiety, depression, and a constant sense of instability.This manipulation can lead to a sense of powerlessness and confusion in the partner.
- **Exploitative Behavior:** Narcissists often exploit their partners for their own gain. This can involve using their partner's resources, emotional energy, and even their self-esteem to bolster their own self-image.
- **Constant Need for Validation:** Narcissists require constant validation and attention. They seek admiration and affirmation from their partners, often at the expense of their partner's own needs and feelings.
- **Inability to Sustain Healthy Relationships:** Due to their self-centered nature and manipulative behaviors, narcissists struggle to maintain healthy and functional relationships. Their pathological tendencies create a pattern of dysfunction that is damaging to their partners.
- **Shifting Identity:** Narcissists often project a façade of who they want their partners to believe they are. This shifting identity can confuse and destabilize their partners' understanding of who they are truly in a relationship with.

A "pathological lover" aptly captures the destructive and toxic nature of narcissistic behaviors within romantic relationships. Especially in the context of Wendy and Peter Pan Syndrome. More specifically, the "Hyper Successful Peter Pan" subtype. This is only an example and not meant to be a generalization of the different types of relationship dynamics that can play out. Remember, this is a fictional term, but we'll use it to picture some common dynamics. So, picture this: The Hyper Successful Peter Pan is someone who appears to have it all together on the outside. He's achieved significant success in different areas of life, like his career or social status. However, deep down, he may struggle with emotional underdevelopment or even show some narcissistic traits. It's like there's a missing piece inside them that they try to fill with attention and admiration from others. [21] Specifically, they might prey on young women for that attention and admiration. They might seek out younger, impressionable partners who are more likely to idolize them without questioning their behavior. They crave constant validation to boost their own ego and self-esteem. For this reason, this subtype will naturally fear strong women. Not because of her efforts to hurt him physically, but because of her unwillingness to tolerate his mistreatment of her mentally and emotionally.

My former partner was quite the Peter Pan. I remembering questioning his relationships once with women substantially younger than him. To which he replied, "She was mature for her age". Reading between the lines, I now recognize that his actions were really exposing how emotionally immature he was for *his*.

In these relationships, a trauma bond based on codependency can develop. A trauma bond is when one person becomes emotionally dependent on the other, even if there's harmful or toxic behavior involved. [22] The young women, in this case, might feel strongly attached to the Hyper Successful Peter Pan due to the material resources, attention and validation he provides. And the Peter Pan? Well, he might manipulate and charm his way into the young woman's life, making her feel like she needs him for validation. It creates this cycle of constantly seeking approval from him, which can be emotionally draining and even abusive over time. Remember, this perspective is just a fictional scenario, but it can help us understand how certain dynamics might play out in real-life relationships. He's the type to use his large disposable income to control his partners and maintain social connections. In narcissistic relationships, everyone and everything is disposable and an intentional means to an end. Heteronormatively speaking, this is often times, but not always, why you will see older men who meet this description with younger women. The term "age gap" is used colloquially to describe significant differences in age between individuals in a romantic or sexual relationship. [23] Predatory narcissistic relationships with younger women, or any individual, are concerning and potentially harmful, particularly when there is a substantial power imbalance or manipulation involved. Such relationships can be emotionally and psychologically damaging to the younger person involved; impacting their overall wellbeing.

Profiling A Narcissist

NUANCES OF NARCISSISM

WENDY & PETER PAN SYNDROME

While it makes psychological and biological sense why older men may find younger women attractive, it begs the question, why would a younger woman find a substantially older man attractive? If not biological, in what ways is this attraction psychological? Could this attraction be a reflection of unhealed father wounds that enable codependency and trauma bonds to exist?

In reality, not all successful people are emotionally underdeveloped or manipulative, and not all young women in relationships with older partners experience trauma bonds or codependency. Every person and relationship is unique. But if you ever find yourself in a situation that feels emotionally draining or harmful, it's crucial to prioritize your well-being. Seeking support from trauma-informed professionals can help you navigate the complexities of such relationships. In any healthy relationship, it's essential to feel valued and respected, with both partners supporting each other's growth and well-being. Remember, you deserve to be with someone who treats you with kindness, empathy, and understanding. At the very least, you deserve a safe relationship free of power dynamics that include the use of covert psychological warfare.

However, it situations where that isn't the case, those with Wendy Syndrome and Peter Pan Syndrome make the perfect symbiotic relationship. Wendy Syndrome and Peter Pan Syndrome are both terms used to describe certain behavioral patterns in relationships, especially in romantic partnerships. Imagine Wendy Syndrome as a concept where one partner, typically the female, takes on a nurturing and caretaking role in the relationship, similar to Wendy Darling from the Peter Pan story. This nurturing behavior often involves supporting and taking care of the partner's emotional needs, just like Wendy looked after Peter Pan and the Lost Boys. [24]

On the other hand, as we now know, Peter Pan Syndrome refers to a behavioral pattern often seen in one partner, typically the male, where they resist growing up and taking on adult responsibilities. Much like Peter Pan, they want to stay young at heart, avoid commitments, and may have difficulty dealing with the challenges of adulthood and maintaining healthy adult relationships.

If a male narcissist witnessed his father physically or emotionally abuse his mother, he is likely to seek out partners with wounded feminine energy. This is someone he can easily exploit as he witnessed his mother's coerced submission enable his fathers aggression. It is essential to prioritize healthy and consensual relationships built on mutual respect, understanding, and equality, regardless of age. Age, finances or social status are common forms of manipulation tactics in these relationship dynamics and should never be used as a means to exploit or control another person. So, how might Wendy Syndrome enable Peter Pan Syndrome? Well, she does so by:

1. **Enabling His Avoidance:** In the dynamic of Wendy Syndrome, the nurturing partner may enable the avoidant behavior of the Peter Pan partner. By continuously taking care of his emotional needs and responsibilities, she unintentionally reinforces his resistance to grow up and take on adult roles.
2. **Nurturing His Dependency and Comfort:** The Peter Pan partner might become dependent on the nurturing Wendy partner for emotional support and comfort. As a result, he may become comfortable with not taking on adult responsibilities because he knows she will always be there to take care of him.
3. **Reinforcing His Lack of Accountability:** Wendy's nurturing nature might shield Peter Pan from facing the consequences of his actions or lack of responsibilities. He may not take accountability for his behavior because he knows she will cover for him.
4. **Stagnating His Personal Growth:** With Wendy constantly catering to Peter Pan's emotional needs, he may not feel the need to work on personal growth or development. This can lead to stagnation in his emotional and psychological maturation. The dynamic can lead to a codependent relationship, where Wendy derives her sense of self-worth from taking care of Peter Pan, and he relies heavily on her to meet his emotional needs.

It's important to recognize that these behavioral patterns are not limited to specific genders, and they can manifest in any relationship dynamic. Additionally, these patterns can be fluid, and individuals may switch roles or exhibit both Wendy and Peter Pan traits at different times. To foster a healthier relationship, open communication, setting boundaries, and encouraging personal growth for both partners are essential. Both Wendy and Peter Pan need to take responsibility for their own emotional well-being and development to create a balanced and fulfilling partnership. As you look back on your interactions with a highly toxic individual, take a moment to consider the emotional and psychological impact it may have had on you. How did those experiences make you feel, and what valuable insights have you gained about yourself through navigating this challenging relationship?

Profiling A Narcissist

NUANCES OF NARCISSISM

10 QUESTIONS TO GAUGE WHETHER YOU ARE OVER FUNCTIONING IN YOUR RELATIONSHIPS

YES. NO

CHECKLIST

AS YOU READ EACH QUESTION, SIMPLY TICK "YES" IF YOU AGREE OR "NO" IF YOU DISAGREE WITH THE STATEMENT.

		YES	NO
01	DO YOU OFTEN TAKE ON MORE RESPONSIBILITIES IN THE RELATIONSHIP WHILE YOUR PARTNER AVOIDS THEM?	☐	☐
02	DO YOU FREQUENTLY FIND YOURSELF TRYING TO FIX YOUR PARTNER'S PROBLEMS OR MAKE THEIR LIFE EASIER?	☐	☐
03	ARE YOU REGULARLY SACRIFICING YOUR OWN NEEDS OR WELL-BEING FOR THE SAKE OF YOUR PARTNER'S COMFORT?	☐	☐
04	DO YOU FEEL RESPONSIBLE FOR MANAGING YOUR PARTNER'S EMOTIONS AND MOOD?	☐	☐
05	DO YOU FIND IT CHALLENGING TO SAY "NO" TO YOUR PARTNER'S REQUESTS OR DEMANDS?	☐	☐
06	DO YOU OFTEN TAKE ON THE EMOTIONAL LABOR IN THE RELATIONSHIP WHILE EXPERIENCING AN IMBALANCE IN RECIPROCITY?	☐	☐
07	ARE YOU THE ONE WHO INITIATES MOST OF THE COMMUNICATION AND PLANNING IN THE RELATIONSHIP?	☐	☐
08	DO YOU OFTEN FEEL MORE LIKE A PARENT THAN A PARTNER, SACRIFICING YOUR OWN NEEDS TO MAKE UP FOR THEIR LACK OF EMOTIONAL INTELLIGENCE OR INCREASED EMOTIONAL IMMATURITY?	☐	☐
09	ARE YOU FREQUENTLY TRYING TO ANTICIPATE AND PREVENT PROBLEMS OR CONFLICTS IN THE RELATIONSHIP?	☐	☐
10	DO YOU HAVE DIFFICULTY DELEGATING TASKS OR RESPONSIBILITIES TO YOUR PARTNER, EVEN WHEN THEY ARE CAPABLE?	☐	☐

A Narcissist thrives off of what you can do for them and how you can make them feel versus appreciating you for who you are. In such cases, they will disempower you from being the best version of yourself, so you can be the version that best serves them. Remember, these questions are meant to help you reflect on your behavior in romantic relationships. If you find yourself answering "yes" to many of them, it could be an indication that you are over functioning and taking on more than your fair share in the relationship. It's important to maintain a healthy balance of giving and receiving in any relationship.

Profiling A Narcissist

NUANCES OF NARCISSISM

The sad truth is, over-functioning can create the illusion that there is more intimacy and connection in a relationship than there really is. The moment you stop overextending, you will notice one of two things: who was reciprocating your energy or who was exploiting it. Now that we understand a bit about the psychology behind male narcissists, let's talk about the correlation between female narcissists and their mothers. Just as we used a gentle disclaimer when discussing male narcissists, it's essential to approach this topic with understanding and empathy, considering the impact of family dynamics on a person's development.

So, picture this: Similar to the dynamics with male narcissists, female narcissist might have grown up with a mother who was either under functioning or over functioning. An under functioning mother may have struggled with emotional issues, making it challenging for her to provide the nurturing support her daughter needed. [25] On the other hand, an over functioning mother might have been overly controlling, setting high expectations for her daughter to meet. As a result, she could have developed a deep sense of insecurity and a constant need for attention and admiration.

In either scenario, the young girl might not have received the healthy emotional guidance and validation necessary for her development. If she felt rejected by her mother and/or disrespected by her father, she may have learned to shut down or lash out in order to meet her needs or conceal them. The "Alice in Wonderland" subtype in relationships are individuals who exhibit a pattern of escaping reality and living in a fantasy world. [26]

This colloquial phrase is used to describe women who exhibit characteristics similar to Alice in Lewis Carroll's novel "Alice's Adventures in Wonderland." In the novel, Alice is a young girl who experiences various adventures in a dream-like and surreal world. They may seem charming, whimsical, and playful, drawing others in with their enchanting allure. However, beneath the surface, their behavior can be toxic and detrimental to the relationship. These women often struggle with a lack of emotional maturity and may use escapism as a coping mechanism. They avoid facing challenges, conflicts, or responsibilities in the real world by retreating into their own dreamlike existence. They may have a tendency to deny or downplay serious issues, preferring to stay in a state of denial rather than dealing with reality.

In relationships, their behavior can be erratic and unpredictable. They may have difficulty expressing their true feelings and needs, leading to a breakdown in communication. Their partners may find it challenging to understand or connect with them, as they seem to be living in a world of their own. Additionally, the "Alice in Wonderland" subtype may exhibit a fear of commitment and intimacy, as they prefer to remain in a state of fantasy rather than fully engaging in a genuine emotional connection. This can lead to a cycle of emotional distancing as they push their partners away.

Ultimately, the toxicity arises from the lack of authenticity and emotional depth in the relationship. The partner of an "Alice in Wonderland" woman may feel emotionally unfulfilled, frustrated by the lack of real connection, and burdened by the constant need to navigate their partner's escapist tendencies. Addressing these toxic patterns often requires open and honest communication, both within the relationship and with the support of a qualified trauma informed mental health specialist. Helping the "Alice in Wonderland" woman confront her avoidance of reality and emotional issues can lead to healthier relationships and personal growth for both partners. However, in order to empower this subtype, one cannot enable it. It's pretty wild how unhealed family dynamics can influence they way we react in relation to others. In Alice's case, having a mother who made her feel overly coddled or criticized influced how she copes with connection and emotional regulation.

Switching gears, now, let's talk about the absent father. An absent father, whether physically or emotionally, can further impact the daughter's sense of self-worth and identity. She might grow up seeking male validation and approval, trying to fill the void left by her father's absence. [27] As she navigates her way into adulthood, these early experiences might lead her to adopt narcissistic traits as a coping mechanism. To compensate for the emotional neglect or lack of validation, she may develop a grandiose self-image and demand constant attention and admiration from others. It's crucial to remember that these patterns are not set in stone, and not every woman who grew up in such circumstances becomes a narcissist. Other factors, such as genetics, individual temperament, and external influences, also play a role in shaping a person's personality.

Profiling A Narcissist

NUANCES OF NARCISSISM

FEMALE NARCISSISTS – THE MANIC PIXIE

Next up on the female narcissist profile is the "manic pixie". The "manic pixie" subtype is a term often used to describe a specific personality archetype commonly portrayed in media and literature. This character type is typically depicted as an eccentric, whimsical, and free-spirited woman who enters the life of a male protagonist to help him break free from his mundane or conventional existence. The term "manic pixie dream girl" was popularized by film critic Nathan Rabin in 2007 to describe such characters, who are often characterized by their quirkiness, unpredictability, and ability to inspire personal growth or change in the male protagonist. [28]

In the context of female narcissism, the concept of the manic pixie subtype becomes interesting when examining how it can align with certain traits or behaviors associated with narcissistic personalities. Female narcissists, like their male counterparts, exhibit a range of traits that revolve around a self-centered focus, a need for admiration, and a lack of empathy. Some female narcissists might adopt or amplify the characteristics of the manic pixie subtype as part of their manipulative strategies to engage and control others, particularly male partners or admirers. Here's how the manic pixie subtype could potentially relate to female narcissism with their exploitation of:

1. **Charm and Charisma:** Female narcissists often possess a captivating charm and charisma that can draw people in. By adopting the traits of the manic pixie dream girl, they might amplify their eccentricity and whimsicality to create an initial magnetic attraction that entices others to become emotionally invested.
2. **Idealization and Devaluation:** Female narcissists are known for idealizing their partners initially and then devaluing them once their needs are met or their partner's utility diminishes. Adopting the manic pixie persona might facilitate this process, as the unpredictable and ever-changing behavior of the character can mimic the cycle of idealization and devaluation that is common in narcissistic relationships.
3. **Manipulative Behavior:** The manic pixie archetype often employs unpredictable behavior and emotional highs and lows, which can be used by narcissists to manipulate and control their partners. By alternating between moments of intense affection and withdrawal, female narcissists can keep their partners emotionally off-balance, making them more susceptible to the narcissist's influence.
4. **Validation and Admiration:** Female narcissists thrive on admiration and validation from others. The manic pixie persona, with its unconventional and attention-grabbing behavior, can attract attention and admiration, fulfilling the narcissist's need for constant affirmation.
5. **Lack of Authentic Connection:** The manic pixie archetype, while charming and intriguing, often lacks depth and authenticity in its relationships. This can mirror the superficial connections that narcissists tend to form, as their interactions are often focused on their own needs rather than genuine emotional exchange.

It's important to note that not all individuals who exhibit traits of the manic pixie subtype are narcissists, and not all female narcissists will adopt this persona. However, the overlap between the two concepts can shed light on the complex ways in which narcissistic traits can manifest and be expressed in various social and cultural contexts.

Approaching this from a compassionate perspective, we can understand that the female narcissist's behavior is often a reflection of her unresolved wounds and the coping mechanisms she developed in response to her upbringing. It doesn't mean we excuse harmful actions, but it helps us empathize with her struggles. Her aloof demeanor doesn't necessarily make her a narcissist, however, it does make many of her behavioral patterns highly toxic, unpredictable and volatile. In other words, unhealthy. If you encounter a female narcissist in your life, remember that setting boundaries is essential. Just like with male narcissists, it's encouraged to prioritize your well-being and protect yourself from manipulative or abusive behaviors. Reflecting on your experience with a highly toxic female, how do you think that interaction might have impacted you emotionally and psychologically? How did it make you feel, and what insights have you gained about yourself through Navigating this challenging relationship?

Profiling A Narcissist

NUANCES OF NARCISSISM

TOXIC MASCULINITY & TOXIC FEMININITY

Alright, so we've been talking about female narcissists and the whole Alice in Wonderland, Manic Pixie thing, right? It's incredible to see how some people use escapism and struggle to grow emotionally. But wait, there's more! Let's dive into the bigger picture of toxic masculinity and toxic femininity traits. By getting a grip on these damaging behaviors in both these men and women, we'll get a better handle on how they negatively impact relationships and society as a whole.

Toxic masculinity and toxic femininity are cultural constructs that describe harmful gender norms and expectations that limit individuals' emotional expression and well-being. [29] It's important to address these concepts with warmth and compassion while recognizing that they can negatively impact people of all genders.

Toxic Masculinity Traits of Male Narcissists:
1. Grandiosity: Male narcissists often exhibit an exaggerated sense of self-importance and superiority, believing they are above others and deserve special treatment.
2. Lack of Empathy: They struggle to understand or care about the feelings and needs of others, focusing mainly on their own wants and desires.
3. Dominance and Control: Male narcissists tend to assert power and control over others, seeking to dominate and manipulate situations to serve their interests. Also, overly competitive about everything.
4. Emotional Suppression: They may have difficulty expressing vulnerable emotions like sadness or fear, as they see them as signs of weakness.
5. Aggression: Some male narcissists resort to aggressive behaviors, verbally or even physically, to assert their dominance and intimidate others.

Toxic Femininity Traits of Female Narcissists:
1. Covert Manipulation: Female narcissists often employ subtle and covert tactics to manipulate and control others, using charm and emotional manipulation to get their way.
2. Victim Mentality: They may portray themselves as perpetual victims, using their vulnerability to elicit sympathy and attention from others.
3. Envy and Competition: Female narcissists can be intensely competitive and envious of others' achievements or successes, seeking to undermine or outdo them.
4. Emotional Intensity: They may use their heightened emotional expressions to keep others engaged and entangled in their dramas, making it difficult to set boundaries.
5. Attention-Seeking: Female narcissists crave constant attention and validation, often resorting to dramatic or attention-grabbing behavior to stay in the spotlight.

It's important to remember that these traits can vary in intensity and manifestation across different individuals, but they all contribute to the toxic dynamics in relationships involving narcissistic individuals.

7 Common Traits That Apply To Both Of Them :
1. They are highly concerned about their looks and keeping up social appearances
2. They hate boundaries and don't take "no" for an answer
3. They flirt with anyone and act single all while being in a relationship
4. They are masters at apologies (if they apologize at all) but struggle with being held accountable
5. They lack emotional intelligence and empathy
6. They exploit and manipulate
7. They are highly competitive with everyone, even those they claim to love

It's crucial to recognize that these traits are not inherent to masculinity or femininity but rather a result of nature and nurture. Embracing healthy masculinity and femininity involves promoting emotional intelligence, empathy, authenticity, and mutual respect among individuals of all genders.

Profiling A Narcissist

NUANCES OF NARCISSISM

5 TYPES OF NARCISSISTS

Now that we have explored the toxic traits associated with both toxic masculinity and femininity in narcissists, let's take this understanding to the next level by diving into the five different types of narcissists. By identifying the specific characteristics of each type, we can gain deeper insights into how these individuals operate and the unique challenges they present in relationships. Understanding the nuances of different narcissistic types will empower us to recognize red flags early on and navigate these complex dynamics with greater awareness and self-preservation. As mentioned earlier, Narcissism is a complex personality trait characterized by an excessive sense of self-importance, a need for admiration, and a lack of empathy for others. While there is not a universally agreed-upon categorization of narcissism, researchers and psychologists have identified different types or subtypes of narcissism based on certain core characteristics. Here are some commonly recognized types of narcissism:

- **Overt Narcissism:** Overt narcissism, also known as grandiose or exhibitionistic narcissism, is characterized by an overt display of grandiosity and attention-seeking behavior. Individuals with overt narcissism often have an inflated sense of self-importance, a strong desire for admiration, and a tendency to dominate conversations and situations. They may engage in self-promotion, seek validation through achievements, and exhibit a lack of empathy towards others. [30]

- **Covert Narcissism:** Covert narcissism, also known as vulnerable or closet narcissism, is characterized by a more subtle and hidden expression of narcissistic traits. Individuals with covert narcissism often struggle with low self-esteem, hypersensitivity to criticism, and a need for constant validation and reassurance. They may display passive-aggressive behavior, manipulate others emotionally, and present themselves as victims while seeking attention and validation. [31]

- **Antagonistic Narcissism:** Antagonistic narcissism, sometimes referred to as malignant or aggressive narcissism, involves a combination of narcissistic and antisocial personality traits. Individuals with antagonistic narcissism display grandiosity, a sense of entitlement, and a disregard for others' feelings or rights. They may engage in exploitative behavior, show a lack of remorse, and demonstrate a tendency towards aggression or manipulation to meet their own needs. [32]

- **Communal Narcissism:** Communal / spiritual narcissism is characterized by a grandiose self-perception associated with being exceptionally caring, helpful, or morally superior. Individuals with communal narcissism often seek validation through acts of generosity, charity, or self-sacrifice. They may have an inflated belief in their own altruism and expect recognition and admiration for their perceived selflessness. [33]

- **Malignant Narcissism:** Malignant narcissism is considered a more severe and destructive form of narcissism, combining narcissistic traits with antisocial and sadistic tendencies. Individuals with malignant narcissism exhibit a combination of grandiosity, a lack of empathy, a thirst for power and control, and a propensity for manipulation, deceit, and exploitation. They may engage in destructive behaviors and have a disregard for the well-being of others. [34]

It's important to note that these categories are not rigid and can overlap or coexist within individuals. Each type of narcissism represents different patterns and manifestations of narcissistic traits, but the specific characteristics and behaviors may vary from person to person. Remember, the assessment of narcissistic traits should be conducted by qualified mental health professionals as this is a genuine personality disorder that should not be used lightly to label those we dislike or who disagree with us.

Profiling A Narcissist

NUANCES OF NARCISSISM

SHAME & NARCISSISM

As we continue our journey together, it's important to pause and reflect on what you have learned about others as well as the lessons you have learned about yourself. I know this can all feel a bit overwhelming, however I am so proud of you for doing the inner work required to heal and grow. When you think about the various personality subtypes and varieties of narcissists, what thoughts or emotions come up for you? Do you see parts of people you know and love within these descriptions? If so, simply pause and take note of your physical and emotional experience as you begin to integrate the information you have just learned. I remember how overwhelming this information was on my own healing journey. However, it was just the medicine I needed to break certain illusions with people whose only desire was to inflict harm. There will be growing pains associated with this journey. However, I'm here to support you every step of the way.

Now that we have familiarized ourselves with the five different types of narcissists, let's shift our focus to exploring the intriguing connection between narcissism and shame. Delving into this topic will shed light on the underlying emotions that often fuel narcissistic behavior. By understanding the role of shame in the narcissistic psyche, we can gain valuable insights into their motivations, coping mechanisms, and defense mechanisms. This deeper understanding will help us navigate the complexities of narcissistic relationships and provide us with a more compassionate perspective.

Shame can be described as a sense of inadequacy, worthlessness, and powerlessness in a given situation. It is triggered by a "perceived" detachment in one's connectedness to others or to oneself. Maltreatment during childhood such as bullying, mental/physical abuse or emotional neglect can increase the risk for Narcissistic Personality Disorder (NPD) in early adulthood. [35] However, a person blaming their childhood trauma on their destructive behaviors can be used as a distraction from actually taking accountability. This can prevent them from healing the abuse they cause to others based on the abuse others have caused to them. Shame based behaviors such as eating disorders, substance abuse or perfectionism can reaffirm destructive beliefs such as:

I am defective (damaged, broken, a mistake, flawed)
I am incompetent (not good enough, inept, ineffectual, useless).
I am unwanted (unloved, unappreciated, uncherished).
I am weak (small, impotent, puny, feeble).
I am nothing (worthless, invisible, unnoticed, empty)

Sadly, shame plays a significant role in the struggles of individuals with Narcissistic Personality Disorder (NPD). It affects their ability to maintain meaningful friendships, experience true intimacy, and impacts their self-esteem. You see, those high levels of narcissistic traits may lead to disruptions in their self-awareness and how they relate to others. This could manifest as low empathy, reduced life satisfaction, emotional unavailability, and grandiosity, among other performative behaviors.

It's a big reason why they find it challenging to confront their emotions and often resort to projecting their shame onto those around them. It's like they reject parts of themselves and push it onto others instead. And you know what? Shame can drive us to shut down or engage in behaviors like pleasing others, trying to be perfect, or seeking attention just to gain approval.

But here's the thing – we're wired for connection, so when we disconnection from ourselves because we feel unworthy, it causes us pain and enables us to disconnect from others. Brene Brown hit the nail on the head when she said, "Our sense of belonging can never be greater than our level of self-acceptance." To build meaningful relationships and tackle shame, we need to be honest with ourselves and not hide our vulnerabilities. This requires doing the inner work to understand how we are, who we are.

When trauma remains unhealed, it can stunt emotional growth and lead to emotionally immature behaviors in narcissists. You might notice them struggling to regulate their emotions, being impulsive, avoiding accountability, and showing a lack of empathy. As we know, they can even resort to emotional manipulation to maintain control or validation.

Recognizing these patterns can help us understand the underlying dynamics and challenges that narcissists face in their relationships and emotional regulation. It sheds light on their emotional struggles and lack of empathy, all stemming from their unresolved trauma. Understanding these aspects can open up opportunities for healing and growth, both for them and those who interact with them.

Profiling A Narcissist

NUANCES OF NARCISSISM

PERFORMATIVE EMPATHY

So far, we've explored things like shame, family dynamics and brain development to better understand narcissistic behavior and its impact on emotional growth. Let's move on to another crucial aspect of understanding human interactions – empathy. Empathy plays a significant role in how we connect with others and form meaningful relationships. Performative empathy is when someone puts on a show of empathy, pretending to care about others' feelings and experiences, but it's all just an act. [36] Performative empathy is what narcissists utilize to create a facade of being a good person in public while causing pain to those closest to them in private. It's like they wear a mask of empathy to gain admiration, sympathy, or to maintain a positive image, rather than genuinely connecting with others on an emotional level.

Narcissists are masters of performative empathy, especially when it comes to personal and professional settings. They have a knack for presenting themselves as kind, caring, and understanding individuals in public, which can make it incredibly difficult for others to see through their charade. They know how to say the right things, offer superficial support, and appear attentive to others' needs when they're being watched. In personal relationships, narcissists may engage in grand gestures, lavish praise, and over-the-top displays of affection when others are around. They want to be seen as the doting partner, the supportive friend, or the loving family member. But here's the heartbreaking truth: behind closed doors, they often reveal their true colors. They may engage in emotional manipulation, gaslighting, and even outright abuse, leaving their loved ones feeling confused, hurt, and invalidated.

My former partner was an expert at this. His behaviors were confusing until I realized they were all calculated. One of the most painful experiences was his ability to weaponize "caring for me" by concealing his feelings of deep contempt for the things I deeply cared about - Like my career, family or even friends.

In professional settings, narcissists can be equally cunning. They excel at networking, charming their colleagues, and creating a positive impression among superiors. They may volunteer for high-profile projects, put on a show of teamwork, and appear like the model employee. However, their true motivations often revolve around personal gain, power, and validation.

They may engage in office politics, sabotage others' progress, and exploit their coworkers' vulnerabilities for their benefit. It's important to note that real life monsters don't hide under your bed or in your closet. These predatory abusers disguise themselves as the perfect partners. They can be leaders, politicians, pastors, CEO's, teachers, brothers, fathers, mothers, sisters and even friends. This is how these predators are able to hide in plain sight. We tend to pedestal a lot of these roles in our life which enables us to overlook how those closest to us can end up hurting us the most.

The purpose of this performative empathy is to create an illusion—a carefully constructed image of goodness and empathy—to protect their ego and maintain control.

Understanding performative empathy can help us recognize the manipulative tactics employed by narcissists to maintain their image and exert influence over their relationships. As we transition into learning about the three primary types of empathy—cognitive, emotional, and compassionate empathy—we'll gain valuable insights into how genuine empathy differs from performative displays. This exploration will shed light on the nuances of human connection and emotional understanding, empowering us to recognize healthy empathy in our relationships and differentiate it from manipulative behaviors associated with narcissism. There are three different types of empathy, and delving into these can provide us with valuable insights into the dynamics of emotional connections, both in ourselves and in those around us.

Profiling A Narcissist

NUANCES OF NARCISSISM

5 TYPES OF EMPATHY

So, empathy is the ability to understand and share the feelings of another person. In the context of narcissistic relationships, it's important to differentiate between healthy empathy and the manipulative use of empathy by narcissists. While there are various ways to categorize empathy, one common framework distinguishes three types: cognitive empathy, emotional empathy, and compassionate empathy. [37]

- **Cognitive empathy:** This type of empathy involves understanding another person's perspective and emotions on an intellectual level. It allows individuals to recognize and intellectually grasp what someone else might be feeling or thinking, even if they don't necessarily experience those emotions themselves. Cognitive empathy helps build understanding and can be a positive quality in healthy relationships.

- **Emotional empathy:** Emotional empathy goes beyond understanding someone's emotions on an intellectual level. It involves personally feeling and sharing in the emotions of others. Emotional empathy allows individuals to connect deeply with others, offering support and validation for their feelings. It is often associated with compassion and can foster stronger emotional bonds in relationships.

- **Compassionate empathy:** Compassionate empathy combines cognitive and emotional empathy with the added element of taking action to help and support others. It involves not only understanding and sharing in someone's emotions but also actively seeking ways to alleviate their suffering and improve their well-being. Compassionate empathy involves a genuine concern for the welfare of others and can lead to acts of kindness and support.

In the context of narcissistic manipulation, some narcissists may possess what is often referred to as "dark empathy" or "empathic mimicry." [38] They can mimic empathy by observing and understanding others' emotions on a cognitive level, but they lack genuine emotional empathy and compassionate empathy. Narcissists may use this understanding of emotions to manipulate and exploit their victims. The deception is used to be disarming. They may mimic emotional reactions or display superficial empathy to gain trust and control over others. This manipulation can be subtle and deceptive, as narcissists exploit their victims' genuine emotional vulnerabilities without truly caring for their well-being. The purpose of this type of empathy is to disarm those around them and leverage listening, disguised as genuine caring. It's a form of information gathering to maintain the upper hand.

Here's the thing, mutual support entails uplifting and encouraging one another's aspirations, emotions, and well-being. It involves being a source of strength, comfort, and validation for each other. However, a narcissist's attempt at projecting past traumas can lead to a dynamic where these individuals unconsciously expect the partner to fulfill unmet needs or provide emotional healing for wounds that are not directly related to the current relationship. This can create undue pressure, resulting in codependency or unrealistic expectations that hinder both partners' personal growth and development. In essence, projecting past traumas onto a current relationship is akin to superimposing a distorted lens through which both individuals are perceived and evaluated. It taints the authenticity of the connection, hindering the potential for genuine intimacy and understanding to flourish. To foster a healthy and fulfilling relationship where genuine empathy is the foundation for safety and support, it's crucial for both individuals to increase their self-awareness and prioritize healing. This involves acknowledging their own traumas, addressing their emotional triggers, and consciously choosing to engage with each other based on the present reality rather than through the lens of past wounds. By doing so, they create a space where trust, respect, and mutual support can truly thrive, leading to a stronger and more harmonious partnership. It's important to note that not all narcissists possess this manipulative form of empathy, and empathy itself is not exclusive to narcissists. However, understanding the potential for manipulative tactics can help individuals recognize and protect themselves from abusive and exploitative dynamics - Especially when it comes to those who display characteristics on the Dark Triad and utilize performative empathy to cover their tracks.

Profiling A Narcissist

NUANCES OF NARCISSISM

THE "NICE" NARCISSIST

To summarize, as we navigate the intricate world of empathy and its various forms, it's essential to address the concept of performative empathy and its connection to narcissism. Narcissists often use performative empathy as a facade to present themselves as the "nice guy" or the caring individual, but beneath the surface lies a more manipulative agenda. Understanding the three primary types of empathy—cognitive, emotional, and compassionate empathy—will provide us with a comprehensive view of genuine empathy and how it differs from the superficial displays often exhibited by narcissists or other highly toxic individuals. By exploring these different empathic qualities, we can gain valuable insights into the emotional dynamics at play in relationships involving narcissists.

Now, we'll tie this all together by delving deeper into the "nice guy" narcissist, uncovering the traits and behaviors that characterize this specific type of narcissism. This is the guy that's most concern about looking good versus genuinely being good. By understanding the tactics used by "nice guy" narcissists (also known as The Covert Narcissist) to manipulate and control their interactions, we can equip ourselves with the knowledge needed to recognize and navigate these relationships more effectively.

Identifying a "nice narcissist" can be challenging because they often possess certain characteristics that make them appear kind and charming to those outside of their inner circle. Here are seven characteristics that can contribute to this perception, making it difficult to recognize their abusive behavior towards those close to them [39] :

1. **Confident and Assertive:** They exude confidence and assertiveness, which can be mistaken for strength and leadership.
2. **Generosity and Gifting:** They might be generous with gifts or favors, which can create a sense of indebtedness in others.
3. **Surface Empathy:** They can display empathy, especially when it benefits them or maintains their positive image.
4. **Good First Impressions:** They excel at making a positive first impression, making it difficult for others to see through their facade. They are adept at social situations, which can create the illusion of a caring and considerate individual.
5. **Manipulative:** They use manipulation tactics to control and exploit others, while keeping it well hidden from the outside world.
6. **Selective Kindness:** They may be selectively kind, only showing kindness when they believe it will be beneficial for them.
7. **Playing the Victim:** They may twist situations to portray themselves as the victim, garnering sympathy and deflecting attention from their abusive behavior.

One of the most heartrending experiences for me to comprehend initially was the gift-giving disguised as an expression of love. My former partner's emotional disconnection led him to resort to extravagant presents and trips as a way to compensate for the emotions he struggled to express. "If I didn't love you, why would I be with you? I am physically present, right? Look, I got you this gift, and I took you on that trip." These were his attempts to tangibly validate his love, while struggling to consistently show it emotionally. And let me tell you, as I healed I realized the grandiose trips were not worth the trauma. Looking at it through a trauma informed lens, I realized that someone's mere physical presence cannot replace the emotional connection that is essential for nurturing a safe and loving relationship. That's why, when a narcissist attempts to apologize or express their love, they would rather offer material items, trips, or a special date night, rather than engage the effort in the one thing you truly long for - providing an emotionally safe and reciprocal relationship. There's an important nuance between someone who can't show up for you and someone who refuses to show up for you. In the case of loving a highly toxic individual, their intentional resistance conveys their conscious unwillingness to do either.

The visible gifts and trips he provided only enabled his facade as those around us genuinely thought we were happy. Because of his relatively public presence, I was highly protective over him and our relationship. I would never dream of allowing anyone to believe otherwise. However, in his presence I discovered my absence. The silence was so loud that it filled the space that my existence would have occupied if my soul believed she were worthy of being safely seen, heard and understood. The crazy thing is, abuse will enable survivors to believe that shutting down is safer than being shamed. In my case, playing along and eating my feelings was easier than accepting our inevitable fate and my current reality - that we were never meant to be and I was in an abusive relationship. Unhealed trauma will enable us to tolerate abusive behavior for fear of losing those we love. However, a healthy relationship will not never enable you to lose yourself in order to keep the other person. A quote that kept me sane during my healing journey was "When you realize none of it was real, you can set yourself free." It was so confusing to have the same person that tells you they love you, acting in hateful ways. The person that pretended to be my biggest supporter and protective savior turned out to also be my biggest oppressor. As I realized none of it was real, I was able to set myself free.

Profiling A Narcissist

NUANCES OF NARCISSISM

NICE GUY SYNDROME

Here'e the thing, a nice narcissist is more than the "nice guy" with an anger issue. It's predatory, premeditated grooming to convince their victims when that they are safe when they are not. The terms "nice guy" and "good guy" are often used to describe men, but they carry different connotations and implications.

The term "nice guy" is often used to describe someone who presents themselves as kind, polite, and well-mannered. However, in some contexts, it has taken on a negative meaning due to certain behavior patterns associated with it. A "nice guy" may be overly passive, seeking validation from others through excessive people-pleasing, or being selectively nice as a means to gain something in return, particularly in romantic relationships. This behavior can come across as insincere, manipulative, or lacking authenticity.

A "good guy," on the other hand, refers to someone who genuinely exhibits positive qualities and treats others with respect and kindness. Unlike the negative implications of a "nice guy," a "good guy" acts with integrity, empathy, and consideration for others without expecting anything in return. An important nuance is that a "good guy" does not allow circumstances to alter his character and consistently operates from a place of selfless compassion. This is not the case for "nice guys". Being a "good guy" involves authentic care for others and an ability to establish healthy boundaries in relationships.

In the self-help book, "No More Mr. Nice Guy" written by Dr. Robert A. Glover, he focuses on addressing the phenomenon of the "Nice Guy Syndrome" and offers insights and practical advice to men who struggle with it. The book "No More Mr. Nice Guy" explores the concept of the "Nice Guy Syndrome," which refers to men who exhibit overly agreeable and people-pleasing behaviors in an attempt to gain approval and avoid conflict. [40] Dr. Robert Glover argues that many men with this syndrome believe that being nice and accommodating will lead to love, success, and happiness, but it often has the opposite effect. Dr. Glover identifies various patterns and traits associated with the Nice Guy Syndrome, such as:

1. **Seeking Validation:** Nice Guys tend to seek validation and approval from others to feel good about themselves, often neglecting their own needs and desires.
2. **Avoiding Conflict:** They avoid confrontation and assertiveness, fearing that it will lead to rejection or abandonment.
3. **Covert Contracts:** Nice Guys often engage in covert contracts, expecting that if they are "nice" to others, they will receive reciprocation or reward in return.
4. **Emotional Dishonesty:** They may suppress their true emotions, believing that expressing vulnerability or anger will make them undesirable.

Emotional dishonesty enables covert contracts. Covert contracts are a concept often associated with the "Nice Guy Syndrome," where individuals make unspoken or hidden agreements with themselves or others, expecting certain behaviors or outcomes in return for their actions. [41] In the context of relationships, covert contracts can be manipulative and lead to disappointment, frustration, and resentment. When Nice Narcissists are faced with criticism or questions about their behavior, they quickly put on their victim hat. It's their defense mechanism.

By playing the victim, they get sympathy, dodge accountability, and manipulate others into feeling sorry for them.
A Covert Narcissist with Nice Guy Syndrome loves to take advantage of a person's nurturing side, pulling off the victim card to get even more support and deflect blame or criticism.

Profiling A Narcissist

NUANCES OF NARCISSISM

Here's how narcissists may use covert contracts against their victims:

- **Manipulative Expectations:** Narcissists may create unspoken agreements with their victims, expecting them to constantly cater to their needs, provide admiration, or fulfill their desires without ever expressing these expectations clearly. The victim might feel pressured to fulfill these covert contracts, not knowing that they exist. Manipulation has more to do with the other person and their inability to meet their own needs in a healthy way.

- **Emotional Blackmail:** Narcissists may use covert contracts to emotionally manipulate their victims. They may hint at what they want without explicitly stating it, leaving the victim to guess and feel responsible for meeting these unspoken expectations. When the victim fails to fulfill these hidden desires, the narcissist may guilt-trip or emotionally punish them.

- **Fueling Dependency:** By creating covert contracts, narcissists can foster dependency in their victims. The victims might feel obligated to meet the narcissist's expectations to maintain the relationship, fearing the consequences of not complying.

- **Maintaining Control:** Covert contracts allow narcissists to maintain control over their victims while avoiding direct communication about their desires and needs. This lack of transparency can keep the victim off balance and uncertain about the narcissist's intentions.

- **Avoiding Accountability:** Narcissists may use covert contracts as a way to avoid taking responsibility for their actions or expressing their true intentions. They can shift blame onto the victim when their expectations are not met, making the victim feel at fault for the relationship's problems.

As we know, trust is the cornerstone that allows individuals to feel safe and secure in sharing their vulnerabilities, thoughts, and emotions. It's the confidence that your partner will hold your feelings with care and treat them with respect. When past traumas are projected onto the present relationship, trust can be eroded. One might become excessively wary or even suspicious, assuming negative intentions from the partner based on experiences from the past. This projection can undermine the potential for the current relationship to flourish, as it becomes overshadowed by the shadows of past wounds.

Respect is also key to acknowledging each other's autonomy, boundaries, and individuality. In a healthy relationship, partners honor and value each other's opinions, decisions, and feelings. When past traumas are projected, there is a risk of imposing unfair expectations, demands, or judgments onto their partner. One might inadvertently seek validation or reparation for past hurts by trying to control the partner's actions or responses. This not only hinders personal growth and autonomy but also fractures the genuine respect that should form the core of a strong relationship. Those who struggle to trust others, will attempt to control them with criticism and contempt. And those who fear vulnerability are committed to enabling toxicity in their relationships.

In essence, covert contracts enable narcissists to manipulate their victims by leveraging unspoken agreements and hidden expectations. Victims may find themselves trapped in a cycle of trying to fulfill these unclear demands, leading to a loss of personal boundaries, emotional exhaustion, and an overall unhealthy dynamic in the relationship. Recognizing covert contracts is essential for victims of narcissistic abuse.

Profiling A Narcissist

NUANCES OF NARCISSISM

As we continue our exploration of narcissism and its impact on relationships, it's essential to understand empathy and its various forms. Empathy is a powerful force that shapes our connections with others. As we now know, there are three primary types of empathy: cognitive, emotional, and compassionate empathy. Additionally, we dabbled into dark empathy, which is a concept closely linked to the dark triad personality traits and how that can be weaponized as they portray the facade of the "nice guy". By examining these aspects, we can gain a deeper understanding of how empathy plays a role in both healthy and toxic relationships, shedding light on the complexities of human behavior and emotional dynamics. So, let's now shift our focus to the interplay between dark empathy and the dark triad traits to uncover more about the intricacies of narcissistic behavior and its impact on those around them.

The Dark Triad - It sounds like something straight out of a superhero movie, but it's actually a psychological concept. The Dark Triad refers to three personality traits: Narcissism, Machiavellianism, and Psychopathy. [42]

These traits are not your typical "rainbows and unicorns" kind of qualities. They involve some pretty concerning characteristics that you'd want to be aware of to avoid getting entangled with these types of individuals.

First up, we have narcissism. Narcissists, as we know, have an inflated sense of self-importance, a constant need for admiration, and a lack of empathy. They're all about themselves, and they'll often manipulate others to serve their own agenda. Look out for those who constantly seek attention, belittle others, and lack genuine empathy.

Next, we have Machiavellianism. Machiavellian individuals are all about manipulation and cunning. They're skilled at using deceit and manipulation to achieve their goals. They have a "ends justify the means" mindset, so they'll do whatever it takes to get what they want, even if it means stepping on others. Keep an eye out for those who are excessively manipulative, deceitful, and lack moral principles.

Last but not least, we have psychopathy. Now, this is where things get really intense. Psychopaths have a complete disregard for the rights and feelings of others. They lack remorse and empathy, and they're often impulsive and prone to thrill-seeking behavior. They're like the "Jokers" of the world, minus the clown makeup. Watch out for those who display a lack of remorse or empathy, engage in impulsive and reckless behavior, and show little regard for the well-being of others.

So, what demographic makes up the Dark Triad? Well, the Dark Triad traits can be found in people from various backgrounds and demographics. It's not limited to a specific group or age range. These traits can manifest in anyone, regardless of gender, race, or profession. However, it's important to note that not everyone who displays some of these traits is a full-blown Dark Triad individual. It's more about the intensity and combination of these traits that define the Dark Triad.

To avoid getting into relationships with Dark Triad personalities, it's crucial to keep an eye out for red flags. Look for signs of extreme self-centeredness, manipulative behavior, lack of empathy, and a disregard for the well-being of others. If someone consistently exhibits these traits, it's a clear warning sign to steer clear and protect yourself. Stay aware, trust your instincts, and surround yourself with people who value and respect you for who you are. Once caught in these vicious relationship dynamics, it can be extremely difficult to find your way out of them. I deeply encourage you to take inventory of the health of your relationships and do not allow love to be the reason you tolerate abusive behavior. Because love doesn't hurt; it's the only thing that heals. This personality type has the desire to do anything but that.

Profiling A Narcissist

NUANCES OF NARCISSISM

Q&A

DO NARCISSIST KNOW THEY ARE A NARCISSISTS?

Narcissists have a personality disorder that makes them think that they don't have a personality disorder. Most narcissists would rate themselves high on having narcissistic traits. However, narcissists lack self awareness and are deeply are shame-avoidant. Therefore seeking professional help to confirm such diagnosis is perceived as counter intuitive to their social facade and survival. This often times perpetuates their problems versus alleviates them.They are masters at making positive first impressions that deteriorate over time. This is why they often times engage in short-term, superficial relationships that feed their insatiable desire for attention and admiration. If left unresolved, they can experience greater relationship difficulties, anxiety, depression, substance abuse or even other personality disorders. To cover their shame, they may engage in other-destructive behaviors such as: Manipulation, lack of empathy, blame shifting, gaslighting, cheating, compulsive lying, criticism and the transactional/covert exploitation of others.

The problem here is the defense mechanisms that keeps one safe cannot be destructive to others. Childhood environment, genetics and neurobiological factors impact this particular personality disorder. If they do seek treatment, it's more likely to be for symptoms of depression, drug or alcohol misuse, or other mental health problems. Because this is a shame-based personality disorder, it cannot be healed through condemnation. But rather, compassion - But like, with boundaries.

However, that is not an invitation to heal someone at the expense of allow them hurting you. One can only heal what they are ready to acknowledge and reveal - not what they choose to conceal. Shadow work provides the introspection needed to integrate their darkness to light.

The reason why it's important to not label everyone you meet as a "Narcissist" is because (1) these judgements can be made prematurely and haphazardly. This new buzz word can become diluted in severity if we toss the label onto everyone that is mean to us or hurts our feelings. Narcissistic tendencies exist on a spectrum of severity and consistency. (2) there are multiple personality disorders that can be confused as Narcissism but are not. Such personality disorders include:

-4 Personality Disorders Confused For Narcissism [43]

1. Borderline Personality Disorder (BPD): Individuals with BPD often struggle with unstable self-image, intense emotions, and difficulties with interpersonal relationships. They may exhibit attention-seeking behaviors and have a fear of abandonment, which can sometimes resemble narcissistic traits.
2. Histrionic Personality Disorder (HPD): People with HPD tend to seek attention and validation, have a strong desire to be the center of attention, and may exhibit dramatic or theatrical behavior. While there can be some overlap with narcissistic traits, HPD is characterized by a pattern of excessive emotionality and attention-seeking beyond just self-centeredness.
3. Antisocial Personality Disorder (ASPD): ASPD is commonly associated with a lack of empathy, disregard for others' rights, and a tendency to exploit or manipulate others for personal gain. Some individuals with ASPD may display narcissistic traits, such as a sense of entitlement, but their behavior is typically more focused on breaking societal norms and disregarding rules.
4. Obsessive-Compulsive Personality Disorder (OCPD): People with OCPD often exhibit perfectionistic tendencies, rigid adherence to rules, and a strong need for control. While there can be some overlap with narcissistic traits, OCPD is more focused on maintaining order and control rather than seeking constant admiration or attention.

Profiling A Narcissist

NUANCES OF NARCISSISM

- Abusers don't abuse everyone
- Abusers don't abuse 100% of the time
- Chronic emotional abuse can be just as damaging as physical abuse. Not all abuse leaves a visible mark
- Those who mistreat others and avoid communication are not setting a boundary - they avoiding accountability and responsibility. Yes, they do know what they are doing. They just don't care.
- Abuse and neglect isn't just about the things they explicitly do - but also the things they implicitly don't do (like provide allyship, thoughtfulness, interest and warmth)
- Blame Shifting: When they will blame you for your reaction versus their actions that caused your reaction
- The more chances you give them, the less they will respect you
- If it forces you to abandon yourself in order to maintain it, it is not love
- You can't have a healthy relationship with someone who doesn't see an issue with their unhealthy patterns
- There's a difference between a mistake and a pattern
- Every-time you lower your frequency to meet someone on their level, you will end up paying for it
- The red flags that you ignore in the beginning will be the reason the relationship ends
- If they put you through difficult times or left you during difficult times, they are not the one
- Just because a person does not know how to control themselves, does not mean you are not good enough
- Attention is not the same as attunement. Attachment is not the same as love. Physical presence is not the same as emotional presence. and the bare minimum is not the same as effort.
- Actions not matching words is abuse
- Lying by omission is still lying as it creates a manipulation tactic known as plausible deniability that allows them to avoid taking responsibility
- Love isn't a reason to tolerate disrespect. Unconditional love is not synonymous with unconditional tolerance.
- Love is never deceitful or toxic. It will empower you to be more of you, not less of you.
- You can leave a toxic relationship but if you don't heal what attracted you to them in the first place, you will repeat the same pattern with a new partner
- Love doesn't require suppression or self sacrifice
- Be aware of those who guilt you into obligation with "If you loved me you do _____" statements
- Be mindful of when the ratio of emotional giving and receiving feels off. Emotional reciprocity is a crucial nuance to take into consideration as those with high narcissistic tendencies tend to be emotional vampires. If they are consistently inconsistent in this area, this is a red flag.
- One sided conversations, support, validation or admiration is a telltale sign that something is off. This does not mean the person is a narcissist, however, their lack so social awareness and emotional reciprocity is an indicator of a frustration that will continue to arise down the road.
- You cannot heal in the same environment that continues to hurt you.
- Your immediate environment is more likely to change you, than you are likely to change it.
- Unhealed relationship wounds can enable our toxic patterns to be disguised as our relational preferences

As I healed from my own wounds, I had to learn how to regain confidence, nurture healthy relationships and call in conscious partnership in a way that felt authentic and aligned. This is why I created the **Masterclass : From Chaser to Chooser** that can be found at www.imanimvmt.com to support those moving out of survival mode, to thriving mode. As we heal and grow, we will no longer chase love to prove our self worth. Instead we will be empowered to choose it from a place of honoring it.

CHECK FOR UNDERSTANDING

Summary of Main Objectives

-Narcissists have brain abnormalities in the thinking and reasoning part of their brain involved in generating compassion for others. Due to nature and nurture experiences in their life, their brain's compassion department never fully developed.

-Narcissistic traits exist on a spectrum and is one of the three personality types associated with The Dark Triad

-This personality disorder is skilled at manipulation and creating a facade of empathy that is disarming to their victims with the intention of exploiting them

- When reflecting on your experience in a narcissistic relationship, what red flags or warning signs did you overlook or dismiss? How do you think these overlooked red flags impacted the dynamics of the relationship and your well-being? Write your answer in the space below.

_____

_____

_____

_____

_____

_____

_____

_____

_____

_____

_____

_____

_____

_____

_____

reflection

CHECK FOR UNDERSTANDING

Consider the reasons why you may have overlooked certain red flags in the narcissistic relationship. What underlying beliefs, desires, or fears might have influenced your ability to recognize and respond to these warning signs? How can understanding these factors empower you to be more vigilant in future relationships?

Write your answer in the space below.

_____
_____
_____
_____
_____
_____
_____
_____
_____
_____
_____
_____
_____
_____
_____
_____
_____
_____

reflection

CHECK FOR UNDERSTANDING

Reflecting on the lessons learned from the narcissistic relationship, what insights have you gained about the importance of trust in your own intuition and the value of honoring your boundaries? How can you cultivate a stronger sense of self-awareness and self-trust to ensure that red flags are not ignored or dismissed in future relationships?

Write your answer in the space below.

_____

_____

_____

_____

_____

_____

_____

_____

_____

_____

_____

_____

_____

_____

_____

_____

reflection

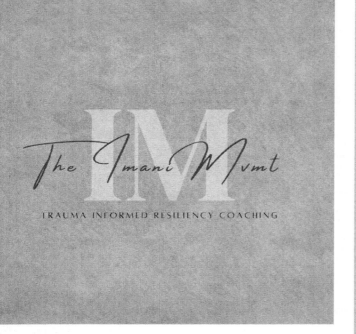

The Imani Mvmt

TRAUMA INFORMED RESILIENCY COACHING

02

Healing The Collective One Individual At A Time

Narcissistic Abuse Cycle

PART 2 OF 3

3 Key Objectives

1)Understanding the Narcissistic Abuse Cycle

2)Emotional Abuse Tactics

3)Strategies to Protect Yourself

INTENTIONS

How did the dynamics of the narcissistic relationship affect your perception of reality and your ability to trust yourself? In what ways do you see these effects manifesting in your current fears, beliefs and behaviors? What does healing look like for you in this next chapter?

Write your answer in the space below.

_____

_____

_____

_____

_____

_____

_____

_____

_____

_____

_____

_____

_____

_____

_____

_____

_____

_____

Remember, reflection is a powerful tool for gaining insight and promoting growth. Give yourself permission to explore your experiences with compassion and curiosity. By delving into these questions, you can deepen your understanding of the impact of the narcissistic relationship and pave the way for healing, growth, and the creation of healthier relationships in the future.

Narcissistic Abuse Cycle

Welcome to the next section of our journey together on navigating narcissism! In this section, we will be delving into a crucial topic: the narcissistic cycle of abuse. Understanding this cycle is essential for protecting ourselves and others from the harmful effects of narcissistic behavior.

The narcissistic cycle of abuse is a repetitive pattern that narcissists often employ in their relationships to maintain control and power over their victims. It involves various phases, each with distinct characteristics and emotional impacts. By learning about this cycle, we can gain valuable insights into how narcissists operate and recognize the warning signs early on.

In this section, we will explore each phase of the narcissistic cycle of abuse, from the idealization and love bombing stage to the devaluation and discard phases. [44] By understanding the tactics used by narcissists during each stage, we can empower ourselves to protect our emotional well-being and set healthy boundaries.

Throughout this journey, we will also focus on effective strategies for safeguarding ourselves against the manipulative tactics of narcissists. Knowledge is power, and by arming ourselves with the information presented in this section, we can cultivate resilience and navigate these challenging relationships more confidently.

So, let's dive into the intricacies of the narcissistic cycle of abuse, gain a deeper understanding of its impact, and equip ourselves with the tools to shield our hearts and minds from its destructive effects. Together, we will emerge stronger and more empowered on our path towards growing and healing.

- **To begin, there's Idealization:** At the beginning, the narcissist sweeps you off your feet. They shower you with love, attention, and admiration. They make you feel like you're the most special person in the world. It's all roses and rainbows, and you feel on top of the world. Lots of love bombing and future faking during this honeymoon period.

- **Next up, we have Devaluation:** Hold on tight because the tables can turn quickly. The narcissist starts to devalue you. They criticize, belittle, and undermine you. It's as if nothing you do is ever good enough. They might even try to control or manipulate you. It's confusing and hurtful. You feel like you're walking on eggshells, desperately trying to please them. You can expect trauma bonds, moving of goal posts, testing behaviors, gaslighting and triangulation here.

- **Woof. As if that's not enough; cue the Discard:** Just when you're at your lowest point, the narcissist might discard you. They abruptly end the relationship or withdraw emotionally. It's like they flip a switch, and you're left feeling abandoned and broken. They may move on to someone else without a second thought. The discard leaves you questioning your worth and feeling utterly devastated. Silent treatment, narcissistic rage, shame and distain is the name of their game.

- **Last, but not least, there is Narcissistic Hoovering:** This refers to a manipulative tactic used by narcissists to draw their previous victims back into a relationship or dynamic after a period of separation or discard. The term "hoovering" is derived from the Hoover vacuum cleaner, symbolizing the narcissist's attempt to suck their target back into their influence. Lots of fake attempts to reconcile, breadcrumbing, overlapping relationships and monkey barring.

But here's the tricky part: the cycle repeats itself. After the discard, the narcissist may come back into your life, repeating the idealization phase, only to eventually devalue and discard you again. It's a never-ending loop that can leave you feeling trapped, confused, and emotionally drained.

In my former relationship, I was unfortunate enough to go through this cycle three times in two years. Oops. I suppose third times a charm! This painful experience is something I would not wish onto anyone. However, it did provide so many valuable insights that I may not have been able to comprehend otherwise. Especially now, as a Trauma Informed Resiliency Coach. When supporting my clients, I can now educate them on the abuse cycle as we work together to pull them out of it. My work doesn't solely include narcissism recovery. In fact, it is only a very small part of it. However, my experience *and* education allows me to provide a unique perspective that enables me to create an environment where my clients feel safe and supported.

In the visual below, we highlight some of the key phases of the Narcissistic Abuse Cycle. This cycle is relatively textbook and therefore highly predictable in nature. That said, the more you understand the nuances of narcissism, the better equipped you will be to protect yourself against it.

The Narcissistic Abuse Cycle [45]

Devaluation

Gaslighting, silent treatment, covert verbal/physical abuse, trauma bonding, testing behaviors, unrealistic expectations, moving goal posts

Love Bombing

Honeymoon / Future Faking

Idealization

Soul Mate Effect / "Twin Flame"

The Cycle Continues

But only if you let it . . .
Release the need to explain
yourself/approval, Gray Rock, set
boundaries

Triangulation

Cheating, competing,
defamation of character,
controlling the narrative

Discard

Breakup, silent treatment,
invalidating behaviors, humiliation,
confusing
narcissistic rage, punishing

Hoovering

Simulating fake attempt to reconcile, narcissistic injury, breadcrumbing

Recognizing the narcissistic abuse cycle is the first step to breaking free from this destructive pattern. It's crucial to prioritize your own well-being, establish boundaries, and seek support from trusted friends, family, or professionals who can help you navigate the challenges of healing and recovery. Remember, you deserve a healthy and loving relationship, free from manipulation and abuse. I'll navigate you through all of confusion in the pages that follow.

Narcissistic Abuse Cycle

IDEALIZATION

UNICORN SYNDROME

Now that we have explored the intricacies of the narcissistic cycle of abuse, we are ready to dive into another fascinating aspect of narcissism: the Narcissistic Unicorn Syndrome. This unique syndrome sheds light on a specific behavior pattern exhibited by some narcissists that can be both perplexing and challenging to navigate. The Narcissistic Unicorn Syndrome refers to the unrealistic and grandiose self-image that certain narcissists harbor about themselves. [46] They see themselves as extraordinary, unique, and above others, making them believe they are somehow "special" and exempt from the usual rules and consequences that apply to everyone else. Not only do they think they are the center of their Universe, they think they are the center of your Universe as well. Delulu, I know.

This term also refers to the belief that there is a mythical, magical solution or person out there who will come and rescue us from our pain and provide us with the perfect love and happiness we've been searching for. It can also refer to our own idealogical belief that we can be the ones to heal them or that we are "special" enough to get them to change. When we overlook their pattern of behavior, we can trick ourselves into believing that they will never do to us, what they have done to others. Breaking this illusion for myself felt like an ego death as the healer in me struggled to believe that I couldn't save the person I loved from himself.

Overtime, I learned that "You cannot save someone who is unwilling to participate in their own rescue." This was a quote I learned from Vienna Pharaon, LMFT. The pain of this realization made me feel devastatingly helpless as the person I loved did everything in his power to push away my help. In fact, overtime it was the very thing he grew to resent me for. In the context of narcissistic relationships, unicorn syndrome can keep individuals trapped in a cycle of trauma bonding when we overlook a toxic person's external value (money, status, physical appearance) at the expense of their internal health (emotional maturity, respect and reciprocity). This gets a little tricky when your attraction to them outweighs your intuition about them. In my case, my unhealed father wounds projected the notion that if I could help him to heal, he could become the man I needed him to be. The parts of myself that I was not yet ready to heal, were the parts of him I was trying to fix. This was codependency at it's finest. I healed the moment I started to love myself more than my inner child's desire to be loved by him.

In this upcoming section, we will delve into the characteristics and behaviors associated with the Narcissistic Unicorn Syndrome, as well as its implications in relationships and daily interactions. By understanding this syndrome, we can gain valuable insights into how narcissists perceive themselves and how it affects their interactions with others. Let's explore this intriguing facet of narcissism and discover how it relates to the overall understanding of narcissistic behavior. By developing a comprehensive view of narcissistic tendencies, we can better equip ourselves to recognize and navigate these challenging dynamics with compassion and awareness. Here's how it works:

1. **Idealization**: At the beginning of a narcissistic relationship, the narcissist often presents themselves as the "unicorn" - charming, attentive, and seemingly perfect. They shower their partner with love and affection, creating an illusion of a fairy-tale romance.
2. **Devaluation**: As time goes on, the narcissist's true colors start to emerge. They may engage in manipulative tactics, emotional abuse, and devalue their partner. However, the trauma-bonded individual clings to the initial idealized image, desperately hoping for the return of that magical love they once believed in.
3. **Fading Magic**: Despite the red flags and mistreatment, the trauma-bonded individual continues to hold onto the belief that the narcissist will change, going back to the idealized version they fell in love with. This hope keeps them locked in the toxic relationship, even though it causes immense emotional pain. Woofers, this one definitely leaves a mark.
4. **Self-Blame and Excuses:** Unicorn syndrome often leads the trauma-bonded person to blame themselves for the narcissist's behavior. They may make excuses for the narcissist's actions, convincing themselves that if they just love harder or do things differently, the magic will return.
5. **Breaking the Cycle:** Recognizing and addressing unicorn syndrome is essential for breaking free from the trauma bond. It involves acknowledging that the mythical perfect love doesn't exist and understanding that the only way to heal is by prioritizing one's own well-being.

Overcoming unicorn syndrome requires self-compassion. It involves shifting the focus from external solutions to internal healing, learning to love and validate oneself, and establishing healthy boundaries in relationships. Let's reflect more on this in the following pages!

Narcissistic Abuse Cycle

IDEALIZATION

UNICORN SYNDROME

IN LIGHT OF OUR EXPLORATION OF NARCISSISM AND THE INTRIGUING CONCEPT OF NARCISSISTIC UNICORN SYNDROME, I INVITE YOU TO REFLECT ON THE FOLLOWING:

HOW DOES GAINING AWARENESS OF THE NARCISSISTIC UNICORN SYNDROME AND ITS GRANDIOSE SELF-IMAGE IMPACT YOUR UNDERSTANDING OF NARCISSISTIC BEHAVIOR AND THE COMPLEXITIES THAT SURROUND IT? HOW MIGHT THIS NEWFOUND KNOWLEDGE HELP YOU NAVIGATE CHALLENGING INTERACTIONS WITH INDIVIDUALS WHO EXHIBIT THESE TRAITS, AND WHAT INSIGHTS HAVE YOU GAINED ABOUT MAINTAINING HEALTHY BOUNDARIES WHILE ENGAGING WITH THEM?

Narcissistic Abuse Cycle

IDEALIZATION

LOVE BOMBING & LIMERENCE

Alright, now that we've explored narcissism and unicorn syndrome, let's delve into another crucial aspect of understanding narcissistic abuse: love bombing. Love bombing might sound like something out of a romantic movie, but it's actually a manipulative tactic used by narcissists to draw people into their web of abuse. Love bombing is like the gateway to the narcissistic abuse cycle. It's when the narcissist goes all out showering their target with affection, attention, and affectionate gestures. A lot of narcissists hate themselves and lack identity, which is why they mirror everything you like, to be who you like in order to reel you in and manipulate you. They make you feel like you're on cloud nine, like you've found your soulmate. It's overwhelming, intense, and oh-so-hard to resist. But here's the catch: love bombing is not genuine love. It's a carefully crafted facade designed to hook you in. Once they've got you wrapped around their finger, the narcissistic abuse cycle begins, and things can take a dark turn. That's why it's essential to recognize love bombing for what it is – a manipulative tactic to gain control and power over you. [47] Understanding this can help us protect ourselves from falling into the trap and getting entangled in a toxic relationship.

So Picture this: You meet someone new, and they come into your life with an overwhelming flood of affection, attention, and compliments. It feels like you've found your soulmate, and everything is perfect. This intense showering of love and adoration is what we call love bombing. Now, love bombing might initially seem like a dream come true. Who wouldn't want to be swept off their feet and feel absolutely cherished? Love bombing works by rapidly establishing a deep emotional connection, often with excessive displays of affection, gifts, trips and flattery. The aim is to create an intense bond and gain control over your emotions and decisions.

Studies show it takes about 6 months to determine if the person you dating is marriage material or not. [48] That said, the first 6 months of deeply observing how a relationship begins is crucial as the narcissistic mask doesn't stay on forever. This comes with its own unique challenges though as love bombing tugs at our deepest wounds and needs for attachment, validation and connection.

However, beneath the surface, just remember there is always hidden agenda. The manipulative nature of love bombing becomes evident when you realize that it's not genuine love and care that motivates the person, but a desire for power and control. They use love bombing as a tool to disarm you, weaken your boundaries, and gain influence over your thoughts and actions. It can feel a lot like love but its limerence.

Limerence is a state of intense infatuation or obsession with another person. [49] It involves strong feelings of attraction, desire, and a heightened focus on the person of interest. Limerence can be all-consuming, leading individuals to think constantly about the other person, experience euphoria when in their presence, and become preoccupied with the idea of being with them. It often leads to a strong desire for reciprocation and validation from the object of affection.

On the other hand, love is a more complex and enduring emotion that involves genuine care, trust, and mutual respect. Love is built on a foundation of understanding, compassion, and a deep emotional connection. Unlike limerence, love evolves over time and involves a deeper emotional bond with the person, where both partners truly know and accept each other's strengths and flaws.

Narcissists use love bombing during the initial phase of a relationship to create an illusion of intense love and affection. Remember, intense sexual chemistry alone is not supplemental for long term relational compatibility.

Narcissistic Abuse Cycle

IDEALIZATION

LOVE BOMBING & LIMERENCE

Physical intimacy is one of the many ways they attempt to suck you in through love bombing and limerence. Their lack of emotional connection will enable them to seek validation in the form of physical connection. As they shower their target with excessive compliments, gifts, attention, and affection to make them feel special and cherished. This intense display of love and attention can be overwhelming and make the person feel like they've found their perfect match. During love bombing, the narcissist becomes an expert at mirroring the target's desires, preferences, and values. They might pretend to share the same interests and dreams, making the target believe they've found someone who truly understands and connects with them. This creates a sense of euphoria and dependency.

However, once the target is fully invested in the relationship, the love bombing phase gradually diminishes, and the true nature of the narcissistic abuse cycle begins, involving manipulation, gaslighting, and emotional harm.

By bombarding you with affection and attention, they create a sense of dependency and attachment. It becomes harder to see their true intentions or notice any red flags that may arise later on. This manipulation can leave you feeling emotionally invested and trapped in a dynamic that revolves around the needs and desires of the love bomber. Remember, only those who feel powerless crave power. Only those who feel weak need to break down others in order to feel strong.

This is why they utilize these manipulation tactics - so they can get what they want without you realizing it. In many ways, they will use this disarming tactic to make you think that saying "yes" to crossing your own boundaries was your idea. For example, a narcissist may love bomb you in order to create a safe enough space for you to become vulnerable in your relationship. They may over extend with grandiose dinners or trips or "acts of service" only to make you feel indebted to them later on as their requests of you lead to more self abandonment. Here, they are grooming you so they can eventually guilt you into blind compliance and obligation in the future.

It's important to remember that love bombing is not a healthy or sustainable foundation for a genuine and loving relationship. True love involves mutual respect, trust, and the development of a connection based on authenticity and shared values. Love bombing, on the other hand, is a manipulative tactic that seeks to control and exploit your emotions. Trust your intuition, establish healthy boundaries, and seek support. It's crucial to stay grounded, take things slow, and maintain healthy boundaries in the early stages of a relationship to ensure genuine love and connection can develop, free from manipulation and abuse.

Remember, genuine love blossoms naturally over time, and it is built on a foundation of trust, respect, and shared experiences. I understand the excitement of finding a new love and wanting to rush into it hopeful and with little to no reservations. An affirmation that helped me to take things slowly is, "If it's meant to last forever, we have the rest of our lives." In other words, if it's meant to last forever, there's no need to rush a relationship as we have nothing but time.

During peak moments of the honeymoon phase, I recall wanting to be around my former partner 24/7. I would willingly lose my sense of self by betraying my own boundaries and prioritizing our relationship over my personal goals and wellbeing. In a very codependent stage of my life, I was engulfed by his larger than life personality that provided an exhilarating sense of adventure and escapism. This made saying "yes" to him easy and enticing. As we quickly built our life together and slowly watched it implode, I realized one of the biggest nuances in our relationship dynamic was found in the way he offered me a beautiful house - while I wanted nothing more than to offer the man I deeply loved a safe and nurturing home. Our goals were in alignment, however, our intentions were not.

Narcissistic Abuse Cycle

IDEALIZATION

LOVE BOMBING & LIMERENCE

REFLECTING ON WHAT YOU NOW KNOW ABOUT THE DIFFERENCE BETWEEN LOVE AND LIMERENCE, IN WHAT WAYS DID THE NARCISSIST OR HIGHLY TOXIC PERSON IN YOUR LIFE FULFILL CERTAIN EMOTIONAL NEEDS OR DESIRES IN THE BEGINNING OF THE RELATIONSHIP? EXPLORE THE ASPECTS OF THE CONNECTION THAT PROVIDED A SENSE OF VALIDATION, EXCITEMENT, OR COMFORT.

Narcissistic Abuse Cycle

IDEALIZATION

LOVE BOMBING & LIMERENCE

LOOKING BACK, WERE THERE ANY RED FLAGS OR SUBTLE SIGNS THAT YOU MIGHT HAVE OVERLOOKED DURING THE EARLY STAGES OF THE RELATIONSHIP? CONSIDER THE DYNAMICS AND INTERACTIONS THAT, IN HINDSIGHT, MAY HAVE HINTED AT POTENTIAL ISSUES WITH THE PERSON'S BEHAVIOR OR CHARACTER. REMEMBER, EXPLORING THESE QUESTIONS FROM A TRAUMA-INFORMED PERSPECTIVE ALLOWS FOR DEEPER SELF-AWARENESS AND CAN EMPOWER YOU TO MAKE HEALTHIER CHOICES IN FUTURE RELATIONSHIPS. UNDERSTANDING YOUR INITIAL ATTRACTION CAN HELP YOU BUILD RESILIENCE AND AVOID PATTERNS THAT MAY LEAD TO HARMFUL DYNAMICS.

Narcissistic Abuse Cycle

IDEALIZATION

TRAUMA BONDS

Tying this all together is one of my favorite quotes: "Love doesn't die a natural death. Love has to be killed, either by neglect or narcissism" by Frank Salvato. Often times, relationships do not end due to a lack of love. But rather, they end due to a lack of connection, safety or neglect. If I am being honest, till this day I never stopped loving him. I just stopped trusting him. Leaving him forced an excruciating period of sadness where I grieved not only our past but a future together we would never have. We were attached by fantasy bonds that allowed us to relish in the illusion of the limerence we once called loved. But I knew I loved him. I saw right through his mask and wanted to love all the parts and pieces of him that he hated so much. Behind his tough exterior was the sweetest, gentlest labor-doodle of a man I had ever met. A gentle giant he was. A side of him only I was allowed to see. And what a beautiful privilege it was. In our best moments, I would hold him in my arms while he fell asleep to head scratches after a long day at work. I loved loving him and miss it very much.

However, loving someone who carries a deep sense of unhealed worthiness wounds can be a heart-wrenching experience fraught with challenges and complexities. Witnessing the person you care about struggle with self-doubt and feelings of inadequacy can evoke a range of emotions, from empathy and frustration to helplessness. The pain lies in seeing them battle an internal war that often appears insurmountable, despite your best efforts to provide support. From a trauma informed perspective, individuals who feel unworthy often struggle to accept love and affection from others, regardless of how genuine and sincere it may be. Because true love feels unfamiliar, they may view this new terrain as being unpredictable and therefore unsafe. They may undermine compliments, dismiss acts of kindness, and hesitate to open themselves up to vulnerability. The roots of this unworthiness can be traced back to past experiences, childhood upbringing, or societal pressures that have etched a negative self-perception into their psyche. The truth is, he was worthy of love because he simply was. An additional truth is, even on my worst days I was not deserving of his abuse. The two seemingly conflicting statements can co-exist; causing confusion and providing clarity at the same time. We call this emotional ambivalence which can often times create cognitive dissonance. In this case, our mind is trying to reconcile letting go while our heart is trying to justify all of the reasons we may wish to hold on.

It's important to note that when loving a narcissist or a highly toxic individual, despite your best efforts to demonstrate love and provide reassurance, their inner dialogue continues to whisper that they are undeserving. This can lead to a painful dance of testing behaviors that push you away while yearning for your presence in hopes that you will fight in order to stay. A dynamic that embodies their internal turmoil. Loving them will require you to lose yourself. If you currently find yourself in this type of relationship dynamic, I encourage you to reflect on not only your reasons for wanting to stay but also the reasons why you feel like you cannot walk away. All answers will reveal themselves when they are meant to. I love you.

Now that we've explored the concepts of love bombing and limerence, it's important to understand how these intense and overwhelming experiences can deepen trauma bonds in relationships with narcissists. As we know, love bombing, with its initial shower of affection and attention, can create an intense sense of euphoria and connection. Limerence, on the other hand, brings about an almost obsessive infatuation with the narcissist.

However, these seemingly passionate experiences are part of the narcissist's manipulative tactics to establish control and create a strong emotional bond with their partner. As the relationship progresses, the intensity of love bombing and limerence may fade, revealing the darker aspects of the narcissistic abuse cycle. The trauma bonds formed during the love bombing phase can be incredibly powerful and challenging to break. The victim becomes emotionally attached to the narcissist, and breaking free from the cycle becomes increasingly difficult. The high highs and low lows of the relationship keep the victim hooked, often leading to confusion, self-doubt, and a sense of emotional dependency on the narcissist.

Understanding the dynamics of love bombing and limerence can shed light on why victims might find it hard to walk away from toxic relationships with narcissists. Recognizing these patterns empowers individuals to take back control of their emotional well-being and seek support to break free from the trauma bonds that keep them entangled in harmful relationships. By learning more about narcissistic abuse and trauma bonds, we can equip ourselves with the knowledge and tools needed to protect our emotional health and build healthier connections in the future.

Narcissistic Abuse Cycle

IDEALIZATION

TRAUMA BONDS

Trauma bonding is the attachment an abused person feels for their abuser, specifically in a relationship with a cyclical pattern of abuse and intermittent positive reinforcement. [50] As it relates to narcissistic partners, love bombing, devaluation, triangulation, discard and hovering are a part of the abuse cycle and are maladaptive defense mechanisms that keep their victim codependent. Many narcissistic or highly toxic individuals up in turbulent homes where their primary caretakers were critical, unpredictable, or exhibited abuse/neglect.

This led to the belief that to meet their needs, they must use such harmful and deceitful strategies to survive. These behaviors become maladaptive into adulthood as the need to hide, lie, control, manipulate, or demand are not helpful tools conducive to supporting a safe environment. The continued use of these maladaptive behaviors is a proactive attempt to safeguard their wounded sense of self. Their emotional inconsistencies train their victim's nervous system to become emotionally addicted to temporary highs and lows. When the highs are so infrequent, their victims tend to disproportionately assign more meaning to them than warranted. This illusion of connection keeps their victims in a state of fear and hope at the same time.

When someone makes you the happiest person in the world and the saddest person at the same time, that is not called love. That is called a Trauma Bond.

The thing about Trauma bonds is that it can feel a lot like Stockholm Syndrome. They share some similarities in terms of the emotional dynamics they create. For example [51]:

- **Emotional Dependence:** Both trauma bonds and Stockholm Syndrome can create a strong emotional dependence on the abuser. In both cases, the victim becomes attached to their abuser as a result of the power dynamics and manipulation involved.

- **Rationalizing and Justifying Abusive Behavior:** Both trauma bonds and Stockholm Syndrome can lead victims to rationalize and justify the abusive behavior of their captors or abusers. They may minimize or make excuses for the harm inflicted upon them, believing that their captor or abuser has valid reasons or even care for their well-being.

- **Protective Feelings Towards the Abuser:** In both trauma bonds and Stockholm Syndrome, victims may develop a sense of protectiveness towards their abuser. This can be a result of psychological manipulation, where the abuser alternates between periods of abuse and moments of kindness or "love bombing." The victim may cling to these moments of kindness, hoping for a change or believing that the abuser truly cares for them.

- **Fear of Leaving or Speaking Out:** Both trauma bonds and Stockholm Syndrome can create a fear of leaving the abusive relationship or speaking out against the abuser. This fear stems from various factors, such as the threat of retaliation, the belief that they are incapable of surviving without the abuser, or a deeply ingrained sense of loyalty or attachment.

It's important to note that trauma bonds and Stockholm Syndrome are complex psychological phenomena, and not all individuals who experience trauma bonds will develop Stockholm Syndrome. However, the similarities lie in the emotional and psychological mechanisms that keep victims tied to their abusers, even in the face of harm and mistreatment. Recognizing the presence of these dynamics is crucial for breaking free from abusive relationships and seeking support to heal from the trauma. Empathy, understanding, and professional assistance can play a vital role in helping individuals navigate their way out of these harmful situations and towards a path of healing and recovery.

Narcissistic Abuse Cycle

IDEALIZATION

TRAUMA BOND VS TWIN FLAME

Furthermore, as we journey through this lifetime, we are often drawn to certain people who spark a deep, intense connection within us. These connections can manifest in different ways, but two that are often misunderstood are trauma bonds and twin flames.

Both trauma bonds and twin flames can feel like a soul-level connection, but it's important to understand the differences between the two. The theory is that twin flames are two beings who were split into different bodies but share the same soul. [52]

Trauma bonds are often rooted in pain and dysfunction. A trauma bonded relationship is reflective of an attachment created by repeated physical or emotional trauma with intermittent positive reinforcement. While twin flames are a mirror of your own soul and are meant to help you grow and evolve.

Trauma bonds are powerful emotional connections that can develop between people who have experienced trauma together. These bonds can be incredibly difficult to break, both physically and psychologically, for several reasons [53]:

1. **Neurological changes:** Trauma can cause changes in the brain's chemistry and structure, which can result in heightened emotional reactions and a sense of dependency on the other person. This can make it difficult to break away from the bond, as the person may feel a strong sense of attachment to the other person.
2. **Repetition compulsion:** People who have experienced trauma may unconsciously seek out relationships or situations that are similar to the traumatic experience. This is known as repetition compulsion, and it can reinforce the trauma bond by creating a sense of familiarity and comfort, even in the midst of dysfunction.
3. **Guilt and shame:** Trauma bonds can also be reinforced by feelings of guilt or shame, as the person may feel responsible for the other person's well-being or feel that they are not worthy of a healthy relationship.
4. **Fear of abandonment:** The fear of being alone or abandoned can also make it difficult to break a trauma bond, as the person may feel that they need the other person in order to feel safe and secure.

Here's the funny thing about toxic relationships: You never think you'll end up in one until you end up in one. One of the hardest parts about all of this is to decipher who in your life is reflective of a repeated pattern from unhealed wounds or an answered prayer from the Universe sent to nurture your healing and growth. The reality is, both can bring up deep emotions and patterns that need to be healed. As you honor yourself and your values, you will be better able to discern who is attempting to bring you back to a version of your past self that you have already elevated from. And who is elevating and empowering you. It's important to approach these connections with awareness and discernment, and to prioritize your own healing and growth.

To help us begin to do so, I'd like to shine a light on a concept known as "pain bodies." The concept of pain bodies was introduced by spiritual teacher Eckhart Tolle. A pain body is essentially a collection of emotional pain that has been accumulated within us over time. [54] It is made up of unpleasant emotions such as fear, anger, sadness, and resentment, and it can be triggered by situations or people that remind us of past emotional pain.

When we are not aware of our pain body, it can influence our behavior and our relationships. We may unconsciously seek out partners who have similar pain bodies, as we feel a familiarity and a sense of comfort with them. Here's the thing: familiarity can feel a lot like safety - even if what is familiar is not safe. Let's explore more of this together!

Narcissistic Abuse Cycle

IDEALIZATION

TRAUMA BOND VS TWIN FLAME

HOW WOULD YOU DESCRIBE YOUR RELATIONSHIP WITH YOUR PARENTS DURING YOUR CHILDHOOD? HOW DID THEIR BEHAVIOR OR EMOTIONAL AVAILABILITY IMPACT YOUR SENSE OF SAFETY AND ATTACHMENT?

Narcissistic Abuse Cycle

IDEALIZATION

TRAUMA BOND VS TWIN FLAME

IN WHAT WAYS DO YOU THINK YOUR EXPERIENCES WITH YOUR PARENTS MIGHT BE INFLUENCING YOUR PRESENT-DAY RELATIONSHIPS? ARE THERE ANY PATTERNS OR THEMES THAT YOU NOTICE IN YOUR INTERACTIONS WITH YOUR PARENTS THAT YOU NOW HAVE WITH YOUR PARTNER [OR FORMER PARTNERS]?

Narcissistic Abuse Cycle

IDEALIZATION

TRAUMA BOND VS TWIN FLAME

REFLECTING ON YOUR CHILDHOOD, WERE THERE SPECIFIC SITUATIONS OR EVENTS THAT LEFT A LASTING IMPACT ON YOU EMOTIONALLY? HOW DO YOU THINK THOSE EXPERIENCES ARE SHAPING YOUR REACTIONS AND RESPONSES TO CHALLENGING SITUATIONS IN YOUR CURRENT RELATIONSHIPS?

Narcissistic Abuse Cycle

IDEALIZATION

TRAUMA BOND VS TWIN FLAME

HOW DO YOU COPE WITH THE PAIN OR EMOTIONAL WOUNDS FROM YOUR PAST? DO YOU FIND YOURSELF SEEKING VALIDATION OR LOVE FROM OTHERS IN A WAY THAT RESEMBLES THE DYNAMICS YOU HAD WITH YOUR PARENTS?

Narcissistic Abuse Cycle

IDEALIZATION

TRAUMA BOND VS TWIN FLAME

WHAT ASPECTS OF YOUR CHILDHOOD DO YOU BELIEVE ARE CONTRIBUTING TO YOUR ATTRACTION TO OR TOLERANCE OF TOXIC INDIVIDUALS? IN WHAT WAYS DO YOU THINK UNDERSTANDING THESE CONNECTIONS CAN HELP YOU BREAK FREE FROM REPETITION COMPULSION AND CREATE HEALTHIER BOUNDARIES IN RELATIONSHIPS?

Narcissistic Abuse Cycle

IDEALIZATION

REPETITION COMPULSION

Integrating the information you now know about yourself as it relates to your emotional pain body can help you to break the cycle of repetition compulsion: patterns of dysfunction and repeated negative experiences in our relationships. Repetition compulsion is a psychological phenomenon in which people unconsciously repeat patterns of behavior or relationships that are similar to past experiences, even if those experiences were negative or traumatic. [55] In other words, people may seek out familiar situations or people that remind them of past experiences, even if those experiences were harmful or unhealthy. In romantic relationships, repetition compulsion can negatively influence the dynamic between partners. For example, a person who grew up in a household with a parent who was emotionally unavailable may unconsciously seek out partners who are also emotionally unavailable, even though this behavior is harmful and unfulfilling. Similarly, a person who experienced abuse or neglect in childhood may unconsciously seek out partners who exhibit similar behaviors, even though this is not healthy or safe.

Repetition compulsion can also contribute to the development of trauma bonds. When we become aware of our pain body, we can start to observe it and detach from it. We can learn to recognize when it is being triggered and to respond to situations in a more conscious and present way. By doing so, we can break free from patterns of pain and dysfunction in our relationships and cultivate healthier, more fulfilling connections with others. We can begin to identify trauma stored in the mind and body in order to call in a healthy partner by:

1. Developing body awareness: Pay attention to your physical sensations and notice how your body responds to different situations or people. Notice areas of tension or discomfort, as these may be indicators of stored trauma.

2. **Seeking professional help:** I'm biased, however this is why I deeply value Trauma Informed work. Consider working with a therapist or other trained professional to help you identify and process past trauma. (Ahem.. hi!) We can guide you through various healing techniques and provide support throughout the process. Specifically Somatic Experiencing (SE).

3. Practicing self-care: Prioritize activities that promote relaxation and reduce stress, such as meditation, yoga, or spending time in nature. This can help to reduce the impact of trauma on your body and mind.

4. Cultivating self-compassion: Be gentle and patient with yourself as you work through past trauma. Practice self-compassion and self-forgiveness, and remind yourself that healing is a process.

5. Focusing on your values and needs: Identify your core values and needs in a relationship, and prioritize these when seeking a partner. This can help you attract partners who are aligned with your values and who support your healing journey.

For those of us who have endured abuse in their homes, the concept of safety takes on a complex hue. The very notion of safety that should ideally bring comfort and solace becomes tainted by memories of pain, fear, and instability. Abusive environments often breed an environment of unpredictability and danger, eroding any sense of security that should exist within the home. When abuse survivors find themselves in situations that seem safe and nurturing, their trauma responses can be triggered.

They may become hypervigilant, expecting the familiar sting of betrayal or harm. The warmth and stability they crave may feel foreign and suspicious, causing them to question the authenticity of love and kindness. This dissonance between the desire for safety and the conditioned fear from their past can create an internal struggle that shapes their relationships. Discover more about yourself in the questions presented in the following pages.

Narcissistic Abuse Cycle

IDEALIZATION

REPETITION COMPULSION

AS MUCH AS WE CRAVE SAFETY, OUR UNHEALED CONDITIONING MAY ACTUALLY ENABLE US TO ALSO FEAR IT.

CAN YOU IDENTIFY ANY SPECIFIC PATTERNS OR BEHAVIORS IN YOUR ADULT RELATIONSHIPS THAT SEEM REMINISCENT OF YOUR EXPERIENCES WITH YOUR PARENTS? HOW DO THESE PATTERNS IMPACT YOUR EMOTIONAL WELL-BEING AND OVERALL RELATIONSHIP DYNAMICS?

Narcissistic Abuse Cycle

IDEALIZATION

REPETITION COMPULSION

HAVE YOU NOTICED ANY REPETITION COMPULSION IN YOUR RELATIONSHIPS, WHERE YOU FIND YOURSELF DRAWN TO PARTNERS WHO EXHIBIT SIMILAR TRAITS OR BEHAVIORS AS YOUR PARENTS? IF SO, WHAT DO YOU BELIEVE ATTRACTS YOU TO THESE INDIVIDUALS?

_____

_____

_____

_____

_____

_____

_____

_____

_____

_____

_____

_____

_____

_____

_____

_____

_____

Narcissistic Abuse Cycle

IDEALIZATION

REPETITION COMPULSION

HOW HAS YOUR PAST PAIN AND UNRESOLVED EMOTIONS FROM CHILDHOOD INFLUENCED YOUR ATTRACTION TO NARCISSISTIC PARTNERS OR INDIVIDUALS WHO MAY EXHIBIT TOXIC TRAITS? IN WHAT WAYS DO YOU THINK THIS DYNAMIC REFLECTS YOUR INNER PAIN BODY SEEKING VALIDATION OR RESOLUTION?

Narcissistic Abuse Cycle

IDEALIZATION

PREDATORY PARTNER SELECTION

Healing from past trauma and understanding our pain bodies is a journey that requires patience and dedication. It's possible to break free from the grip of past pain and create a healthy, fulfilling partnership with commitment and support. The more you understand yourself and your patterns, the better equipped you will be to defend yourself against a narcissist or highly toxic person. That's because these predators are extremely tactical about the character traits intentionally exploit. That said, let's delve into the complex dynamic between empaths and narcissists. While it's essential to avoid generalizations, certain factors can make empaths more vulnerable to getting entangled in such relationships. Empaths, with their highly empathetic and caring nature, may attract narcissists who see them as perfect prey. The disempowerment of an empath becomes what empowers the narcissist. Factors such as unhealed trauma, low self-esteem, and anxious attachment styles can make empaths more susceptible to these dynamics. Having weak boundaries and accepting the bare minimum in relationships may expose empaths to exploitation by narcissistic partners. Their willingness to overperform emotionally and do the emotional labor allows narcissists to escape accountability, while empaths ignore red flags and compromise their own well-being for the sake of the relationship.

Historically, empaths may have played the role of the "enabling empath" as a means of protection. However, healing and growth involve transitioning from enablement to empowerment. Empaths must learn to value themselves, set boundaries, and embrace their needs and opinions. That's because Narcissists feed off the empaths' desire to please and self-sacrifice, making them perfect partners for exploitation. To break free from this cycle, empaths must practice the opposite of what enables a narcissist by learning to value themselves, recognize their worth, and not compromise their well-being for the sake of a relationship. By becoming empowered empaths, they can foster healthier and more balanced connections with others. Here's the thing, Narcissist look for individuals with:

1. **Emotional openness and vulnerability:** Empaths often have a deep emotional openness, making them more willing to invest in and connect with others on an emotional level. Narcissists, who crave attention and admiration, can exploit this vulnerability by initially showering the empath with affection and admiration, creating a sense of closeness.
2. **The desire to fix and heal others:** Empaths have a natural inclination to help and heal others. Narcissists, aware of this quality, may manipulate empaths by presenting themselves as wounded or in need of healing, thereby drawing the empath into a caretaker role within the relationship. Your softness and sensitivity is what they will later weaponize against you to enforce shame and submission.
3. **The tendency to prioritize others' needs:** Empaths tend to prioritize the needs and feelings of others over their own, often putting their own well-being on the back burner. Narcissists take advantage of this selflessness by exploiting the empath's willingness to accommodate and please them.
4. **The fear of conflict and confrontation:** Empaths typically avoid conflict and value harmony in relationships. Narcissists, on the other hand, often engage in manipulative behaviors and create a dynamic of control. This mismatch in conflict resolution styles can make it challenging for empaths to assert their boundaries and address problematic behavior.

It's important to note that while empaths may be susceptible to narcissistic relationships, anyone can become involved in such dynamics, men, women, children, the smart, the weak and the strong. Building awareness, setting boundaries, and developing self-care practices can help empaths protect themselves from unhealthy relationships and foster healthier connections based on mutual respect and empathy. From a trauma informed perspective, when we are choosing partners from an unhealed lens or an unconscious lens, we subconsciously seek out people who reaffirm our subconscious beliefs about ourselves and the world. If we struggle with self worth, we will find people and partners that reaffirm that we are not worthy of love, honesty or reciprocation. Those of us who over function will usually find ourselves surrounded by individuals who exploit this tendency so they can under function.

The codependent partner who is used to people pleasing and performing, has a subconscious belief that if they heal their partner, their partner will be able to meet their needs down the road. This is a reflection of repetition compulsion mirroring their unresolved childhood experiences into their adult relationships. They over extend by giving so much love and support at their own expense, which gives them a sense of control and predictability but also emotional depletion and lack of reciprocity. This, paired with the narcissist's fake apologies and intermittent positive reinforcement, such as kindness, closeness and affection deepens the trauma bonds and dangles a carrot of hope in front of the victim. This is a painful and soul crushing experience to go through. The thing about narcissists is they know who to love, just not how to love. As for enabling empaths, they know how to love, they just have a hard time deciphering who to love and believing they are worthy of receiving it.

Narcissistic Abuse Cycle

IDEALIZATION

EMPOWERED EMPATH VS ENABLING EMPATH

Let's take a closer look at how narcissists intentionally use predatory partner selection to exploit individuals with empathic and caring traits. As we know, they have a keen eye for identifying people who are highly self-sacrificing, caring, and enabling. These traits make them the perfect targets for the narcissist's manipulation and control. Narcissists seek out partners who will put their needs and desires above their own, creating an ideal situation where they can be the center of attention and have their harmful behavior go unchecked. They exploit the empathy and kindness of their partners, using it as a means to control and dominate the relationship. An enabling empath is more likely to fall into the trap set by the narcissist, as they may prioritize the narcissist's needs over their own, ignore red flags, and overlook abusive behavior. This pattern of behavior enables the narcissist to continue their harmful actions without facing consequences.

On the other hand, an empowered empath is one who has learned to value themselves, set boundaries, and recognize their own worth. They refuse to compromise their well-being for the sake of the relationship and are more likely to recognize and address the narcissist's manipulative tactics. An empowered empath is less susceptible to falling victim to the narcissist's predatory partner selection because their boundaries are too difficult for a narcissist to break down. Understanding the difference between an enabling and an empowered empath is crucial in breaking free from the cycle of abuse and manipulation. By recognizing their own value and worth, empowered empaths can foster healthier and more balanced relationships, free from the exploitation of narcissistic individuals. In relationships between narcissistic individuals and enabling empaths, there can be a complex interplay of codependent needs. Enabling Empaths and Narcissists usually attract one another as a result of trauma bonding over similar dysfunction in their childhood. However, the enabling empath leverages their hurt in order to heal others. While the Narcissist is unaware of their pain and projects their hurt, onto others.

An Enabler - Usually a partner/spouse of the narcissist, enablers "normalize" and even perpetuate the narcissist's grandiose persona, extreme sense of entitlement, and haughty attitude and behavior toward others by absorbing the abuse and acting as an apologist for it. Enablers are always avoiding conflict and attack while often also seeking rewards such as affection, praise, power, gifts, or money. Enablers may be under the delusion that they are the only ones who can truly understand the narcissist and oftentimes sacrifice or scapegoat their children to placate the narcissist. Narcissists only surround themselves with people who enable their behavior, ignore it or encourage it. This allows them to avoid doing any inner work that requires taking accountability for their hurtful actions.

Those who try to defend themselves against a narcist are often scapegoated as they defy the status quo. Therefore, many victims of narcissistic abuse, or close family and friends who are privy to it remain silent, even when they know the truth. This was the case in my relationship. That's why knowing how you are, who you are is so important. The wounds that you don't heal become what a toxic person leverages for control and exploits for personal gain. The thing about these types of relationship dynamics is that once you know what enables them to survive, you can begin to do the exact opposite of that in order to empower yourself to thrive. That means if self abandonment or people pleasing allowed a Narcissist to exploit and control you, then standing up for yourself and putting yourself first is how they begin to lose their power.

Nothing scares a bully more than when you begin to stand up for yourself. Remember, the more you feel empowered, the more you take an away their power. If you being happy and healthy results in them feel helpless and powerless, here's your permission slip to ruin their day.

Narcissistic Abuse Cycle

IDEALIZATION

EMPOWERED EMPATH VS ENABLING EMPATH

When you begin to address your codependent patterns, your healing can begin. Keep in mind, Both partners are codependent. The enabling empath has the need to give and please. While the Narcissist feels entitled to take and receive. The Narcissist is codependent too and has the fear of abandonment and being exposed. They are dependent on the codependents need to self sacrifice so they dont have to do the work on themselves. When the co-dependent stops self sacrificing, they are no longer of need for the narcissist who begins to look for new supply.

I get it, this part can be extremely scary though. This fear was my exact dilemma. Especially when we are deep in a trauma bond with someone we love that claims to love us in return. While every individual and relationship is unique, here are some potential mutually codependent needs that may arise:

- **Validation and Self-Worth: Narcissistic** individuals often seek constant validation and admiration to bolster their fragile self-esteem. On the other hand, enabling empaths may seek a sense of self-worth through their ability to meet the needs and expectations of others.

- **Control and Security:** Narcissists may crave control over others and their environment as a means to feel powerful and secure. Enabling empaths, on the other hand, may seek security by being overly accommodating, enmeshing themselves in their partner's needs and desires.

- **Emotional Fulfillment:** Narcissists may seek emotional validation, attention, and a sense of significance from their empathic partners. Meanwhile, enabling empaths may find fulfillment by nurturing and meeting the emotional needs of their partners, sometimes at the expense of their own well-being.

- **Avoidance of Abandonment and Rejection:** Both narcissistic individuals and enabling empaths may have deep-rooted fears of abandonment and rejection. They may unconsciously seek validation and assurance from each other, creating a cycle of dependency to alleviate these fears.

- **Enabling and Co-dependency:** Narcissists and enabling empaths can unknowingly enable each other's unhealthy behaviors. The narcissist's need for control and admiration can be fulfilled by the empath's tendency to prioritize their partner's needs over their own, creating a co-dependent dynamic that reinforces their respective patterns.

The chart below highlights the differences and similarities that bind these codependent patterns between both the enabling empath and the narcissist.

Empath	Similarities	Narcissist
Giver : Wants to feel needed	Highly Emotionally Reactive, Addiction To Chaos	Taker : Wants to feel important
Extremely empathetic, emotionally hypersensitive		Lacks empathy/accountability
Overly concerned with the needs & feelings of others	**Wants:**	No concern for the needs/feelings of others
Intent: To be needed (confuses caretaking & sacrifice	Connection, Certainty, To Be Needed	Wants conformity and admiration
with loyalty & love)		Takes zero blame, lacks remorse
Chronic fear of upsetting others/obsessive thoughts	**Fears:**	Lacks self awareness, unlikely to change
Self aware & able to make changes	Abandonment, Rejection, Vulnerability, Intimacy	Intent: wants some to boost ego/self confidence
Absorbs the energies in their environments		Grandiose/Entitled/Attention Seeking
Highly sensitive & intuitive	**Trauma Traits In Relationships:**	Surface level friends
Easily overwhelmed & startled	Insecure, Difficulty Trusting, Low Self Worth, Resentment	Public/Private Image Management

Narcissistic Abuse Cycle

IDEALIZATION

EMPOWERED EMPATH VS ENABLING EMPATH

YES. / NO

CHECKLIST

AS YOU READ EACH QUESTION, SIMPLY TICK "YES" IF YOU AGREE OR "NO"
IF YOU DISAGREE WITH THE STATEMENT.

		YES	NO
01	DO THEY TAKE RESPONSIBILITY FOR THE *CONSEQUENCES* OF THEIR BEHAVIOR WITHOUT PROJECTING RESENTMENT OR BLAME? AN APOLOGY WITHOUT CHANGED BEHAVIOR IS JUST A PATTERN OF MANIPULATION.	☐	☐
02	ARE THEY ABLE TO RESPOND HEALTHILY TO DISAPPOINTMENT OR WHEN THINGS DON'T GO THEIR WAY?	☐	☐
03	ARE THEY *EQUALLY* AS RESPECTFUL OF YOUR EMOTIONS, NEEDS AND PREFERENCES?	☐	☐
04	DO THEY RESPECT YOUR BOUNDARIES WITHOUT MAKING YOU FEEL GUILTY FOR HAVING THEM?	☐	☐
05	DO THEY RECIPROCATE THE SAME HONESTY, LOYALTY AND RESPECT THAT THEY EXPECT?	☐	☐
06	DO THEY RESPECT YOUR "NO"?	☐	☐
07	DO *YOU* RESPECT YOUR "NO"?	☐	☐
08	DOES LOVING THEM REQUIRE COMING UP WITH NEW WAYS TO COPE WITH THE THINGS THEY'RE DOING THAT HURT YOU?	☐	☐
09	DOES BEING IN THIS RELATIONSHIP ALLOW YOU TO SLEEP PEACEFULLY AT NIGHT?	☐	☐

The goal of healing from your wounds is not to learn how to hate those that hurt you, but to learn how to love the parts of yourself that continue to tolerate being hurt. I love you.

Narcissistic Abuse Cycle

IDEALIZATION

A LOVE LETTER TO AN EMPATH - FROM AN EMPATH

Dear Brave, Beautiful, Compassionate Empath,

When you find yourself tolerating abuse from others, it's essential to recognize that their actions reflect their own wounds, and your acceptance of it reflects your own. Fearing abandonment, you may stay in an abusive relationship, prolonging the inevitable pain. But as your partner diminishes your shine and blames you for not being the same, the self-abandonment you experience hurts even more when amplified by the anticipated abandonment from your abuser. When your need for their approval surpasses your depth of self-love, this will inevitably lead to self-abandonment. Contrary to what they will tell you, it's crucial to understand that you are not selfish for wanting to be treated well. You are not crazy for creating distance in response to disrespect. And you are not weak for being hurt by harmful behavior.

Your healing journey begins when you stop asking your partner why they keep hurting you and start asking yourself why you keep allowing it. In moments of silent suffering, when you begin to wonder if you deserve better, the truth is that you do. Attracting a partner who doesn't need to be saved allows you to deeply honor your intrinsic value beyond what you can do for others and how good you can make them feel.

Loving yourself shifts your perspective, as you start seeing people differently. You no longer seek people who are not good for you, and you stop ignoring the bad in people to keep them in your life. Instead, you accept the version of themselves they show you without feeling the need to beg, fix or change them into who you want them to be. The moment you begin to feel indifferent is the moment when the emotional experience inside of you will become different. Your neutrality ignites the demise of their distorted reality. Recognizing that the parts of your partner that you need to change are the parts within yourself that needs changing.

Remember, lowering your frequency to meet someone else on their level always comes with a cost. Even if you aren't hurting others, continuing a relationship with someone who harms you enables you to indirectly hurt yourself.

Finally, it's important to honor your standards from the beginning, as the red flags you ignore early on may be the reasons why the relationship ends in the future. This doesn't mean withholding love or kindness, but rather being selective with whom you decide to give your love away to. There's no need to be guarded when you remain grounded or hardened when your beauty is in your softness and sensitivity. Relationships become toxic because of the actions and behaviors we engage in to make the incompatible - compatible. Unfortunately, no amount of doing the inner work will make the wrong person right for you.Understanding these dynamics can help you break free from toxic patterns and build healthier relationships in the future.

Remember, you are worthy of love and respect, and it starts with loving and respecting yourself.

If I could go back in time to heal my younger self, this is what I would tell her. And if I can do my part in helping you to heal, this is exactly what I wish to tell you.

With love,

Isabella Imani

Narcissistic Abuse Cycle

IDEALIZATION

As we continue to journey through the world of narcissistic relationships, we encounter the transformative shift from enabling Empaths to empowered Empaths the more we heal and grow. This crucial transition involves redirecting our outward focus towards inward self-love and self-care. By prioritizing our own healing instead of fixating on healing the narcissist, we reclaim our power and encourage their potential for self-healing as well.

I get it, narcissistic relationships can be complex and emotionally draining. They often leading us into the codependent dance of a trauma bond. In these moments, we may find ourselves struggling with "hopium addiction." This term refers to the persistent hope that the narcissist will change or that the relationship will magically improve despite evidence to the contrary. [56] However, this hopeful stance can keep us trapped in a cycle of disappointment and emotional turmoil.

In a narcissistic relationship, the narcissistic partner often engages in manipulative and abusive behaviors, causing emotional distress and harm to the other person. However, the person experiencing this toxic relationship may become addicted to the hope that things will get better. They may cling to the belief that if they just try harder, love more, or meet the narcissist's demands, the relationship will eventually become healthy and fulfilling. This was once my painful reality.

This hope can be incredibly powerful and can keep individuals trapped in abusive dynamics for extended periods of time. It becomes an addiction because the person may find it difficult to let go of this hope, even when faced with ongoing mistreatment and disappointment. The problem with this type of cognitive distortion is that it leads us to believe that our partner has changed into something they are not. Something for the worse. So we hold out hope that our tireless efforts will somehow transform them back into the warm and kind person we fell in love with. The problem here is that they never actually changed. They just got more comfortable with showing you who they really are.

Hopium addiction can be detrimental to one's well-being as it perpetuates a cycle of false hope, enabling the narcissistic partner to continue their abusive behaviors unchecked.

Listen, narcissists are individuals driven by a desperate need for admiration and affirmation, paradoxically sabotage their own pursuit of love. This self-sabotage stems from a twisted narrative they carry deep within – one that convinces them they are fundamentally unlovable. For them, the idea of true and unconditional love clashes with their internal belief system, rendering it incompatible with their self-image. In their efforts to prevent the inevitable "discovery" of their unworthiness, narcissists engage in behaviors that undermine the very relationships they desire. They may push away their partners, create conflicts out of trivial matters, or engage in manipulative tactics to maintain a sense of control. This self-sabotage can be viewed as a defense mechanism, a way to preemptively protect themselves from the pain of rejection that they anticipate.

For abuse survivors, finding safety can be an intricate journey of reconciling past trauma with present experiences. In the case of narcissists, their self-sabotage is a manifestation of their internal conflicts. While love holds the potential for healing, it also serves as a mirror that reflects the wounds, vulnerabilities, and complexities that shape human relationships. It is important to note that these dynamics can be complex and multifaceted. However, highlighting the multitude of ways these dynamics can play out conveys real life examples of how you can shift from an enabled version of yourself to a more empowered version as it relates to hope and healing.

Narcissistic Abuse Cycle

IDEALIZATION

HOPIUM ADDICTION

REFLECTING ON YOUR EXPERIENCE WITH THE NARCISSIST OR HIGHLY TOXIC PERSON MAKING PROMISES TO CHANGE, HOW DID YOU INITIALLY REACT TO THEIR WORDS? HOW DID THEIR PROMISES IMPACT YOUR HOPE FOR A HEALTHIER RELATIONSHIP?

_____

_____

_____

_____

_____

_____

_____

_____

_____

_____

_____

_____

_____

_____

_____

_____

_____

Narcissistic Abuse Cycle

IDEALIZATION

HOPIUM ADDICTION

HOW DID THE CONCEPT OF "HOPIUM" PLAY A ROLE IN YOUR DECISION TO STAY IN THE TOXIC RELATIONSHIP? WHAT EMOTIONS OR THOUGHTS KEPT YOU HOLDING ONTO HOPE DESPITE THEIR REPEATED PATTERNS OF BEHAVIOR?

Narcissistic Abuse Cycle

IDEALIZATION

HOPIUM ADDICTION

DURING YOUR TIME WITH THE NARCISSIST OR HIGHLY TOXIC PERSON, DID YOU NOTICE ANY SPECIFIC TRIGGERS OR SITUATIONS THAT REIGNITED YOUR HOPE FOR CHANGE? HOW DID THESE MOMENTS INFLUENCE YOUR PERCEPTION OF THE RELATIONSHIP?

_____

_____

_____

_____

_____

_____

_____

_____

_____

_____

_____

_____

_____

_____

_____

_____

_____

Narcissistic Abuse Cycle

IDEALIZATION

HOPIUM ADDICTION

LOOKING BACK, HOW DID STAYING IN THE TOXIC RELATIONSHIP AFFECT YOUR SENSE OF SELF-WORTH AND EMOTIONAL WELL-BEING? HOW DID IT IMPACT YOUR ABILITY TO SET AND MAINTAIN HEALTHY BOUNDARIES?

Narcissistic Abuse Cycle

IDEALIZATION

HOPIUM ADDICTION

NOW THAT YOU RECOGNIZE THE IMPACT OF "HOPIUM" AND HOW IT PROLONGED YOUR STAY IN THE TOXIC RELATIONSHIP, WHAT ARE SOME WAYS YOU CAN CULTIVATE SELF-COMPASSION AND SELF-EMPOWERMENT MOVING FORWARD? HOW CAN YOU USE THIS KNOWLEDGE TO BUILD RESILIENCE AND PROTECT YOURSELF FROM SIMILAR DYNAMICS IN THE FUTURE?

Narcissistic Abuse Cycle

DEVALUE

Listen, hopium addiction is just the tip of the iceberg for these skilled manipulators. It can be an extremely painful experience as it feels like the slightest glimmer of hope is just enough to make you feel like you're chasing a carrot at the end of a stick or playing a game of soccer with constantly shift goal posts. In their twisted perception of reality, they test just how much abuse you can take so they can gauge your willingness to stay. Because once a narcissist develops feelings for you, their biggest fear is that you will abandon them once you find out the truth of who they really are. As their feelings start to grow, so does their inner turmoil. The idea of vulnerability and surrendering their heart becomes a source of great pain and fear for them.

Their feelings of love may stir up feelings of resentment within them, which can be confusing and hurtful. It's not that they don't see your value; on the contrary, they are fully aware of the power your love holds. Yet, their own insecurities lead them to treat you differently because your inner beauty makes them feel broken. And your shine dims their light. They may become harsh or mean to the person they love the most – you – and it's not because you lack worth, but because they are grappling with their fear of losing control. It's almost as if they perceive your closeness as a threat to their carefully constructed facade.

Their behavior towards you may seem contradictory and confusing. They may start to treat you like the enemy, devaluing your significance in their life. Beneath this facade of indifference lies their deep-seated fear of being exposed and ultimately abandoned. Because they prioritize protection over authentic connection, their biggest nightmare is that if you see through their mask, you will leave them. Because of this, they will go out of their way, to do anything that leaves them feeling emotionally exposed and vulnerable. Which is often times why they reject you before you can reject them, and leave before they are left. Childish, right? That's because it is. Cue the discard phase of the Narcissistic Abuse Cycle.

In narcissistic relationships, the victim often experiences chronic stress and emotional turmoil due to manipulation, gaslighting, and emotional abuse by the narcissistic partner. This ongoing stress triggers the release of cortisol, and the body becomes conditioned to this heightened state of arousal. Narcissistic abuse can have a significant impact on the body's stress response system, leading to what some refer to as "cortisol addiction." [57] Cortisol is a hormone released by the body in response to stress, and it plays a crucial role in the fight-or-flight response. However, prolonged exposure to high levels of cortisol can be detrimental to physical and mental health. [58] Over time, the body may become "addicted" to the cortisol rush, seeking out situations that create drama or conflict to maintain that heightened state.

Moreover, narcissists may intentionally create situations of chaos or tension, causing the victim to experience a constant cycle of stress and relief. This rollercoaster of emotions can reinforce the victim's addiction to cortisol, as they become accustomed to the adrenaline rush and may perceive it as a form of excitement or intensity or passion. Cortisol addiction can have severe consequences for both physical and mental health. It can lead to symptoms such as chronic fatigue, anxiety, irritability, difficulty concentrating, and disrupted sleep patterns. Additionally, prolonged exposure to stress hormones can weaken the immune system and increase the risk of developing various health issues. [59]

In a twisted attempt to reel their victims in with a sprinkle of hopium addiction to soothe their cortisol addiction, narcissists may disguise their cruel behaviors behind the facade of kind ones. For example, they may suggest "healing together" through the weaponized use of couples therapy.

Now, why would they suggest such a thing? These skilled manipulators go to therapy for attention and validation for their self imposed areas of victimization. The very act of going to therapy reinforces their "good guy" facade. To the trained eye, the "conflicts" the narcissist claims the desire to fix are the symptom. However, the root cause of seeking a couples therapist is found in narcissists behaviors that enabled the conflicts to arise in the first place. Now I'm not saying this is the case in all toxic relationships, however this was the case in mine.

Picture this: you muster up the courage to seek help, hoping that therapy will be the magic wand to fix the cracks in your relationship. But here's the twist – your narcissistic partner sees it as an opportunity to gain more control and manipulate the situation to their advantage. Narcissists are skilled actors who can put on a convincing show in therapy sessions. They may present themselves as the victim, expertly deflecting blame and shifting the focus away from their own harmful behavior. They might charm the therapist, seeking validation and support for their twisted perspective, leaving you feeling unheard and invalidated. As I mentioned earlier, most narcissists enter therapy for attention which is why only a highly skilled mental health professional will need to know how to be empathetically confrontational.

In the realm of narcissistic manipulation, weaponizing incompetence can be a subtle yet effective tactic used to maintain control and deflect accountability. Here's a fictional story that illustrates how this dynamic can play out: Once upon a time, in a big and bustling city, lived a woman named Sarah and her partner, TJ. Unbeknownst to Sarah, TJ had a deep-seated narcissistic personality that thrived on power and control. He had a knack for exploiting his own "incompetence" as a means of evading responsibility for his actions.

Their relationship, initially filled with passion and promise, began to unravel over time. Sarah noticed that TJ would conveniently forget to mention crucial details in his stories, often omitting lies that painted him in a better light. These discrepancies would come to light when Sarah pieced together the truth, prompting her to bring up these issues during couples therapy. 20 examples of covert lies and manipulative actions that TJ utilized in his relationship to create triangulation and secure more narcissistic supply in his relationship with Sarah included:

- **Comparing with Exes:** Making subtle comparisons between their current partner and ex-partners, highlighting the supposed virtues of their past relationships to evoke jealousy and insecurity.
- **Flirting with Others:** Engaging in subtle flirtatious behaviors with others in the presence of their partner, creating feelings of inadequacy and competition.
- **False Concern:** Pretending to be concerned about their partner's well-being, but using it as an opportunity to gather information for manipulation or to appear caring in front of others.
- **Selective Sharing:** Sharing personal information with third parties about their partner's weaknesses, secrets, or insecurities to diminish their image.
- **Social Media Mind Games:** Posting ambiguous or attention-seeking content on social media to trigger jealousy and insecurity in their partner.
- **Triangulation with Exes:** Maintaining contact with ex-partners and subtly mentioning their interactions to make the current partner feel threatened.
- **Creating Doubt:** Deliberately providing conflicting information to sow seeds of doubt and confusion in their partner's mind.
- **Withholding Affection:** Alternating between periods of affection and emotional distance to keep their partner off balance and seeking validation.
- **Guilt-Tripping:** Using guilt as a tool to manipulate their partner into conforming to their desires or decisions.
- **Silent Treatment:** Employing the silent treatment to create anxiety and make their partner eager to win back their attention and approval.
- **Gaslighting:** Manipulating reality by denying facts, events, or conversations to make their partner question their own memory and sanity.
- **Projecting Insecurities:** Accusing their partner of behaviors they themselves engage in, effectively projecting their own insecurities onto their partner.

Narcissistic Abuse Cycle

DEVALUE

- **Love Bombing Others:** Showering attention and affection on new acquaintances or friends to evoke jealousy and insecurity in their partner.
- **Playing Victim:** Presenting themselves as the victim in situations where they are clearly at fault, garnering sympathy and support from others.
- **Undermining Achievements:** Downplaying or dismissing their partner's accomplishments to create self-doubt and dependency on their validation.
- **Mixed Messages:** Giving mixed signals, such as complimenting and criticizing in the same conversation, to keep their partner uncertain and seeking approval.
- **Seeking Validation from Others:** Constantly seeking validation from others in their partner's presence to diminish their partner's role and importance.
- **Favoritism:** Openly showing favoritism toward other people, subtly suggesting their partner is not as valued or appreciated.
- **Emotional Manipulation:** Using emotional outbursts or breakdowns as a way to control and manipulate their partner's reactions and behavior.
- **Subtle Insults:** Veiling insults as jokes or playful comments, designed to demean and create self-doubt in their partner.

Sarah was hopeful that therapy could provide a safe space for open communication and growth. However, TJ saw it as yet another platform to exercise his manipulation. During therapy sessions, whenever Sarah raised concerns about his omissions and lies, TJ would play the card of incompetence. He would shrug, feign confusion, and utter phrases like, "I didn't think it was important" or "I must have forgotten." His seemingly innocent demeanor left Sarah questioning her own perceptions.

To Sarah's astonishment, their couples therapist, Randi, appeared to give TJ the benefit of the doubt. She empathized with his forgetfulness and emphasized the importance of understanding each other's perspectives. This allowed TJ to continue his narrative of "innocent mistakes" and "harmless forgetfulness," leaving Sarah feeling unheard, invalidated and gaslit. As sessions progressed, Sarah's frustration grew. TJ's manipulation tactics were pushing her to the brink of self-doubt. The therapist's seemingly impartial approach began to wear on her confidence, making her wonder if she was truly overreacting.

TJ capitalized on this doubt, further eroding Sarah's sense of reality. In this story, the weaponization of incompetence by the male narcissist, TJ, showcases how he cunningly used his "forgetfulness" to evade accountability and maintain control. The therapist's naive and deeply misguided approach inadvertently enabled TJ's manipulation, leaving Sarah trapped in a cycle of doubt and frustration. It serves as a cautionary tale, highlighting the importance of recognizing and addressing such dynamics, both within relationships and within the therapeutic setting, to prevent the insidious effects of narcissistic manipulation from taking hold. Listen, abusiveness has little to do with psychological challenges and everything to do with values and beliefs.

When it comes to understanding the nuances of someones intentions and actions, there's a difference between a mistake and a habit. And there comes a point in time when their intentions no longer matter when the impact of their actions continue to create a dynamic that is unsafe, inconsistent and unreliable - narcissistic or not. This distinction is crucial as narcissists are skilled at making you question your intuition and manipulating you into believing that you are insecure. This is one of many examples of how they will weaponize your intuition by calling it an insecurity.

Unfortunately, couples therapy can become a battlefield where the narcissist uses their manipulative tactics to gaslight, undermine, or discredit your experiences and emotions. They may twist the therapist's words, downplay your concerns, or even turn the therapist against you. It's crucial to recognize that this is not your fault. Narcissists are master manipulators, and their goal is to maintain power and control. Remember, therapy should be a safe space for both partners to express their emotions and work towards healthier dynamics. But when dealing with a narcissist, that safe space can be violated.

Narcissistic Abuse Cycle

DEVALUE

PERFORMATIVE THERAPY ~ WEAPONIZED INCOMPETENCE

HAVE YOU EVER BEEN INVALIDATED BY A THERAPIST REGARDING YOUR EXPERIENCES WITH NARCISSISTIC ABUSE? IF SO, HOW DID IT FEEL WHEN YOU EXPERIENCED INVALIDATION FROM YOUR THERAPIST WHILE DISCUSSING YOUR EXPERIENCES OF NARCISSISTIC ABUSE?

_____

_____

_____

_____

_____

_____

_____

_____

_____

_____

_____

_____

_____

_____

_____

_____

Narcissistic Abuse Cycle

DEVALUE

PERFORMATIVE THERAPY - WEAPONIZED INCOMPETENCE

CAN YOU DESCRIBE THE SPECIFIC INSTANCES OR STATEMENTS MADE BY YOUR THERAPIST THAT LED YOU TO FEEL INVALIDATED IN THE CONTEXT OF YOUR TRAUMA?

_____

_____

_____

_____

_____

_____

_____

_____

_____

_____

_____

_____

_____

_____

_____

_____

_____

Narcissistic Abuse Cycle

DEVALUE

PERFORMATIVE THERAPY – WEAPONIZED INCOMPETENCE

IN WHAT WAYS DID THE INVALIDATION FROM YOUR THERAPIST IMPACT YOUR ABILITY TO TRUST AND OPEN UP ABOUT YOUR EXPERIENCES OF NARCISSISTIC ABUSE?

Narcissistic Abuse Cycle

DEVALUE

PERFORMATIVE THERAPY - WEAPONIZED INCOMPETENCE

HOW DO YOU THINK YOUR PAST EXPERIENCES OF NARCISSISTIC ABUSE MIGHT HAVE INFLUENCED YOUR REACTIONS TO THE THERAPIST'S INVALIDATING BEHAVIORS?

Narcissistic Abuse Cycle

DEVALUE

PERFORMATIVE THERAPY – WEAPONIZED INCOMPETENCE

REFLECTING ON YOUR CURRENT NEEDS, WHAT KIND OF SUPPORT AND VALIDATION DO YOU BELIEVE WOULD BE MOST BENEFICIAL FOR YOUR HEALING JOURNEY IN THE AFTERMATH OF NARCISSISTIC ABUSE?

_____

_____

_____

_____

_____

_____

_____

_____

_____

_____

_____

_____

_____

_____

_____

_____

_____

_____

Narcissistic Abuse Cycle

DEVALUE

PERFORMATIVE THERAPY

In the context of my relationship with a highly toxic individual, I wasn't aware of his level of deceit until almost a year into our relationship. Often times, you don't know a person is lying until you catch them in a lie. Even then, they don't suddenly tell the truth. They just tell a bigger lie. Until this day, it's difficult to decipher the extent of his lies because he was so skilled at telling half truths. Over time, his attempts at performative therapy would enable him to use my deepest vulnerabilities against me. All while blaming my past traumas for my reactions to his actions, instead of owning up to his behavior that triggered those reactions in the first place.

Sadly, our therapist would side with him. All the while, I had a running list of his undeniable lies and subtle microaggressions. Whenever I brought up the facts of how he hurt me, the conversation would some how shift into how I can better manage my feelings and to create a "safe space" that enables him to want to express his. Her wildly misguided and misogynistic mentality of forcing a woman to do the emotional labor for a man who had no problem causing emotional harm was infuriating. It left me feeling unsafe and unheard. Imagine screaming underwater, only to have your voice drowned out by the weight of the ocean – that's how our sessions often felt. Overtime, that's how our entire relationship felt. It became easier to remain silent than to be continuously shamed. The paralyzing helplessness enabled a freeze response that would take my brain and body over a year to begin to heal from.

Over 16 months into our relationship I discovered a dating app on his phone. This was due to a private message I received from a woman on social media attempting to match with him. When confronted, he coerced me into firing my therapist who sided with my emotional experience. While our couple's therapist justified his behavior all because he weaponized incompetence and chronic "forgetfulness". In hindsight, this funny, (not so funny) blame shifting example is just one of many that almost deserves a round of applause for how skillfully and successfully manipulative it was. He was, an expert illusionist. Talk about pulling a David Blaine.

The entire experience was incredibly invalidating as she would witness him bully me into an apology or shame me into submission with his cruelty and contempt. My attachment system was on fire as this enabled our trauma bonds to deepen. Our couples therapist at the time was highly unskilled at conflict resolution. Therefore it was easier to get me to submit to the situation versus to get him to take accountability for the actions that caused it. Despite the countless emails I sent documenting his actions, she completely invalidated my experience, forcing me to doubt myself advocacy. In many ways, she's a significant factor that kept me in an abusive relationship; and why it was an act of God to leave it. Despite my best efforts, I will never forgive the way she stood by and allowed the abuse to happen.

Her constant invalidation and victim-blaming left me feeling as if I was losing my mind. This phenomenon is often called "Crazy Making," which we'll explore later in the cycle of abuse. Narcissists have a knack for weaponizing therapy and psychological terms to appear empathetic, especially when it comes to manipulating boundaries and evading accountability.

It's important to remember that therapy doesn't guarantee inner growth – it's a part of the process. True inner growth involves the integration of education, paired with the consistency of changed behavior. It's the difference between behavioral modification (short term) and behavioral change (long term). Another favorite quote of mine is, "An apology without changed behavior is just manipulation." -Unknown. When dealing with narcissists or highly toxic individuals, pay attention to their actions aligning with their words. Narcissists excel at apologies but fall short when it comes to taking personal accountability over an extended period of time.

Here's the thing, every time you forgive them, the honeymoon period gets shorter and shorter. That's because someone who is at war with themselves can never truly provide peace. Narcissists would rather control others versus control themselves. They would rather hurt others than heal themselves. They would rather manipulate others than build confidence and character. They would rather conceal the truth of who they are instead of heal from it. But that's the thing, liars never heal. If you think about it, someone that has to lie about who they are in order to be loved by others is an indication of someone who truly hates themselves.

Unbeknownst to him, the biggest reason I found the strength to leave was because of his mother's secret intervention. She, in many ways, saved my life. Because of his public presence, I fiercely protected our relationship, keeping the full extent of the abuse from those closest to us. I didn't want them to worry about me. And I also didn't want them to hate him. But she understood what I was going through, because she had faced a similar situation with his father.

Narcissistic Abuse Cycle

DEVALUE

PERFORMATIVE THERAPY

That said, Narcissists can weaponize therapy as a form of performative behavior to manipulate and scapegoat their partner in various ways:

- **Manipulative Charm:** In therapy sessions, narcissists may present themselves as charming, articulate, and composed. They may manipulate the therapist into believing that they are the victim or that their partner is the cause of all the problems in the relationship.
- **Blame-Shifting:** Narcissists are skilled at shifting blame onto others, including their partners. They may use therapy as a platform to blame their partner for all the issues in the relationship, portraying themselves as innocent victims.
- **Gaslighting:** Narcissists often gaslight their partners, making them doubt their own reality and experiences. In therapy, they may distort events and manipulate the narrative to make their partner appear irrational or unstable.
- **Triangulation:** Narcissists may involve third parties, such as friends or family members, in therapy sessions to gain allies and reinforce their version of events. This can further isolate and scapegoat their partner.
- **Lack of Accountability:** Narcissists are reluctant to take responsibility for their actions and may refuse to acknowledge their harmful behaviors. Instead, they might project their faults onto their partner or deny any wrongdoing.
- **Performative Behavior:** In therapy, narcissists may engage in performative behavior to create a false impression of self-awareness and willingness to change. However, their intentions are often insincere, and they may not genuinely work towards improving the relationship.
- **Manipulative Tactics:** Narcissists may use therapy sessions to gather information about their partner, which they can later use against them or exploit their vulnerabilities.

Because of my personal experience with a highly toxic individual, I can recognize the signs of abuse when working with my clients. I often see in a one-sided relationship with a narcissist, resentment can slowly build up in one partner while the narcissist intentionally avoids engaging in difficult conversations that truly matter to the other partner. The narcissist is unwilling to invest the emotional effort required for meaningful communication and accountability in the relationship. As the other partner attempts to address important issues, the narcissist may deflect blame and make the person feel guilty for even bringing up their concerns. This pattern of blame-shifting creates a toxic dynamic where the partner becomes hesitant to raise any further concerns or feels like they are walking on eggshells to avoid triggering conversations that lead to aggressive retaliation from a narcissist.

The more the narcissist avoids taking responsibility, the less the other partner feels comfortable bringing up their feelings or needs. This dynamic places the other partner in a double bind/double standard position. On one hand, they can choose to stay silent, suppressing their feelings and desires, and in turn, enabling the relationship to remain stagnant and unfulfilling. On the other hand, if they decide to stand up for themselves and express their needs, they risk the possibility of the narcissist becoming even more defensive, dismissive, or even retaliatory. In other words, they can risk staying silent and things remaining the same or risk voicing their pain and losing the relationship or being retaliated against. Either way, the Narcissist or highly toxic person is still less likely to change, and more likely to continue to deflect blame and shame. The narcissist's avoidance of difficult conversations and accountability demonstrates their unwillingness to prioritize the quality and growth of the relationship. They may prefer to maintain control and avoid any challenges to their ego or sense of self-importance. This leaves the other partner feeling invalidated and unimportant in the relationship.

Remember, a healthy and fulfilling relationship requires open communication, empathy, and mutual effort from both partners. If one partner consistently avoids difficult conversations and refuses to take responsibility, it may be an indication that the relationship is not truly balanced and nurturing. Putting oneself first and prioritizing emotional well-being is crucial in such circumstances. It's crucial for the partner of a narcissist to recognize these manipulative tactics and set clear boundaries during therapy. If you suspect that your partner is weaponizing therapy or using it to scapegoat you, consider seeking individual therapy for yourself to gain support and perspective. Remember, therapy should be a safe space for healing and growth, and it's essential to be in a therapeutic environment that supports your well-being and empowers you to address your needs. If you are dealing with a coach, therapist or even group of friends who have never experienced narcissistic abuse, they will miss the mark and underestimate the severity of the abuse every time. That's because someone's mere education about narcissism is not supplemental for their actual experience in overcoming it.

According to World Renowned Couples Therapist, Esther Parel, "A good clinician sees the invisible and sometimes hears the inaudible." It's not your job to convince people of your pain or to tolerate those who victim blame. As you heal and grow, you will learn to walk away instead of beg others to believe you or treat you better.

Narcissistic Abuse Cycle

DEVALUE

In the spirit of supporting your well-being and ensuring that you're never caught in the web of gaslighting, especially in the context of therapy or an unhealthy relationship, I've put together a list of thoughtful questions. These questions are your compass, guiding you as you advocate for yourself and take an active role in your healing journey. As someone who values the person within and serves as a trauma-informed coach, I deeply encourage those I love, including my clients, to empower themselves through education and self-advocacy. It's my belief that a compassionate and effective guide—whether they be a coach, therapist, friend, partner, parent, or leader—should nurture open dialogue and embrace constructive disagreement. Your discernment is invaluable. It's vital to engage with individuals you respect and who embody the lifestyle you aspire to achieve. Remember, seeking advice from those who've never ventured beyond their comfort zones can inadvertently slow down your personal growth and healing process.

- Have you been to therapy or have worked with a mental health specialist before?
- What is your educational and personal experience with mental health and wellness?
- What tools / frameworks do you most commonly use / teach?
- How should I communicate if something isn't working for me?
- What's your cancellation / communication policy?
- How will we meet and how often will we meet?
- How can I get in touch with you between sessions?
- What will we do if I/we feel stuck or disagree in session?
- Have you worked with individuals like me/us before?
- What are your credentials and ongoing educational / personal development goals?
- How will we measure progress?
- Do you offer / teach practical somatic healing modalities?
- Do you have a spiritual practice? If so, what does that look like?
- Can you describe what client success looks like and the game plan for the next 3-6 months together looks like?
- How can we structure in tools and frameworks in each session?
- How do you structure sessions to reinforce education and practical integration?
- What cultural competency, anti racism or gender biases trainings have you taken and how often do you take them?
- How do you educate your clients on the various healing modalities out there so they can become better equipped to manage their mental health and emotionally regulate?
- How do you regulate your nervous system when you find yourself triggered during sessions?
- Share an instance when your misjudgment of a client's situation led to detrimental outcomes.

In all fairness, I don't assume malice on the part of our therapist. Instead, I suspect that internalized biases might have colored her perception of what behaviors women should or should not tolerate within a relationship. It's crucial to acknowledge that within a woman's softness, there also resides immense strength. Surrendering does not equate to a woman's blind submission, and her delicacy should never be weaponized or confused with docility.

Words like "submissive" and "docile" often masquerade as descriptions of "femininity," but these definitions are skewed. They are also labels that have been placed upon those who've experienced oppression. Let's reflect on why these definitions are problematic and continue our journey of self-discovery and empowerment together. As we know, equality begins in the home. And empowerment is reflected in the way we shine (*or fail to*) our deepest, most intimate relationship.

Remember, mental and emotional health is not just for moments when you are struggling. It can be used as a tool to learn new interpersonal skills, unlearn harmful ones or to remove emotional blockages preventing you from reaching your goals. It is important to connect with a specialist that can meet you where you are and has the skills to move you to where you want to be.

Narcissistic Abuse Cycle

DEVALUE

As we transition from the nuances of performative therapy, I want you to picture this: You're caught up in a whirlwind of confusion and self-doubt, feeling like you're losing your grip on reality. That's what crazy making is all about. Crazy making is when someone, often a narcissist or manipulative individual, intentionally messes with your mind. [60] They use sneaky tactics to make you question your own sanity and perception of reality. It's like they're playing mind games with you, and it can leave you feeling like you're going, well, crazy.

So, how do they do it? They might twist your words and manipulate the truth, leaving you second-guessing your memory or what actually happened. They might gaslight you, making you believe that your feelings and experiences are invalid or exaggerated. They might even deny things they said or did, making you question your own sanity.

It's like they're in a constant dance of deception, where they spin the truth and distort reality to fit their narrative. They might make you feel like you're overreacting, being too sensitive, or even imagining things. The goal of crazy making is to gain power and control over you. By making you doubt yourself and your perception of reality, they can manipulate you more easily. It's a way for them to maintain dominance and keep you off balance. When in doubt, ask yourself: is this relationship driving me forward, or driving me crazy? Because here's the thing: You're not crazy. You're not imagining things. Your feelings and experiences are valid. Trust yourself and your instincts. Surround yourself with supportive people who can help you see through the manipulation.

This is important to note as the nuances of narcissism persist even in crazy making with the actor-observer bias. The actor-observer bias is an interesting psychological phenomenon. It's all about how we tend to explain our own behavior and the behavior of others in different ways, depending on whether we're the one doing the action (the actor) or the one observing it (the observer). When we're the actor, we often attribute our behavior to external factors – like, "I was late because traffic was terrible." But when we're observing someone else, we tend to attribute their behavior to internal factors – like, "They're late because they're always so disorganized." [61] Now, let's connect this to narcissistic abuse. Narcissistic abuse involves manipulative behaviors from someone who seeks to control and dominate another person. The actor-observer bias can come into play here in a few ways:

1. **Self-Victimization:** Narcissists might use the actor-observer bias to their advantage. They might excuse their hurtful behavior by blaming external circumstances, while accusing their partner of having internal flaws that caused the situation. For instance, if they're yelling, they might say, "I only acted this way because you pushed me to it!"
2. **Manipulative Shifting of Responsibility:** Narcissists might use the bias to manipulate their victims. They could do something hurtful and then blame the victim for "provoking" them or claim the victim is exaggerating the harm.
3. **Perception of Reality:** Victims of narcissistic abuse might struggle with the observer role. Friends and family might not see the manipulative behavior since the narcissist often presents a charming façade to the outside world. This can lead to the victim questioning their own perceptions and reality, due to the contrasting behavior they experience.

The actor-observer bias can contribute to the power dynamic in narcissistic relationships. It can make it harder for the victim to recognize the abuse, as they might attribute the narcissist's behavior to external factors or even blame themselves. It's a tricky psychological twist that can play a role in keeping the abusive cycle going. Recognize the signs of crazy making and set boundaries. Don't let their mind games drive you to the brink. Stay grounded in your truth and seek validation from trusted sources. Keep a journal, document incidents, and remind yourself of your worth. Narcissist are experts at making you question your reality, even when cold hard proof is available. The intermittent truth telling paired with their performative empathy allows them to groom their victims into submission.

Narcissistic Abuse Cycle

DEVALUE

PROFILING AN EMOTIONAL LIABILITY

Because Narcissists possess a knack for orchestrating a disturbing dance of manipulation, during the crazy making process, they have perfected the art of distorting reality as they skillfully create confusion, uncertainty, and self-doubt in their victims. This intricate manipulation is designed to break down a person's sense of self and gradually groom them into submission, fostering a dangerous cycle of control. To truly grasp the nuances of narcissism, it's crucial to recognize certain triggers that can set off narcissists, ones that might not have the same impact on individuals with healthier emotional dynamics. These insights shed light on the complexity of narcissistic behavior and help illuminate the intricate web they weave around their victims.

So, what are ways to identify if you're dealing with a Narcissist or Highly Toxic Individual?

Things That Trigger A Narcissist But Not Healthy People:
-When you tell them no
-When they are in the presence of someone who either has more money, status or is better than them or has more than them in any way
-They don't get what they want
-The lose the control or attention of their supply / victims
-When someone tells them the truth about themselves with feedback or holds them accountable
-When they are ignored
-When someone disagrees with them or doesn't pedestal them
-When they feel rejected or criticized
-When someone proves them wrong or challenges them
-When they are exposed or held accountable and are exposed for the behaviors they did in fact do

You Know You Are Dealing With An Emotional Liability When:
-You express your feelings and it ends in an argument
-They blame you for your reaction vs take responsibility for their actions that caused your reaction
-They shut you out to avoid accountability and responsibility
-They get mad at you for appropriately getting mad at them
-You find yourself walking on eggshells to avoid their emotional outbursts
-They discard and disrespect you after a disagreement or discussion
-They call you "too sensitive" for expressing how you feel
-Narcissists are triggered when questioned about the truth. Honest people have nothing to hide and provide reassurance

A person's response to various situations can reveal a lot about their character and emotional makeup. A telltale sign of a highly toxic individual will be communicated in the way someone responds reactively with emotional volatility, escapes accountability, or dismisses emotional validity. These three behavioral traits often intertwine, forming a manipulative strategy that toxic individuals employ to secure their dominance and control over others. Recognizing these patterns is essential for protecting oneself from emotional and psychological harm. As the saying goes, "What you allow, will continue". Establishing boundaries, developing emotional intelligence, and learning to identify healthy relationships are crucial steps in safeguarding against the impact of toxic individuals. Especially if the individual you are dealing with has a history of pathological lying and utilizing other manipulation tactics. One tactic to be mindful of is their ability to weaponize your love for them against you.

Narcissistic Abuse Cycle

DEVALUE

PATHOLOGICAL LYING & OTHER MANIPULATION TACTICS

Trust me, I know how devastating and heartbreaking it is when some people can wield the powerful words "I love you" like a double-edged sword. Narcissists are experts at using these words to keep their victims under their spell, making them believe that love is the reason to stay, even when the lack of it is a reason to leave. Love is never deceitful, abusive or selfish. That's not love. And love doesn't hurt. It's the only thing that heals. When a narcissist says "I love you," it can reawaken those deep childhood wounds. It's like a haunting echo of the past, where those who were meant to protect us, neglects us.

It's pretty twisted, but despite my former partner's name calling, abusive yelling or icing me out with the silent treatment, I wasn't actually afraid of him. At the time, I was most afraid of *losing* him. His big, beautiful muscles he would persuade me would protect me, were - in actuality - quite useless. Especially when the only thing I needed protection from was his egoic volatility, emotional instability and escapism tendencies. (*Sigh* He worked so hard for those.)

Any male that takes pride in not hitting a woman, but instead, does everything in his power to break her soul by weaponizing her own love for him against her, is not a man. That's a monster. No strong man goes out of his way to make the woman who loves him, feel weak. Or tries to destroy her when he feels angry.

If we grew up in unstable homes, our caregiver's neglect and emotional unavailability may have created a void, and now the narcissist preys on that vulnerability. They twist love into a painful dance, making you feel like you're not worthy of genuine affection and care if you are not performing enough for it. It's as if they know exactly how to press those old pain points, leaving you feeling powerless and trapped. But here's the thing – you don't have to let their manipulation define your worth or dictate your choices. You deserve a love that nurtures, respects, and cherishes you. You are worthy of a love that heals those old wounds and helps you grow. It takes immense courage to recognize the patterns and break free from the cycle.

In relationships with narcissists, it's essential to be aware of the countless manipulation tactics they employ - in addition to weaponizing your love for them against you. These tactics can include mirroring, where they reflect back what you want to hear or see [62], playing dumb to gain an advantage, using word salad to confuse and distract [63], and employing crazy-making behaviors that leave you feeling disoriented [64]. They may withdraw emotionally, refusing to address the issues at hand, while focusing on your reaction rather than taking responsibility for their actions.

As we know, often, their apologies are insincere, with no real change in behavior, and they may discard you after any disagreement. Moreover, they invalidate your experiences and emotions, using your vulnerabilities against you to maintain control. The use of double standards, double binds, and reactive abuse further complicates the dynamics. Narcissists may employ intimidation and control resources such as money, home, car, or family to keep you under their power.

One of the most difficult tactics to recognize is the pathological lying. For example, let's highlight pathological lying and its connection to a child's upbringing. Imagine a situation where a parent confronts their child about lying. If the parent reacts with anger and punishment, the child may feel scared, leading them to deny the truth to protect themselves from the pain of rejection. The parent's approach of sending the child to their room until they confess can backfire, as it may make the child even more skilled at hiding the truth or telling bigger lies to avoid the pain of punishment.

This pattern can carry into adulthood, especially when dealing with narcissists or toxic individuals. A child that learned to lie becomes adult who struggles to tell the truth. Narcissists and other highly toxic humans can act like grown children, covering up their lies with even bigger lies or playing dumb to manipulate the situation in their favor. Plausible deniability and lying by omission is still lying. However in their mind, a half truth is still their valid version of the truth. A Narcissistic partner does not have a problem with lying. They often have a problem with being held accountable for their actions once you find out the truth.

Listen, lying is not only a form of emotional manipulation but also a destructive form of emotional regulation. When we lie, we rob others of their power to make informed choices and decisions based on what is good for them, so it benefits what is best for us. This is the exact definition of taking advantage of someone's trust. We may lie out of fear of not getting what we want or losing what we have, leading to relational betrayals. Not all betrayals in toxic relationship dynamics are infidelity. However infidelity is an example of a relational betrayal. More on this later. In short, you should never lie to someone who trusts you. Or trust someone who continuously lies to you. Naturally, a Narcissist will become offended when you don't believe their lies. *Sigh*

To help us to address pathological lying, Chris Voss, a former FBI negotiator, and Evy Poumpouras, a former Secret Service agent, both offer strategies for detecting deception and catching someone in a lie. Their approaches are grounded in understanding human behavior, reading verbal and nonverbal cues, and asking strategic questions. Here are some of their recommended strategies:

Chris Voss's Strategies [66]:
1. **Labeling:** Voss suggests using labels to acknowledge someone's emotions and thoughts. This technique encourages the person to either confirm or correct the label, potentially revealing inconsistencies in their response.
2. **Mirroring:** Mirroring involves subtly mimicking the other person's body language and speech patterns. This can establish rapport and make them more comfortable, potentially making it easier to notice shifts in behavior or inconsistencies.
3. **Calibrated Questions:** Asking questions that encourage the person to divulge more information can help reveal inconsistencies in their story. These questions are open-ended and require more than a simple "yes" or "no" response.

Evy Poumpouras's Strategies [67]:
1. **Baseline Observations:** Pay attention to the person's baseline behavior, noting their usual mannerisms, speech patterns, and body language. Deviations from this baseline could signal deception.
2. **Microexpressions:** Look for fleeting facial expressions that occur involuntarily, revealing hidden emotions. These microexpressions can be subtle signs of deception.
3. **Verbal Clues:** Poumpouras emphasizes listening for changes in tone, pitch, and word choice, which can indicate nervousness or discomfort.

Next, Ask Open-Ended Questions:
1. Can you tell me more about your involvement in this situation?
2. How did you come to that conclusion?
3. Can you describe your thought process leading up to that decision?
4. What were your feelings when that occurred?
5. Walk me through the events that led to this outcome.

Followed By, Closed-Ended Questions:
1. Did you really say that?
2. Were you present at that place and time?
3. Did you have any involvement in this incident?
4. Is this version of events accurate according to your memory?
5. Did you communicate with them about this matter?

When dealing with narcissists, it's important to remember that they are adept manipulators and might resort to more elaborate forms of deception. Their pathological lying is deeply ingrained, often serving their need for control and admiration. While these strategies can help you detect inconsistencies, it's also vital to trust your intuition and carefully assess the larger context of their behavior.

Pathological lying is just one aspect of narcissism, and addressing it requires careful consideration of the broader dynamics and potential impact on your well-being. Honesty is crucial for building trust and meaningful connections. In order to be trusting of an individual, they must be trustworthy. By concealing the truth, Narcissists and other highly toxic individuals hinder their own healing and growth. Lying implies that what others might know will hurt the deceitful parts of us we active choose to hide. Embracing honesty and creating a safe space for open communication are vital for breaking free from these destructive patterns and fostering healthier relationships.

Narcissistic Abuse Cycle

DEVALUE

PATHOLOGICAL LYING & OTHER MANIPULATION TACTICS

NOW THAT YOU UNDERSTAND A BIT MORE ABOUT PATHOLOGICAL LYING AND OTHER MANIPULATION TACTICS, HOW HAS PATHOLOGICAL LYING IMPACTED YOUR EXPERIENCES OF NARCISSISTIC ABUSE OR TOXIC RELATIONSHIPS? HOW DO YOU NAVIGATE TRUST AND HONESTY WITHIN THESE DYNAMICS?

Narcissistic Abuse Cycle

DEVALUE

IN WHAT WAYS DO YOU SEE PATHOLOGICAL LYING AS A COPING MECHANISM FOR THE NARCISSIST OR TOXIC INDIVIDUAL? HOW DOES THEIR USE OF LIES AND DECEPTION AFFECT YOUR EMOTIONAL WELL-BEING AND SENSE OF SAFETY?

Narcissistic Abuse Cycle

DEVALUE

PATHOLOGICAL LYING & OTHER MANIPULATION TACTICS

HOW HAS ENCOUNTERING PATHOLOGICAL LYING IN A NARCISSISTIC RELATIONSHIP AFFECTED YOUR ABILITY TO TRUST AND CONNECT WITH OTHERS OUTSIDE OF THAT RELATIONSHIP? HAVE YOU NOTICED ANY PATTERNS OR TRIGGERS IN YOUR INTERACTIONS WITH PEOPLE AFTER EXPERIENCING SUCH ABUSE?

Narcissistic Abuse Cycle

DEVALUE

PATHOLOGICAL LYING & OTHER MANIPULATION TACTICS

WHAT STRATEGIES HAVE YOU FOUND HELPFUL IN IDENTIFYING AND RESPONDING TO PATHOLOGICAL LYING WITHIN THE CONTEXT OF NARCISSISTIC ABUSE? HOW DO YOU PRIORITIZE YOUR EMOTIONAL WELL-BEING AND SET BOUNDARIES WHEN DEALING WITH SOMEONE WHO CONSISTENTLY MANIPULATES THE TRUTH?

Narcissistic Abuse Cycle

DEVALUE

NARCISSISTIC CONTRADICTIONS

Navigating a relationship with a narcissist can be confusing af due to their consistent use of double standards and contradictions. As we delve deeper into navigating the complex landscape of narcissism, it's essential to gain a comprehensive understanding of the intricate web of covert manipulation tactics and pathological lying that often define their behavior. Armed with this awareness, we can now transition our focus towards a particularly insightful technique: recognizing and utilizing contradictory statements to shed light on the inconsistencies that underlie their actions. This approach allows us to pierce through the veneer of deception and grasp the inner workings of narcissistic behavior.

Here are 18 ways they often display this behavior:

1. **Expecting Praise, Yet Rarely Giving It:** Narcissists often crave admiration and compliments, but they rarely offer the same in return.
2. **Demanding Honesty, Yet Concealing Truths:** Narcissists may demand complete honesty from their partner but frequently engage in deception and half-truths themselves.
3. **Seeking Empathy, Yet Lacking Empathy:** They desire empathy and understanding for their emotions but struggle to show genuine concern for their partner's feelings.
4. **Needing Space, Yet Becoming Clingy:** Narcissists may demand space and independence but can quickly become clingy and possessive when their partner asserts independence.
5. **Wanting Control, Yet Avoiding Responsibility:** They seek to control various aspects of the relationship but tend to avoid responsibility for their actions and choices.
6. **Desiring Loyalty, Yet Betraying Trust:** Narcissists expect unwavering loyalty but may betray their partner's trust through lies or infidelity.
7. **Criticizing Imperfections, Yet Refusing Accountability:** They are quick to point out their partner's flaws but rarely take responsibility for their own shortcomings.
8. **Demanding Flexibility, Yet Resisting Change:** Narcissists may expect their partner to adapt to their needs but resist change or compromise themselves.
9. **Seeking Validation, Yet Dismissing Opinions:** They crave validation and agreement but often dismiss or belittle their partner's opinions, achievements or ideas.
10. **Valuing Independence, Yet Seeking Enmeshment:** Narcissists may value their independence but frequently seek to control and manipulate their partner, creating an enmeshed dynamic.
11. They expect others to prioritize their needs but show little consideration for others' feelings or desires.
12. Narcissists expect forgiveness for their actions but hold grudges against those who have wronged them.
13. They may claim to be selfless and giving but are often selfish and focused on their own interests.
14. Narcissists may play the victim to gain sympathy and attention, even if they are the ones at fault.
15. Narcissists demand privacy and autonomy but invade others' boundaries and violate their privacy.
16. They expect others to be accountable for their actions but rarely take responsibility for their own behavior.
17. They blame others for their reactions to their harmful actions.
18. They may seek approval and validation from everyone, even strangers, but disregard the feelings and opinions of close friends and family.

Recognizing these patterns can help individuals identify the toxic dynamics present in their relationship with a narcissist. Especially as they double down on their contradictions with the use of gaslighting.

Narcissistic Abuse Cycle

DEVALUE

Gaslighting is a manipulative psychological tactic used by individuals to make someone doubt their own perceptions, memories, and reality. [68] It is a form of emotional and psychological abuse where the gaslighter seeks to gain power and control over the gaslightee by undermining their confidence and sense of self. The term "gaslighting" originates from a play and subsequent film adaptation titled "Gas Light," in which a husband uses manipulative tactics to make his wife believe she is going insane. Gaslighting involves a series of actions, behaviors, and statements that collectively erode the victim's trust in their own judgment. The gaslighter may:

1. **Deny Reality:** They might deny that events or conversations took place, even if there's evidence to the contrary.
2. **Twist the Truth:** The gaslighter might distort facts, manipulate details, or provide a skewed version of events to confuse the victim.
3. **Withhold Information:** By selectively sharing information or keeping crucial details hidden, the gaslighter maintains control over the narrative.
4. **Project:** They accuse the victim of behaviors or feelings that they themselves are engaging in, making the victim doubt their own intentions.
5. **Trivialize Feelings:** The gaslighter undermines the victim's emotions, belittling their reactions as irrational or exaggerated.
6. **Shift Blame:** They deflect responsibility for their actions and project it onto the victim, making them feel guilty for things they didn't do.
7. **Isolate:** Gaslighters might isolate the victim from friends, family, or other sources of support to ensure they rely solely on the gaslighter's perspective.

The ultimate goal of gaslighting is to make the victim doubt their own reality and become dependent on the gaslighter's version of events. Over time, the victim's self-esteem, confidence, and ability to trust their own perceptions can become severely damaged. Gaslighting is a particularly insidious form of manipulation that can occur in personal relationships, workplaces, and various social contexts such as political gaslighting, historical gaslighting, medical gaslighting, gender bias gaslighting or even social justice gaslighting.

Below are 13 common gaslighting phrases that narcissists might use. However, it's important to note that not everyone who uses these phrases is necessarily a narcissist, and context is essential in understanding gaslighting.

1. "You're just overreacting, I never did that."
2. "You're too sensitive."
3. "You're imagining things."
4. "I never said/did that. If I'm so terrible why are you still here then?"
5. "You're crazy/insane. I think you misunderstood what happened."
6. "You're always playing the victim. Stop feeling sorry for yourself."
7. "You're just trying to make me look bad."
8. "You must be remembering it wrong."
9. "You're just being dramatic. It's not that big of a deal."
10. "You're making things up, you're the one that's lying."
11. "You're so insecure. I was just joking. It's not that big of a deal."
12. "You're being irrational. I "forgot" to tell you that happened."
13. "You're always exaggerating. That didn't happen. Do you have proof?"

Often times, Narcissists will call you crazy for questioning their actions that turned out to be true. They will prey off of your insecurities and make you question your intuition by betraying your trust, lying to you and avoiding accountability. Remember, gaslighting is a manipulative tactic that seeks to undermine your perception of reality and make you doubt yourself. If you consistently encounter these phrases and feel confused, belittled, or invalidated, it may be a red flag of gaslighting behavior. A healthy person doesn't tolerate games or desires to play them. Trust your instincts and seek support from trusted friends, family, or professionals to help you navigate such situations. One of the best defense mechanisms against gaslighting is going "Gray Rock".

Narcissistic Abuse Cycle

DEVALUE

GRAY ROCK METHOD

Going "gray rock" is a boundary-setting and conflict-avoidance strategy that can be effective in dealing with narcissists. It simply means making yourself dull and nonreactive, like a colorless unmoving rock. In gray-rock mode, you engage minimally with the narcissist and his/her circus of enablers/flying monkeys. [69]

Every time you negatively respond to someones anger, you become a physical manifestation of it. Do not show or share your thoughts or feelings. You do not need to react to antagonism and manipulation. In short, you make yourself of little interest to the narcissist as possible. Limit contact, decrease you emotional reactions, arguing or explanations. This only encourages them. Any attention, even negative attention makes them feel powerful and relevant. Remember, silence is not the same as stupidity. And remaining silent is not the same as being silenced. As you heal and grow you will recognize that not every action deserves a reaction. Sit back and watch what they show you. They are revealing to you their character, their intentions, who they really are.

In doing so, you will be better able to discern between your feelings for them and the facts about them. Discerning between your feelings and facts is crucial when identifying and tracking manipulative behavior from a narcissist. Here are three steps to help you in this process:

- **Recognize Emotional Triggers:** Pay attention to moments when you feel emotionally charged or upset. Take a step back and ask yourself, "What are the facts in this situation?" Separate your emotions from the objective reality of the situation. By acknowledging your emotional triggers, you can start to distinguish between your own feelings and the manipulative tactics employed by the narcissist.

- **Validate Your Experience:** Validate your emotions and experiences as valid and important. Trust your instincts and intuition. It's common for narcissists to gaslight and make you doubt your own perceptions. Even if you don't have hard evidence to support your intuition, trust what your nervous system is telling you. It's your job to create distance from a threat if you feel like you are in danger or being disrespected. Instead of trying to control the way the treat you, work towards controlling what you will and will not tolerate. You can't control their actions but you can control your reactions. Remind yourself that your feelings matter and have value.

- **Document Manipulative Behavior:** Keep a record or journal to document instances of manipulative behavior from the narcissist. Write down specific incidents, behaviors, and their impact on you. This helps create a factual record of the manipulation, making it easier to identify patterns and gain clarity. I usually make a running list of facts that I can reference when I am feeling emotionally dysregulated. It also serves as a reminder when you might doubt yourself in the future.

Remember, discerning between your feelings and facts requires practice and self-awareness. It's a valuable skill in navigating the complexities of a narcissistic relationship and protecting your emotional well-being. The goal is to recognize their abusive behavior in order to leave a harmful situation versus trying to stay and make a bad situation good. As difficult as it may be, you have to stand up for yourself. Even if that means secretly leaving. You cannot allow someone to mistreat you just because you love them. Their trauma is not an excuse for them to allow them to traumatize you. In abusive relationships that feel like a life or death situation, find ways to escape in secret by seeking the support of trusted family, friends, law enforcement and therapists. The domestic abuse hotline number is 800-799-7233.

Remember, you deserve to be in a relationship where your voice is heard, your experiences are validated, and your emotional well-being is valued. Stay strong, trust your instincts, and surround yourself with a supportive network as you navigate the challenges posed by a narcissistic partner. Your well-being matters, and healing and growth are possible. If you find yourself in this situation, using the Gray Rock method will help you to protect yourself from the narcissists intentional attempt at crazy making and using word salads to confuse you. Use the questions on the following page to help you to address the difference between your intuition guiding you and your anxieties guarding you.

Narcissistic Abuse Cycle

DEVALUE

TRUSTING YOUR INTUITION

INTUITION AND ANXIETY CAN SOMETIMES BE CONFUSED, BUT THERE ARE KEY DIFFERENCES BETWEEN THEM. INTUITION IS A DEEP SENSE OF KNOWING OR UNDERSTANDING WITHOUT THE NEED FOR LOGICAL REASONING OR EVIDENCE. IT IS OFTEN DESCRIBED AS A GUT FEELING OR A SENSE OF INNER WISDOM. ON THE OTHER HAND, ANXIETY IS A STATE OF UNEASE, FEAR, OR WORRY THAT ARISES IN RESPONSE TO PERCEIVED THREATS OR UNCERTAINTIES. BY REFLECTING ON THESE QUESTIONS AND PAYING ATTENTION TO YOUR BODY'S RESPONSES, YOU CAN START TO DIFFERENTIATE BETWEEN GENUINE INTUITIVE NUDGES AND ANXIETY-DRIVEN WORRIES. IT'S IMPORTANT TO LISTEN TO YOUR INTUITION WHILE ALSO ADDRESSING AND MANAGING ANY ANXIETY THAT MAY ARISE TO MAKE DECISIONS THAT ARE ALIGNED WITH YOUR BEST INTERESTS AND OVERALL WELL-BEING.

THINK OF A TIME (PAST OR PRESENT) WHERE A HIGHLY TOXIC PERSON MADE YOU QUESTIONED YOUR INTUITION. WRITE YOUR RESPONSES TO EACH REFLECTION QUESTION IN THE SPACE BELOW.

IS/WAS THE FEELING BASED ON ACTUAL EVIDENCE OR CONCRETE INFORMATION? INTUITION OFTEN ARISES FROM A PLACE OF INNER KNOWING WITHOUT NEEDING EXTERNAL PROOF. ANXIETY, ON THE OTHER HAND, MAY BE TRIGGERED BY IRRATIONAL FEARS OR WORRIES THAT LACK SUBSTANTIAL EVIDENCE.

Narcissistic Abuse Cycle

DEVALUE

TRUSTING YOUR INTUITION

DOES/DID THE FEELING PERSIST OR SUBSIDE OVER TIME? INTUITION IS OFTEN A CONSISTENT AND STEADY GUIDANCE, WHEREAS ANXIETY TENDS TO BE MORE FLUCTUATING AND CAN ESCALATE OR DECREASE IN INTENSITY BASED ON VARIOUS FACTORS.

Narcissistic Abuse Cycle

DEVALUE

HOW DOES/DID THE FEELING IMPACT YOUR OVERALL WELL-BEING AND SENSE OF CLARITY? INTUITION USUALLY BRINGS A SENSE OF CLARITY, AND ALIGNMENT WITH YOUR VALUES AND DESIRES. ANXIETY, ON THE OTHER HAND, OFTEN LEADS TO INCREASED STRESS, CONFUSION, AND A FEELING OF BEING OVERWHELMED. YOU ONLY QUESTION THE RIGHT THING TO DO WHEN IT'S THE HARD THING TO DO.

Narcissistic Abuse Cycle

DEVALUE

The devaluing stage in a narcissistic relationship is undeniably one of the most challenging and tumultuous phases of the narcissistic abuse cycle as it can leave you questioning your intuition as you are overwhelmed with anxiety. During this period, the narcissist's behavior becomes chaotic and confusing with both overt and covert nuances associated with emotional and psychological abuse. It can be incredibly difficult to decipher whether the person you love is intentionally being malicious or is simply absent-minded or unaware. However, the mind games and manipulations are intentionally orchestrated with precision to keep you in a perpetual state of confusion. This constant state of uncertainty serves their ultimate goal: maintaining power and control over you.

In the devaluing stage, you may find yourself questioning whether the love and affection you once received were genuine or merely part of the narcissist's elaborate facade. They skillfully blur the lines between love and hate, leaving you feeling emotionally trapped and vulnerable. The gaslighting, blame-shifting, and projection techniques they employ are meant to further erode your sense of reality and self-worth. As they meticulously plan their moves, the narcissist remains two steps ahead, making it challenging for you to fully comprehend their motives and intentions. This calculated strategy is designed to ensure they always have the upper hand in the relationship. By exploiting your vulnerabilities and keeping you off-balance, they manipulate your emotions, creating a toxic environment that perpetuates their control. One of the most significant lessons I've taken to heart is refraining from asking myself, "Why are they treating me poorly?" I've also let go of the habit of coming up with excuses for their harmful actions. Instead, I've come to terms with the fact that irrespective of their awareness or intention, they were indeed treating me in a way that didn't align with my values. This realization has enabled me to start acknowledging the person before me for who they truly are, rather than projecting my desires onto them of who I wanted them to be for me.

Below is a list of over 50 examples of words used to describe a healthy and unhealthy relationship dynamic. In the space below, highlight all of the healthy and unhealthy words associated with the state of your relationship with a highly toxic person in your life (past or present). Next, I want you to make note of the frequency, intensity and duration of time each negative characteristic lasts in a two week span. Evaluate your relationships and adjust accordingly.

Healthy Relationship		Unhealthy Relationship	
• Trusting	• Fun-loving	• Manipulative	• Conditional love
• Respectful	• Empowering	• Controlling	• Power struggles
• Supportive	• Loyal	• Abusive	• Disconnected
• Loving	• Inspiring	• Disrespectful	• Resentful
• Communicative	• Accepting	• Demeaning	• Escalating conflicts
• Equal	• Boundary-respecting	• Distant	• Violation of boundaries
• Empathetic	• Shared values	• Dishonest	• Imbalanced power dynamics
• Nurturing	• Growth-oriented	• Toxic	• Financially exploitative
• Safe	• Balanced power dynamics	• Volatile	• Emotionally unavailable
• Caring	• Authentic	• Jealous	• Invalidating
• Honest	• Constructive conflict	• Codependent	• Lack of growth or stagnation
• Open	resolution	• Insecure	• Dishonesty
• Reliable	• Mutual support	• Unpredictable	• Lack of reciprocity
• Secure	• Individual autonomy	• Dismissive	• Dependency
• Collaborative	• Emotional availability	• Inconsistent	• Lack of accountability
• Affectionate	• Mutual admiration	• Isolating	• Infidelity
• Understanding	• Space for personal growth	• Violent	• Emotional manipulation
• Balanced	• Financially responsible	• Unfaithful	• Unresolved trauma
• Encouraging	• Emotional intimacy	• Coercive	• Lack of communication
• Compassionate	• Reciprocal love	• Possessive	• Lack of trust
• Committed	• Consistent	• Domineering	• Lack of empathy
• Intimate	• Forgiving	• Selfish	• Contemptuous
• Patient	• Non-judgmental	• Gaslighting	• Blaming
• Appreciative	• Team-oriented	• Neglectful	• Unsupportive
• Independent (while	• Harmonious	• Dismissive	
maintaining connection)	• Resilient	• Irresponsible	

Narcissistic Abuse Cycle

DEVALUE

Navigating relationships with narcissists can be a complex journey, unveiling stark differences between healthy, unhealthy, and abusive dynamics. In a healthy relationship, there's mutual respect, open communication, and a willingness to support each other's growth. In contrast, an unhealthy dynamic with a narcissist involves an imbalance of power, manipulation, and disregard for the other person's feelings. Here, emotional and psychological boundaries are often violated. When it came to my former partner, his anger wasn't the issue. It was the destructive actions he used to convey it. His inability to control his emotions projected an almost perverse entitlement that he used to justify controlling my emotions instead. It was this entitled belief system that allowed him to remain abusive and unable to convey compassion or remorse. However, it was my unprocessed worthiness wounds that enabled me to think I was deserving of it.

Being in an abusive relationship with a narcissist is characterized by a deliberate pattern of control, emotional torment, and exploitation. In these relationships, the narcissist's need for dominance trumps empathy, resulting in relentless manipulation, gaslighting, and emotional abuse. Victims often grapple with diminished self-worth, confusion, and isolation, trapped in a cycle that erodes their mental and emotional well-being. Remember, the momentary moments of happiness are not worth the long term harm. The difference between healthy and unhealthy relationships is the way conflict is handled. Unhealthy relationships begin the same way healthy relationships do; with love, kindness and affection. However, in unhealthy relationships, the bad begins to disproportionately outweigh the good until all resemblance of love and trust has been deeply eroded.

In the chart below, I highlight some key differences to be aware of.

Healthy Relationship	Unhealthy Relationship	Abusive Relationship
1. Mutual respect and equality.	1. Lack of respect and equality.	1. Power and control dynamics.
2. Open and honest communication.	2. Poor communication or communication breakdown.	2. Frequent emotional, verbal, or physical abuse.
3. Trust and transparency.	3. Jealousy, possessiveness, or controlling behaviors.	3. Manipulative tactics and gaslighting.
4. Supportive and caring behavior.	4. Disregard for boundaries and personal autonomy.	4. Fear and intimidation.
5. Shared decision-making and compromise.	5. Lack of support or dismissive behavior.	5. Isolation and controlling behavior.
6. Individual autonomy and personal boundaries are respected.	6. Power imbalances and unequal decision-making.	6. Extreme jealousy and possessiveness.
7. Emotional and physical safety.	7. Frequent arguments or constant tension.	7. Denial or minimization of abusive behavior.
8. Growth and personal development are encouraged.	8. Emotional manipulation or guilt-tripping.	8. Inability to express opinions or make decisions without fear.
9. Healthy conflict resolution and problem-solving.	9. Isolation from friends and family.	9. Physical harm and potential danger to one's well-being.
10. Emotional intimacy and connection.	10. Unresolved conflicts and repetitive negative patterns.	

Our upbringing leaves an incredible mark on how we perceive relationships. If we grew up in emotionally abusive or neglectful environments, those toxic behaviors can become ingrained and normalized. This normalization blinds us to recognizing unhealthy or abusive patterns in our romantic relationships. The very behaviors that should raise alarms might instead trigger a sense of familiarity, subconsciously linking them to love and acceptance. Breaking free from this cycle requires us to unravel the past, relearn healthy dynamics, and muster the courage to redefine what we deserve in love. It's a journey of self-discovery and healing, leading us toward relationships that nurture our well-being rather than perpetuate old wounds. Answer the reflection questions on the pages that follow to learn more about your interactions with highly toxic or Narcissistic individuals.

Narcissistic Abuse Cycle

DEVALUE

HEALTHY VS UNHEALTHY RELATIONSHIPS

IN WHAT WAYS DOES THE BAD OUT WEIGH THE GOOD? OR THE GOOD OUTWEIGHS THE BAD? BECAUSE OF THIS, IN WHAT WAYS DO/DID YOU FIND IT HARD TO LEAVE OR CREATE DISTANCE?

_____

_____

_____

_____

_____

_____

_____

_____

_____

_____

_____

_____

_____

_____

_____

_____

_____

_____

Narcissistic Abuse Cycle

DEVALUE

REFLECTING ON YOUR EXPERIENCE IN THE NARCISSISTIC RELATIONSHIP, CAN YOU IDENTIFY SPECIFIC MOMENTS OR EVENTS THAT MARKED THE TRANSITION FROM A HEALTHY DYNAMIC TO AN UNHEALTHY AND ABUSIVE ONE? HOW DID YOU FEEL DURING THESE PIVOTAL MOMENTS, AND WHAT EMOTIONS DID YOU OBSERVE IN THE OTHER PERSON?

Narcissistic Abuse Cycle

DEVALUE

HEALTHY VS UNHEALTHY RELATIONSHIPS

HOW DID THE NARCISSISTIC PARTNER'S BEHAVIOR CHANGE AS THE RELATIONSHIP PROGRESSED INTO AN UNHEALTHY AND ABUSIVE STATE? WERE THERE ANY PARTICULAR PATTERNS OR RECURRING THEMES IN THEIR ACTIONS OR COMMUNICATION THAT YOU NOTICED? HOW DID THESE CHANGES IMPACT YOUR EMOTIONAL WELL-BEING AND OVERALL SENSE OF SELF?

Narcissistic Abuse Cycle

DEVALUE

HEALTHY VS UNHEALTHY RELATIONSHIPS

IN RETROSPECT, DO YOU RECOGNIZE ANY RED FLAGS OR WARNING SIGNS THAT YOU MAY HAVE OVERLOOKED OR DISMISSED DURING THE EARLY STAGES OF THE RELATIONSHIP? HOW DO YOU THINK THESE INITIAL SIGNS CONTRIBUTED TO THE EVENTUAL SHIFT TOWARDS AN ABUSIVE DYNAMIC? WHAT INSIGHTS HAVE YOU GAINED ABOUT YOURSELF AND YOUR BOUNDARIES AS A RESULT OF THIS EXPERIENCE?

Narcissistic Abuse Cycle

DEVALUE

SELF GASLIGHTING & DISMISSIVE POSITIVITY

I saw a quote once that said, "Sometimes red flags are not always about the other person. When you start making excuses for their mistreatment or unhealthy behaviors, the red flags become about you." -Unknown. Admittedly, this would have made me a walking red flag. This is how I enabled my ego to betray my heart. Whoops. The difficult reality about abusive relationships is that many of us who were raised in abusive homes, may have difficulty spotting covert abuse due to its normalization. It is this level of normalization that can lead to desensitization.

When leaving my abusive relationship, I felt so much shame as if I were abandoning him in the process. I even experienced shame from those who couldn't understand why I stayed "if it were so bad." When processing the aftermath of an abusive relationship, it's important to address why you stayed, but also why you felt like you couldn't leave. Often times this is the root of our trauma responses that can be traced back to unhealed wounds from childhood.

In order to justify staying and overlooking his abuse, I used to make excuses for his behavior or minimize the impact his actions had on me - just as he did. In other words, I started to treat myself the way he treated me.

Gaslighting ourselves in relationships can be a harmful defense mechanism that allows us to justify someone's toxic behavior by downplaying its negative impact. Here are ten examples of how we might engage in self-gaslighting with dismissive positivity:

1. **Excusing their hurtful comments:** Telling ourselves that they didn't mean it or that they were just having a bad day, rather than acknowledging the emotional harm caused by their words.
2. **Minimizing their controlling behavior:** Downplaying their need for control as a sign of concern or care, even when it infringes upon our independence.
3. **Ignoring their emotional unavailability:** Making excuses for their lack of emotional support, telling ourselves that they are just not good at expressing their feelings.
4. **Rationalizing their lies:** Convinced that they lied to protect us or avoid unnecessary conflict, even when their dishonesty erodes trust.
5. **Accepting their aggressive behavior:** Believing that their anger or aggression is justified because of external stressors, rather than recognizing it as a form of abuse.
6. **Dismissing their manipulation:** Convinced that they are just looking out for our best interests, rather than recognizing their self-serving motives.
7. **Overlooking their disrespect:** Explaining away their disrespectful actions as a result of a bad mood or a misunderstanding.
8. **Ignoring their dismissive attitude:** Justifying their lack of interest in our opinions or feelings as mere differences in communication styles.
9. **Excusing their neglect:** Blaming ourselves for not being "good enough" to deserve their attention, rather than holding them accountable for their lack of effort in the relationship.
10. **Normalizing their silent treatment:** Telling ourselves they need space or time to process, rather than recognizing the silent treatment as a form of emotional abuse.

By engaging in dismissive positivity, we inadvertently enable and perpetuate the toxic behavior of others, and more importantly, deny ourselves the opportunity to acknowledge the harmful impact it has on our well-being. It's crucial to practice self-awareness and confront these tendencies to break free from the cycle of self-gaslighting and establish healthier boundaries in relationships. Your conscious attempt to stay is a manifestation of your subconscious attempt to receive love. There's no shame in that. Just compassion. In the pages that follow, let's dive into some reflection questions to help you to understand not only why you engaged in justifying behaviors but also, why you felt like you had to.

Narcissistic Abuse Cycle

DEVALUE

SELF GASLIGHTING & DISMISSIVE POSITIVITY

REFLECTING ON YOUR EXPERIENCES WITH NARCISSISTIC ABUSE, CAN YOU IDENTIFY ANY FACTORS THAT MADE YOU FEEL LIKE YOU COULDN'T LEAVE THE RELATIONSHIP? HOW DID THESE FACTORS IMPACT YOUR SENSE OF SAFETY AND WELL-BEING?

Narcissistic Abuse Cycle

DEVALUE

SELF GASLIGHTING & DISMISSIVE POSITIVITY

HOW DID THE NARCISSISTIC ABUSER MANIPULATE YOUR EMOTIONS AND PERCEPTIONS TO MAKE YOU BELIEVE THAT STAYING IN THE RELATIONSHIP WAS THE ONLY OPTION? WHAT WERE SOME OF THE MIND GAMES OR TACTICS THEY USED TO KEEP YOU TRAPPED?

_____

_____

_____

_____

_____

_____

_____

_____

_____

_____

_____

_____

_____

_____

_____

_____

_____

_____

Narcissistic Abuse Cycle

DEVALUE

SELF GASLIGHTING & DISMISSIVE POSITIVITY

CAN YOU IDENTIFY ANY INTERNAL BELIEFS OR SELF-DOUBTS THAT MAY HAVE INFLUENCED YOUR DECISION TO STAY IN THE ABUSIVE RELATIONSHIP? HOW DID THESE BELIEFS SHAPE YOUR UNDERSTANDING OF YOUR WORTH AND WHAT YOU DESERVED IN A PARTNERSHIP?

_____

_____

_____

_____

_____

_____

_____

_____

_____

_____

_____

_____

_____

_____

_____

Narcissistic Abuse Cycle

DEVALUE

In the graphic below we highlight the push/pull relationship dynamics of the Narcissistic Abuse Cycle [70]. As tension builds, there is only matter of time before there as an acute explosion within the relationship that forces a victim to protect themselves by acquiescing to the abuser to abandoning them. This graphic indicates the nuances of narcissism that can be addressed in a relatively cyclical and predictable pattern of emotions and behaviors. By understanding the intricacies associated with reach stage of the cycle, you can begin to raise your level of self awareness in order to break free from it.

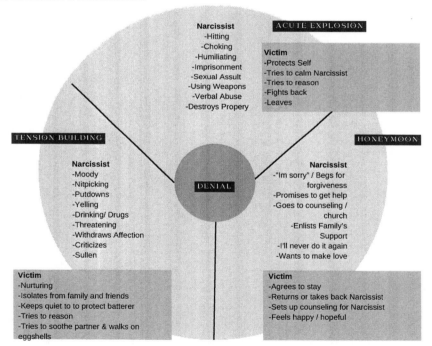

Narcissist
-Hitting
-Choking
-Humiliating
-Imprisonment
-Sexual Assult
-Using Weapons
-Verbal Abuse
-Destroys Propery

ACUTE EXPLOSION

Victim
-Protects Self
-Tries to calm Narcissist
-Tries to reason
-Fights back
-Leaves

TENSION BUILDING

Narcissist
-Moody
-Nitpicking
-Putdowns
-Yelling
-Drinking/ Drugs
-Threatening
-Withdraws Affection
-Criticizes
-Sullen

DENIAL

HONEYMOON

Narcissist
-"Im sorry" / Begs for forgiveness
-Promises to get help
-Goes to counseling / church
-Enlists Family's Support
-I'll never do it again
-Wants to make love

Victim
-Nurturing
-Isolates from family and friends
-Keeps quiet to to protect batterer
-Tries to reason
-Tries to soothe partner & walks on eggshells

Victim
-Agrees to stay
-Returns or takes back Narcissist
-Sets up counseling for Narcissist
-Feels happy / hopeful

Narcissistic abuse can create incredibly complex and painful push-pull relationship dynamics in each phase of the abusive cycle. At the outset, victims often find themselves irresistibly drawn to the charm and charisma of their abuser, only to later experience the emotional manipulation and cruelty that characterizes the abusive phase. The push-pull dynamic can ensnare victims further, making it difficult to break free. In moments of vulnerability and self-doubt, they may acquiesce to their abuser's actions, hoping to regain the fleeting moments of affection and kindness they once experienced. This pattern can be deeply damaging, eroding a victim's self-esteem and sense of agency. With the right support and resources, survivors can eventually break free from this cycle, heal, and rebuild their lives with healthier, more respectful and reciprocal relationships.

Narcissistic Abuse Cycle

DEVALUE

STONEWALLING & THE SILENT TREATMENT

As we journey through the discard phase of the narcissistic abuse cycle, it's crucial to take a moment and reflect on the profound impacts this phase can have on survivors. Here's a summary of some key points to consider:

- The dicard phase is often filled with emotional turmoil, confusion, and feelings of abandonment as the narcissist abruptly ends the relationship or withdraws affection and attention.
- Survivors may experience intense grief and loss, even though the relationship was toxic, due to the trauma bond and emotional attachment formed during the idealization phase.
- The narcissist may engage in gaslighting and manipulation during the discard to make the survivor doubt their reality and worth, furthering their control over the victim.
- Discarded survivors may struggle with feelings of unworthiness, self-blame, and a sense of not being good enough for the narcissist, which can have long-lasting effects on their self-esteem.
- It's common for survivors to question themselves and replay events, trying to understand what they did wrong or how they could have prevented the discard, perpetuating a cycle of self-doubt.

As we continue on, let's transition to learning a bit more about the nuances of narcissism and how they weaponize stonewalling and the silent treatment against their victims. You know, it's heartbreaking to see how some people can use love as a weapon, especially those with narcissistic tendencies. It's like they have this Dr. Jekyll and Mr. Hyde act – one moment, they're kind and charming, and the next, they're using silent treatment or stonewalling as a way to punish those who love them.

It's tough to wrap our heads around it because love should be a force that brings people closer, not push them away. But narcissists have a way of manipulating emotions, taking advantage of the love and care that others have for them. When they experience narcissistic injury, that's when their dark side emerges. They use the silent treatment or stonewalling as a form of emotional abuse, leaving their loved ones feeling confused, hurt, and desperate for their affection.

And here's the thing – they know what they're doing. Though they may not be emotionally self aware enough to intentionally identify their behavior with psychological terms, they are well aware of their manipulative tactics. They know that by pushing their loved ones away, they can control them, keep them on edge, and maintain a sense of power over them. That's why you must educate yourself on the nuances of narcissism so you can identify and protect yourself against their manipulative tactics. Especially when the hot and cold behavior is used to intentionally confuse you.

It's not just the silent treatment or stonewalling; they're experts at using kindness as a weapon too. They will shower you with affection and love when they want something or when they are fearful you might leave. It's all a game to keep you hooked, to prevent you from seeing the truth about their hurtful behavior. But here's the thing – as we learn to love ourselves more, as we become more attuned to our emotions and needs, we start to see through their facade. We begin to recognize the manipulative patterns and the emotional roller coaster they intentionally impose and are better able to redirect our energy. That's when we can finally break free from their grasp. We can walk away from the toxicity, knowing that we deserve genuine love and respect. It's not easy, and it might be a journey with ups and downs, but the more we love ourselves and trust our instincts, the stronger we become. It's important to talk about how some narcissists use the silent treatment as a hurtful weapon against their victims. The silent treatment can be a form of emotional abuse, and it can leave the person on the receiving end feeling confused, rejected, and even questioning their self-worth.

When a narcissist resorts to the silent treatment, it's like they're cutting off communication and withdrawing all emotional connection. They do this to gain power and control over their victim, leaving them feeling vulnerable and anxious. It's a manipulative tactic designed to make the victim feel like they've done something wrong, even when they haven't by leveraging ambiguity, distance, anxiety, blame and shame. [71]

One of the best defenses against the silent treatment is empowering yourself with a good offense. Instead of dwelling on their silence and trying to please them, try to shift your focus inward. Take this time to prioritize self-care, surround yourself with supportive friends or family, and engage in activities that bring you joy. It's not easy, but remember that you are not defined by their actions or lack of communication. Find ways to enjoy peace in their silence, knowing that their behavior is a reflection of their internal struggles, and not a reflection of what you deserve. You deserve to be treated with respect and kindness, and if someone is using the silent treatment as a form of emotional manipulation, it's crucial to set healthy boundaries to help you navigate through this challenging situation.

Narcissistic Abuse Cycle

DEVALUE

As we delve deeper into the dynamics of narcissistic abuse, it's crucial to explore the tactics employed by narcissists, such as the silent treatment and stonewalling, which can cause immense emotional pain and distress in their victims. These manipulative behaviors deprive victims of emotional responsiveness and validation, leaving them feeling invalidated and soul crushingly confused.

To gain further insight into the impact of such emotional withdrawal and invalidation, we will now transition to learning about two significant experiments: the "Still Face Experiment" and Harry Harlow's "Surrogate Mother Experiment." These experiments provide valuable insights into the consequences of attachment styles and the inherent human need for emotional connection.

By examining the results of these experiments, we can better understand how early caregiving and emotional bonding play a crucial role in shaping our attachment styles. This knowledge will shed light on why victims of narcissistic abuse may choose to stay in abusive relationships, despite the harm inflicted upon them, as attachment is hardwired into our nervous system.

That said, let's explore these experiments and their implications to gain a deeper understanding of the profound impact of abuse and the importance of healthy attachment in our lives. So, the "Still Face Experiment". It's this mind-blowing study from the '70s by Dr. Edward Tronick that shows how early attachment and emotional connection play a huge role in a baby's development. In the experiment, a caregiver interacts warmly with the baby, creating a safe and secure feeling. But then, without warning, the caregiver switches to a "still face" mode, showing zero emotion or response to the baby's attempts to engage. [72]

Over the course of the experiment, experimenters witness the baby getting visibly upset and tries everything to get a reaction from the caregiver, like smiling, cooing, or reaching out. But when all efforts fail, the little one gets even more distressed, feeling frustrated, sad, shutting down and sometimes even withdrawing.

From this experiment, we learn how crucial attachment and emotional responsiveness are for a child's healthy growth. Babies rely on their caregivers for emotional regulation, validation, and a sense of safety. When that connection is disrupted, it can seriously mess with their emotional development and their ability to trust others later on. But here's where it gets even more interesting. Let's link this experiment to narcissistic abuse, especially when they use stone-walling and the silent treatment. Narcissists are masters at manipulation, and these tactics are their go-to moves to mess with their victims. The silent treatment is like the "still face" phase for adults.

Sadly, in my toxic relationship, he knew I would get anxious when he iced me out as I made every attempt to apologize for my reactions to his deceitful actions. He would weaponized silence and distance against me to shame me into submission. It's wild! When this happens to abuse victims, the victim feels so much distress and tries everything to get some emotional responsiveness from the narcissist, just like the baby in the experiment. But the narcissist stays cold and unresponsive, making it even worse for the victim.

You know what else they do? They use the silent treatment to gaslight their victims and make them doubt themselves. Victims might blame themselves for the emotional distance and feel like they're at fault, which just feeds the narcissist's control over them. Recognizing how these tactics work is crucial. It shows us how harmful emotional invalidation can be and how vital healthy attachment is in any relationship. This understanding paired with Harry Harlow's experiment amplifies the validity of these findings.

Narcissistic Abuse Cycle

DEVALUE

Harry Harlow's experiment with monkeys, also known as the "Surrogate Mother Experiment," is a classic study in attachment theory that sheds light on the importance of early caregiving in the development of attachment styles. In the experiment, baby monkeys were separated from their biological mothers and raised with two surrogate mothers. One surrogate mother was made of wire and had a feeding bottle, while the other was soft and nurturing but lacked the feeding bottle. The baby monkeys had a basic need for nourishment, which was provided by the wire mother, but they also had an inherent need for comfort and emotional support, which they sought from the soft and nurturing mother. The results of the experiment were fascinating and demonstrated the significance of attachment in a child's development. The baby monkeys spent most of their time clinging to the soft and nurturing mother, seeking comfort and security, even though the wire mother provided nourishment. This behavior showed that the monkeys prioritized emotional connection and comfort over their basic need for food. This experiment highlights the fundamental role of attachment in our lives. From infancy, we are wired to seek emotional connection and bonding with our caregivers. Attachment is not just about fulfilling physical needs; it's about forming a deep emotional bond that provides us with a sense of safety, security, and belonging. When we relate this to victims of narcissistic abuse, we can see how their need for attachment and connection can sometimes lead them to choose an abusive attachment over no attachment at all. [73]

That said, unhealed attachment trauma casts a long shadow over our responses to abuse, especially within relationship dynamics involving narcissists. According to John Bowlby, our attachment styles, formed in early life, deeply influence how we perceive and respond to interactions, even when they're harmful. These responses vary significantly across attachment styles, shedding light on how we navigate the complex terrain of narcissistic relationships [74]:

Secure Attachment:
- Recognizes abuse and unhealthy behavior, and seeks to address it openly.
- Sets and enforces boundaries to protect emotional well-being.
- Willing to confront the narcissist or end the relationship if necessary.
- May experience pain but seeks healing and growth from the experience.

Anxious Attachment:
- Tends to internalize blame for the abuse, assuming it's their fault.
- Seeks validation and reassurance from the narcissist, often becoming stuck in a cycle of seeking approval.
- May have difficulty leaving the relationship due to fears of abandonment.
- Struggles with self-esteem and self-worth as a result of the abuse.

Avoidant Attachment:
- Tends to dismiss or downplay the abuse, distancing from emotional pain.
- May rationalize the narcissist's behavior as a way to avoid facing the truth.
- May struggle with opening up about the abuse, even to close friends or family.
- May prioritize self-reliance over seeking help or support.

Disorganized Attachment:
- Experiences extreme confusion and emotional turmoil due to abuse.
- Alternates between seeking closeness with the narcissist and pushing them away.
- May engage in self-destructive behaviors as a response to the abuse.
- Struggles with a profound internal conflict regarding their feelings and responses.

The emotional manipulation and control exerted by narcissists can create a strong bond with their victims, even though the relationship is toxic and harmful. Victims may stay in abusive relationships because the emotional attachment is so deeply ingrained in their nervous system. The fear of being alone or abandoned can outweigh the pain of the abuse, leading them to endure the mistreatment in the hope of maintaining some form of connection. Understanding the significance of attachment and our inherent need for emotional connection can help us comprehend the complexities of narcissistic abuse and why victims may struggle to break free from such relationships. It also emphasizes the importance of healing and seeking support to develop healthier attachment styles and form more fulfilling and secure relationships in the future.

Narcissistic Abuse Cycle

DEVALUE

Q & A

WHAT HAPPENS WHEN YOU FIGHT BACK?

The Narcissist will experience Narcissistic Injury. Individuals with narcissistic personality disorder typically suffer invalidating emotional injury during their early years that interferes with the healthy development of a stable identity, sense of self-esteem, and emotional empathy. Conditional caregiving because of loss, rejection, abuse, neglect, or overindulgence (or a messy mix of those things) and a possible genetic predisposition is thought to be at the root of narcissistic injury, leading to foundational feelings of worthlessness. Becuase of this, when you fight back, they often become The "Victimized" Abuser. This is specific to Covert Narcissists who exhibit narcissistic injury. One of the important nuances to narcissistic abuse is that its not just about what they do to you (yell, belittle, gaslight, cheat) but also what they don't do to you (stand up for you, support you, putting other people's needs above yours, acting indifferent). In their twisted reality, they will judge your character based on how you react to their abuse. If you get upset and angry, rightfully so, they will label you as "crazy" or "emotionally unstable". This testing behavior is what keeps them safe but is ultimately what becomes unsafe for you. This is due to their lack of Object Constancy: People with narcissistic personality disorder suffer from a lack of object constancy, or the ability to sustain in real time an awareness of overall positive feelings and past positive experiences with people in their lives when they are disappointed or hurt by them in some way. When triggered, the narcissist's continuity of perception collapses into present-moment reactive emotion. If his/her child forgets to do a chore, for example, the narcissist father may become enraged and punish him/her, seeing the behavior as spiteful or irresponsible even if the child is usually conscientious.

WHAT HAPPENS WHEN YOU DISCARD AN ABUSIVE NARCISSIST FIRST?

Losses in love hurt a Narcissist as they move from pain to rage after the ending of a relationship. If you were the one who was strong enough to get away, even for legitimate reasons - such as your mental, emotional or physical safety, this type of antagonizer will still find ways to play the victim as a result of their own projected abuse. Defensive detachment is a coping mechanism that some people, including narcissists, may employ when they feel rejected or face the possibility of being left by someone they are in a relationship with. It's like a shield they put up to protect themselves from emotional pain and vulnerability. When a narcissist senses rejection or the potential end of a relationship, they might resort to defensive detachment as a way to cope with their feelings of hurt and fear. They create emotional distance and may withdraw affection, attention, or empathy. It's not that they don't feel the impact of the situation, but they try to shield themselves from further emotional injury by detaching emotionally.

In this state, a narcissist may act aloof, dismissive, or even cold towards the person who is considering leaving them. They might avoid engaging in deep emotional discussions and resort to deflecting or blaming the other person for any problems in the relationship. The goal is to protect themselves from feeling inadequate or abandoned. Keep in mind that while defensive detachment is a way for narcissists to cope, it can be challenging and painful for those on the receiving end. It's important to remember that the behavior of a narcissist is not a reflection of your worth or lovability.

Remember, Narcissistic Personality Disorder (NPD) is a personality disorder that usually goes misdiagnosed or undiagnosed with symptoms that include: An excessive need for admiration, disregard for others' feelings, lack of empathy, an inability to handle any criticism, and a sense of entitlement. As a result, anyone who possesses this disorder lives in a program of cognitive distortions that prevent them from taking responsibility for the outcome of their maladaptive actions. Vindictive retaliation stemming from resentment, possessiveness and jealousy results in manipulative coping mechanisms to regain a sense of self importance by using: Smear Campaigns Against Their Victims, Extreme Mood Swings, Power Imbalances, Extreme Hot & Cold Behavior Jekyll and Hyde Hoovering, Extreme Feelings of Guilt, Shame, Anger, Abandonment and Anxiety.

Protecting the narcissist by lying to people so they will like them while they lie to people so others will hate you is called flipping and blame shifting. Ultimately the lies that you tell in order to protect them will be the same lies they use in order to discredit you during the discard stage of your relationship.

IF THEY DON'T LOVE ME, WHY DON'T THEY JUST LEAVE ME?

Why would they? By maintaining a relationship with you, they have conquered the partner of their dreams who is willing to tolerate their disrespect and mistreatment. This means your unlimited narcissistic supply. They don't want a person that will challenge them when they are being abusive when they already have someone who they have conditioned to be comfortable with being abused. Why would they be incentivized to change if they know you will never leave? If accountability goes out the window as soon as they apologize, why would they take your boundaries seriously if you don't? You can't force people to treat you respectfully. However, you can decide what you will tolerate when you are disrespected.

Narcissistic Abuse Cycle

DISCARD

NARCISSISTIC INJURY, NARCISSISTIC RAGE

As we journey together through the intricate realm of narcissism, we've made significant strides in comprehending the deceitful layers of this personality disorder. I'm so proud of you for making it this far! From unraveling the unsettling technique of gaslighting to understanding the tumultuous phases of the discard, love bombing, and the bonds formed through trauma, we've delved into the calculated dance that characterizes narcissistic relationships. As we continue our exploration, our path leads us toward delving into another critical aspect: narcissistic injury and narcissistic rage. These phenomena shed light on the profound sensitivity underlying narcissists' façades and the explosive reactions that often follow. Understanding these dynamics provides us with a more holistic understanding of narcissism, equipping us to navigate its complexities with greater insight and resilience. Our journey is far from over, but with each step forward, we gain a deeper understanding of the insidious world of narcissism and its impact on both individuals and relationships.

So, narcissistic injury. This refers to the emotional hurt or perceived threat to a narcissist's self-esteem and grandiose self-image. Narcissistic personalities often react with rage when their underlying feelings of vulnerability and shame are triggered. It occurs when something challenges or contradicts their inflated sense of self-importance, superiority, or specialness. This injury can result from criticism, rejection, failure, humiliation, loss of power, loss of control or any situation where the narcissist feels that their self-image is being threatened. [75] When a narcissist experiences narcissistic injury, they often respond with what is known as narcissistic rage.

Narcissistic rage is an intense and explosive emotional reaction that serves to protect the narcissist's fragile ego and self-image. It can manifest in various ways, such as anger, aggression, verbal attacks, or other physically or emotionally destructive behaviors. [76] They tend to take even small slights, which most people would easily brush off, as intensely humiliating. When this happens, their fabricated "perfect" self and overblown feelings of entitlement are threatened, setting off a wild rage response. When I confronted my former partner about the photos and messages I found on his phone before making the final decision to end our relationship, he never apologized for his actions. He just blamed me for my response. Someone's inability to accept responsibility for their actions will always result in them struggling to apologize for the harm they have caused to others. That doesn't mean they are right. It just means they are wildly incapable of maturely processing the emotions associated with being in the wrong. Narcissistic rage is terrifying, sometimes physically violent, and goes far beyond normal anger. It is emotionally and physically traumatizing for those on the receiving end, particularly children, who naturally blame themselves for adults' reactions. Narcissistic rage can be triggered by real or perceived threats to the narcissist's self-esteem, and it can be disproportionate to the actual situation.

To provide more context, let's take it back to our fictional couple with the complex relationship dynamic: TJ and Sarah. As we know, TJ possesses strong narcissistic traits, while Sarah is learning about these behaviors to better navigate the relationship. One day, Sarah confronts TJ about a matter she feels strongly about. TJ, being a narcissist, immediately interprets this as a challenge to their self-importance. TJ's pride takes a hit, and they start feeling vulnerable and uncomfortable. This is what psychologists call a "narcissistic injury." TJ's initial response is a mix of defensiveness and anger. Sarah's challenge contradicted the image of superiority TJ holds about themselves. Feeling threatened, TJ's insecurity and shame bubble to the surface, causing them to react emotionally. This is the onset of what we call "narcissistic rage." In a fit of rage, TJ lashes out at Sarah, raising their voice and belittling Sarah's perspective. The intensity of their reaction might even seem disproportionate to the situation. TJ's aim is to regain a sense of control and reassert their grandiose self-image. As Sarah learns about narcissism, she recognizes this pattern. Instead of getting caught up in the argument, Sarah decides to disengage and give TJ space to cool down. This time, Sarah doesn't let TJ's rage manipulate her own emotions. Understanding the interplay between narcissistic injury and rage helps Sarah navigate the relationship more effectively. She realizes that beneath TJ's grandiose exterior lies a fragile ego, and learning to address the underlying vulnerability becomes key to fostering a healthier connection.

Narcissistic Abuse Cycle

DISCARD

PSYCHOLOGICAL SPLITTING & RAGE EYES

In this example, the narcissist's reaction is often defensive and aimed at reasserting their superiority and control over others. They may attack or belittle the person they perceive as causing the injury, or they may engage in manipulative tactics to regain a sense of power and dominance. Narcissistic injury and narcissistic rage are interconnected phenomena that often stem from the emotional immaturity of narcissists. When a narcissist experiences perceived criticism, rejection, or threats to their fragile self-esteem or self-image, they undergo narcissistic injury. This injury is like a blow to their ego, and they struggle to handle the emotional distress that comes with it. Instead of processing these emotions in a healthy way, narcissists resort to a defense mechanism known as psychological splitting. Psychological splitting is a coping strategy where the narcissist perceives situations and people in extreme black-and-white terms. [77] They have difficulty integrating both positive and negative aspects of themselves or others into a cohesive whole.

So, when they encounter any form of criticism or injury, they tend to see the person responsible as either all good or all bad, with no middle ground. All while idealizing themselves as all-good. It's like categorizing people into two extreme categories—angelic or demonic—without acknowledging the shades of gray that make up our complex human experience. This cognitive distortion fuels their narcissistic rage. In this state of rage, narcissists lash out in an attempt to regain a sense of power and control over the situation. They may engage in aggressive behaviors, hurl hurtful insults, or even engage in manipulative tactics to exact revenge or seek validation. It's important to understand that narcissistic injury and rage are not typical reactions to life's challenges. Instead, they are manifestations of deep-seated emotional vulnerabilities and an inability to cope with perceived threats to their grandiose self-image.

Now, why is splitting considered a sign of emotional immaturity? Well, here's the scoop. Emotionally mature individuals understand that people are multifaceted, with a range of qualities and behaviors. They recognize that someone can have both positive and negative aspects. They embrace the complexity of human nature and can hold space for contradictory feelings and experiences. On the other hand, individuals who engage in splitting tend to struggle with emotional maturity. They have difficulty integrating and reconciling opposing qualities or experiences in themselves and others. It's like they're stuck in an all-or-nothing mindset, unable to embrace the gray areas. And guess what? Narcissists love to exploit this tendency. They use splitting to their advantage when discarding their victims. At first, they may idealize their victims, putting them on a pedestal, showering them with attention and affection. But when the victim inevitably falls short of the unrealistic expectations set by the narcissist, the dynamic flips. The narcissist engages in devaluation, where they suddenly perceive the victim as all bad, unworthy, or flawed. They may begin to look down on you with distain. They are unable to hold positive feelings towards you when they hold negative feelings about themselves. At this point of the emotional discard, they may completely emotionally withdraw from you and it's very unlikely the relationship will be able to recover. It's like they're playing a game of emotional ping pong, bouncing between extremes to keep their victims off-balance and under their control. Understanding the role of splitting in narcissistic relationships can help us recognize the manipulative dynamics at play. It reminds us that the way the narcissist perceives us is distorted, and their actions are not a reflection of our true worth.

Next, cue the Narcissistic Rage Eyes. The term "narcissistic rage eyes" is not a formal psychological term but is rather a colloquial way of describing the striking and aggressive facial expression that narcissists may display during these moments. The eyes of a person experiencing narcissistic rage may appear cold, intense, and devoid of empathy. Their menacing gaze can be piercing and intimidating, conveying a sense of anger and contempt. It's like the lights are on but no one is home. They could be inches away from you physically but emotionally, you will feel worlds apart. It's important to note that narcissistic rage is a destructive and unhealthy response to perceived threats, and it can lead to emotional manipulation, verbal abuse, or even physical aggression. Dealing with someone who exhibits narcissistic rage can be challenging and emotionally draining.

Remember, it's not your job to teach others how to act but it is your right to revoke access to those who fail to act right.

Narcissistic Abuse Cycle

DISCARD

TRIANGULATION, MODONNA-WHORE COMPLEX & EROTICIZED RAGE

As we delve deeper into the dynamics of narcissistic abuse, it becomes evident that narcissistic injury can be a significant trigger for narcissistic rage during the discard phase of the abusive cycle. The emotional immaturity of narcissists often leads them to react explosively when their fragile self-esteem is wounded. This rage can manifest in various harmful ways, leaving the victim emotionally devastated. One manipulative tactic employed by narcissists during this phase is triangulation, where they introduce a new person or interest to create a sense of competition and insecurity in the relationship. [78] Let's explore how these tactics come into play and the impact they have on the victim's emotional well-being.

To begin, triangulation is used to create tension, confusion, or competition within the relationship. It's like they're playing a twisted game of emotional chess. Why do they do it? Well, it's all about control and manipulation. Pretty on brand, right? Also, it's their destructive form of emotional regulation. When a narcissist feels insecure and inferior in their relationship, they will seek validation outside of their partnership in the form of narcissistic supply as a form of escapism. This exiting strategy allows them to create just enough emotional distance from their relationship to shield themselves from the pain of rejection while also cushioning their next target in preparation for the discard phase.

Take The Madonna-Whore Complex for example. The Madonna-Whore complex is a psychological phenomenon that was first coined by Sigmund Freud. It refers to a mindset in which an individual, typically male, divides women into two distinct categories: the "Madonna" figure, who is seen as pure, virtuous, and maternal; and the "Whore" figure, who is considered sexually alluring, but morally corrupt. This complex can lead to a difficulty in reconciling sexual desires and romantic feelings within a single partner. Narcissists may exploit the Madonna-Whore complex to manipulate and control their heterosexual partners during the discard phase. [79]

By compartmentalizing their partners into these polarized categories, narcissists can effectively dismiss their current partner's sexual appeal and desirability. As they become infatuated with new sources of supply, narcissists tend to idealize these new individuals, placing them in the "Whore" category and attributing heightened sexual attractiveness to them. This contrasts with their existing partner, whom they have already began to devalue. This manipulation serves to erode the self-esteem and self-worth of the current partner, making them feel inadequate and undesirable. The narcissist's shift of attention and affection towards the new supply also creates a sense of competition and jealousy, further fueling the emotional turmoil experienced by their current partner. By exploiting the Madonna-Whore complex, narcissists maintain their power and control over their partners, exploiting their vulnerabilities for their own satisfaction.

When combined with narcissism, the Madonna-Whore complex takes on a particularly insidious form. One of the ways they achieve this is through the weaponization of eroticized rage. Eroticized rage is a term that describes a complex and disturbing psychological phenomenon where intense anger and aggression become intertwined with sexual arousal and desire. [80] This fusion of emotions can result in a potent and destructive mixture that has the potential to be both psychologically damaging and physically harmful. In the context of narcissistic relationships, narcissists can indeed weaponize eroticized rage to manipulate and control their partners. As they channel their shame through their sexuality, they are unconsciously seeking out both relief and revenge.

Narcissists often utilize emotional intensity, aggressive behavior, threatening language, or even physical gestures that convey their power. By channeling anger and aggression into a sexual context in the form of intimidation and control, they create a volatile mix that can be difficult for their partners to navigate. This could involve playing on guilt, fear, or shame to elicit certain reactions or behaviors. By alternating between episodes of eroticized rage and moments of affection or reconciliation, the narcissist creates a cycle that keeps their partner emotionally off-balance. This can lead the partner to become more dependent on the narcissist for emotional stability and validation that further enables isolation and dependency. The intense and confusing blend of anger and sexualization can lead to a fragmented sense of self for the partner. This makes it difficult for the partner to maintain a clear understanding of their own emotions, which in turn makes them more susceptible to the narcissist's manipulation.

As someone who has overcome childhood sexual abuse, this was one of the most difficult experiences for me to heal from. During our time away in Italy, while the emotional abuse was at its peak, the man I loved would disregard my soul as he disrespected my body. Only to discarded me afterwards. This was an excruciatingly painful experience. At the time, I didn't have the words to explain what was happening. All I knew was that it felt wrong, confusing and violating. Narcissists are skilled at using emotional triggers to manipulate their victims, and eroticized rage is one of the most potent tools in their arsenal. This involves tapping into the complex emotions surrounding the Madonna-Whore dynamic to induce intense feelings of guilt, shame, and confusion within their partners. Sadly, it works. However, as you heal and grow, you will begin to realize their actions are not a reflection of your worth, but rather, a reflection of their character.

Narcissistic Abuse Cycle

DISCARD

TRIANGULATION & MONKEY BARRING

I know this is a lot to take in. Pulse check! Are you doing okay? Trust me, just as overwhelmed as you might be reading this, imagine how it felt writing it! Sadness. Anger. Gratitude. Reminiscent. Healed. Whole. The thing about healing from toxic relationships is, when we reflect on our story, we realize that it was only one chapter in a very beautiful life. And that chapter played a crucial role in shaping how we are, who we are today. The only thing that matters is the meaning you give to your experiences that allows you to heal or enables you to continue to hurt. As I healed, I realized my strength wasn't going to be found in becoming resentful.

But rather, it was going to be revealed in the way I allowed this experience to make me resilient. And guess what? Resiliency is possible for you too! As someone who has a passion for helping you to heal, I can tell you that on the other side of all of this pain, there's not only peace, but happiness as well. This took time and patience. It took darkness and light. It took isolation and a slow integration. It took almost a year of celibacy and deep inner work. It wasn't easy, but let me tell you, it was absolutely worth it.

Listen, people with narcissistic personality disorder depend emotionally on others to sustain their sense of identity and regulate their self-esteem. They get their narcissistic supply either by idealizing and emulating others or by devaluing and asserting their superiority over others. Anyone they can manipulate—a partner, child, friend, or colleague—is a potential source of supply. Without suppliers, narcissists are empty. Narcissists thrive on power and attention. It's their way of making you feel insecure and questioning your worth. They want you to feel like you're not good enough- like you have to compete for their love. But here's the thing, the game ends when you decide to stop playing.

As we continue on our journey, I want to tie this all together with a term my former partner's mother taught me called "Monkey barring". Monkey barring is a manipulative tactic used by narcissists during the discard phase of the abusive cycle. It involves creating form of triangulation where the narcissist introduces a new person or interest into the dynamic with the primary goal of securing additional emotional supply before ultimately leaving their current victim. During this phase, the narcissist may instigate jealousy, insecurity, and the fear of abandonment in their current partner. They can keep you on your toes, always vying for their affection and approval. [81]

This emotional turmoil serves the narcissist's purpose of obtaining more attention and validation from both the current victim and the new person they're involving in the situation. The term "monkey barring" is derived from the behavior of monkeys swinging from one branch to another. In this context, it illustrates how the narcissist jumps from one relationship or potential source of supply to another, without considering the emotional impact on their current partner. [82] The victim may feel desperate to win back the narcissist's affection and loyalty, unaware that the narcissist is intentionally manipulating their emotions and using the presence of another person to extract more supply through overlapping relationships. Pretty mean, right?

With a narcissist, they are likely to emotionally cheat on you before they physically cheat on you. They will also emotionally detach from you before fully attaching to someone else. It's not about you. It's about their deep-rooted insecurities and need for constant validation. Compartmentalizing allows them to justify their competing thoughts : cheating on you while still loving you. Understanding triangulation is crucial because it helps you see through the manipulation. It allows you to recognize that it's not your fault and that you deserve better. Remember, a healthy relationship is built on trust, respect, and genuine love, not mind games and emotional roller coasters. You deserve more than the triangulation they put you through. Especially when they attempt to triangulate you with new supply, friends or even family members.

Narcissistic Abuse Cycle

DISCARD

TRIANGULATION & MONKEY BARRING

That said, it's a heartbreaking reality that sometimes, even family members who are aware of the abusive behavior of a narcissist may turn a blind eye to the abuse. Why does this happen? Well, the dynamics within a narcissistic relationship can be complex and manipulative, and it's not just the direct victims who are affected. Family members, too, can become entangled in the web of the narcissist's tactics. One common way this occurs is through triangulation, where the narcissist manipulates and divides relationships by pitting individuals against each other. They may play the role of the victim, painting themselves as misunderstood or mistreated, while also love bombing others to gain their loyalty and support. This manipulation can leave family members feeling torn and confused.

They may fear the narcissist's wrath if they speak up or go against their wishes. The narcissist may also employ tactics to undermine the credibility of anyone who tries to expose their abusive behavior, leaving family members feeling isolated and powerless. Additionally, the love bombing aspect of narcissistic relationships can be enticing. Narcissists can be charming, charismatic, and skilled at presenting an idealized version of themselves. They may shower family members with affection, attention, and praise, creating a false sense of security and attachment. In these situations, family members may choose to turn a blind eye to the abuse as a means of self-preservation.

They may fear the repercussions of speaking out or believe that their own relationship with the narcissist will be jeopardized if they acknowledge the abuse. It's important to approach this issue with empathy and understanding. This doesn't justify the behavior, however family members who turn a blind eye to the abuse are not necessarily condoning or endorsing the narcissist's behavior. They may be trapped in their own cycle of manipulation and fear as well.

Eventually, the narcissist will discard their current victim, often leaving them heartbroken and confused, as they move on to the new source of supply. The cycle of abuse continues, as the narcissist seeks new victims to fulfill their insatiable need for admiration and validation. It's essential for individuals who have experienced this type of manipulation to recognize the pattern and understand that the narcissist's behavior is not a reflection of their worth or value. Educating oneself about narcissistic abuse and manipulation can help victims break free from the cycle and begin the healing process.

As they make their devastating departure during the discard phase, you would be right to assume their inability to do so peacefully. Cue the smear campaign. This is basically when someone, typically a narcissist, tries to tarnish another person's reputation by spreading false information, rumors, or exaggerated stories about them. [83] It's a calculated and manipulative tactic used to undermine the victim's credibility, isolate them from support networks, and gain control over the narrative.

Imagine this: You've been involved with a narcissist, and things didn't go well. Suddenly, you start hearing whispers and rumors circulating about you—things that you know are completely untrue or twisted versions of the truth. A narcissist will tell lies about the victim in order to shame the victim into submission from telling the truth. Yes, it's true that when you expose a narcissist's actions and reveal the truth about what they did to you, they often retaliate against you to protect their reputation. I read somewhere that after a relationship with a narcissist ends, the abuser will usually talk about the victim, while the victim will usually talk about the abuse. This fear of retaliation is one of the reasons why many victims are afraid to leave or speak up about the abuse they endured. I also experienced this fear firsthand. The victim blaming, invalidation, and retaliation are all painful aspects that I went through, even from people who were aware of my relationship but unaware of the hidden emotional abuse I endured. Speaking up about my experiences didn't guarantee support or understanding, as some people chose to remain neutral. To many abuse survivors, this further invalidates their experience and feelings. It reminded me of Martin Luther King Jr.'s powerful words, "There comes a time when silence is betrayal. Remaining silent about the things that matter can be destructive to our lives and well-being. In the end, it's not just the hurtful words of our enemies that leave a lasting impact, but the silence of our friends and acquaintances who choose not to stand by us in our time of need."

Narcissistic Abuse Cycle

DISCARD

When Narcissists engage in a smear campaign, they do so to bolster their own image while painting their victims as the "bad guys." They want to control the narrative, ensuring that others see them as blameless and the victim as the one at fault. It's a way for them to manipulate people's perception and maintain their power and control over the situation. When a toxic person can no longer control you, they will try to control the way people view you in an attempt to protect their wounded ego and escape personal accountability. This is their attempt to deflect their feelings of inferiority. They are not trying to convince others that you're a bad person as much as they are trying to convince themselves that you're a bad person in order to justify the things they did to you. Everything that went wrong was your fault, and everything that went right was because of their efforts. These campaigns can take various forms, from spreading gossip among friends and family to posting damaging content on social media or even reaching out to your workplace or community. The aim is to discredit and isolate the victim, making it harder for them to find support or seek validation for their experiences. The nuance of smear campaigns is that victims will tell the truth about the abuse that took place, whereas a narcissist will lie about it. These are common, lesser known nuances of navigating narcissism to be aware of.

The "Narcissistic Prayer" is a phrase often used to describe a pattern of thinking or mindset commonly observed in narcissistic individuals. It goes something like this: "That didn't happen. And if it did, it wasn't that bad. And if it was, it's not a big deal. And if it is, it's not my fault. And if it was, I didn't mean it. And if I did... You deserved it." [84] This prayer, so to speak, encapsulates the way narcissists tend to deflect responsibility, downplay their actions, and refuse to acknowledge or take accountability for the harm they may have caused. It's a way for them to rationalize and justify their behavior, even when faced with evidence or consequences. An acronym for this manipulative technique is known as DARVO. DARVO stands for Deny, Attack, and Reverse Victim and Offender. [85] It is a manipulative tactic commonly used by narcissists in relationships to deflect accountability and maintain control over their victims.

First, the narcissist denies any wrongdoing or responsibility for their actions. They may gaslight or distort the truth to make the victim doubt their own perceptions or memories of events. Next, the narcissist launches a counterattack by attacking the victim. They may criticize, belittle, or blame the victim for the problems in the relationship. This serves to shift the focus away from their own behavior and manipulate the victim into feeling guilty or responsible for their response. Lastly, the narcissist reverses the roles, portraying themselves as the victim and the actual victim as the offender. They may play the victim card, claiming that they are being unfairly accused or mistreated. This further manipulates the victim and elicits sympathy or support from others. It can be highly damaging to the victim's self-esteem, emotional well-being, and ability to trust their own perceptions. I remember going through this exact moment and feeling so helpless. Going Gray Rock was the best defense mechanism I had. Between supportive messages from his family and private emails documenting the abuse to our therapist in real time, I didn't need the world to validate my truth in order for my experience to be true or valid. The moment I realized that forcing an admission from an abuser was just a subconscious form of seeking their approval, I was able to stop defending myself in order to fully detach.

Dealing with a smear campaign can be incredibly challenging. It can leave you feeling confused, frustrated, and hurt. However, it's important to remember that the lies and rumors being spread are not a reflection of who you are as a person. They are tactics used by the narcissist to maintain control and deflect responsibility. In order to move from being a victim, it's important to allow yourself to be a villain in someone else's delusional story. I know this feels unfair. That's because it is. But your safety and sanity are more important than trying to convince those who are committed to hurting you, to help you to heal. Above all, stay true to yourself and your own values. You deserve not to carry the weight of constant explanation for those who were present during your pain but absent during your recovery journey. It's understandable if friends who maintain ties with your abuser under the guise of "keeping the peace" or "staying impartial" have inadvertently made a choice. A choice that aligns with the abuser. It's important to recognize that this kind of unintentional support creates a safe haven for your abuser, turning it into an unsafe environment for you.

Ultimately, the truth will always be revealed, and you'll emerge stronger and more resilient from the experience. As my personal trainer once said, "Don't be afraid to be the villain in someone else's story if they are only a clown in yours." It's important to recognize that this pattern of thinking is characteristic of narcissistic individuals. Understanding the Narcissistic Prayer can help us identify these thought patterns and protect ourselves from being manipulated or gaslit by narcissistic individuals - especially during the Smear Campaign.

Narcissistic Abuse Cycle

DISCARD

ABUSE BY PROXY & FLYING MONKEYS

Now, let's transition our discussion to explore another insidious tactic used by narcissists known as "abuse by proxy." This form of manipulation involves the narcissist enlisting other people, such as friends, family members, or even strangers, to perpetuate their abuse and control over the survivor. We will delve into the dynamics of abuse by proxy, its impact on survivors, and strategies for dealing with this challenging aspect of narcissistic abuse. [86]

In this context, "proxy" means using someone else as an intermediary or agent to harm, intimidate, or exert power over the victim. This tactic allows the narcissist to distance themselves from the direct consequences of their actions, making it harder for the victim to identify the true source of the abuse. This can be painful to the victim as it invalidates their experience, forcing them to prove their pain to people who are doubting them. In this case, silence is compliance.

There are several ways abuse by proxy can manifest in a narcissistic relationship:

1. **Flying monkeys**: The narcissist enlists friends, family members, or other allies (commonly referred to as "flying monkeys") to do their bidding. These individuals may unknowingly or willingly participate in gaslighting, spreading rumors, or carrying out other forms of emotional harm on behalf of the narcissist. [87]
2. **Smear campaigns:** The narcissist spreads false or damaging information about the victim to tarnish their reputation and credibility. They may use mutual acquaintances, social media, or other channels to disseminate these falsehoods. A person with a lot of unprocessed shame will lie in order to be loved. Which is often why they will attempt to destroy the victim with lies in retaliation for them telling the truth. At the end of a toxic relationship, the abuser will often times lie about the victim, while the victim will often times talk about the abuse.
3. **Triangulation**: The narcissist involves a third person (real or imaginary) to create conflict and jealousy within the relationship. This can lead to emotional distress and insecurity for the victim.
4. **Legal maneuvers**: The narcissist may use the legal system to harass or intimidate the victim, filing frivolous lawsuits or making baseless accusations.
5. **Online harassment:** The narcissist may use online platforms, anonymous accounts, or fake profiles to cyberbully and harass the victim, causing emotional distress.
6. **Coercive control:** The narcissist may manipulate others to monitor, control, or spy on the victim, infringing on their privacy and autonomy.
7. **Parental alienation:** In cases involving children, the narcissistic parent may try to turn the children against the victim, causing emotional harm and disrupting the parent-child relationship.

One of the most painful aspects of Abuse by Proxy is when they enlist their group of Flying Monkeys. Flying Monkeys may sound like a scene from "The Wizard of Oz," but in the context of a narcissistic relationship, it's quite a different story. Let me explain it to you in everyday terms. Flying monkeys are the sidekicks, the loyal followers, or the enablers that narcissists recruit to do their bidding. They are the people who support and reinforce the narcissist's toxic behavior, often without even realizing it. You can think of them as the narcissist's little army.

Now, you might wonder, why do narcissists need flying monkeys? Well, it all comes down to control and manipulation. Per usual. Narcissists thrive on power and attention, and having a group of people who blindly support them gives them an even greater sense of control. These flying monkeys often carry out the narcissist's dirty work. They might spread rumors, engage in character assassination, or even launch personal attacks on the narcissist's behalf. They are like the messengers of the narcissist's toxicity.

Narcissistic Abuse Cycle

DISCARD

ABUSE BY PROXY & FLYING MONKEYS

But here's the heartbreaking part: the presence of flying monkeys can cause significant psychological harm to the victim. Imagine being surrounded by a group of people who side with the narcissist, who undermine your experiences, and who make you question your own sanity. It's isolating, disorienting, and deeply painful. The victim may feel invalidated, gaslighted, and overwhelmed. Their self-esteem takes a hit, and they may start doubting their own perceptions and reality. It's a form of psychological abuse that can lead to anxiety, depression, and a loss of self-worth. Recognizing the role of flying monkeys is crucial because it helps victims understand that they are not alone and that the problem lies with the narcissist, not with them. It encourages them to seek safe support from trusted friends, family, or professionals who can provide validation and help them rebuild their sense of self.

So, if you find yourself in a situation where you're dealing with flying monkeys, remember that their actions are a reflection of the toxic dynamics orchestrated by the narcissist. The most manipulable types make the best flying monkeys. They may be ex's, mutual friends, colleagues, children or other relatives. Speaking up about abuse or injustice takes immense courage, and it's natural to hope for understanding and support from those around us. However, it's essential to acknowledge that not everyone may respond as we expect or desire. Some people may struggle to comprehend the gravity of the situation or may choose to remain neutral to avoid conflict.

Neutrality in the face of abuse is not only enabling the abuser but invalidating the victim - leaving survivors feeling unheard and dismissed. It's painful when those we thought would stand with us decide to stay on the sidelines, seemingly indifferent to the harm that has been inflicted. Especially if people who are aware of the abuse continue to associate with the abuser, it can further exacerbate the sense of betrayal and isolation experienced by the survivor. This form of enabling, known as abuse by proxy, allows the abuser to continue their harmful behavior unchecked.

You know, sometimes when we're on the path of healing, it's easy to second-guess ourselves, especially when we've been through experiences that have shaken us to the core. It's in these moments that we need to hold onto a fundamental truth: your truth is valid, and your voice carries immense significance. What you've been through, what you feel, and how you perceive things matter deeply.

But you know what else matters? The people you choose to have around you during this journey. Seeking out those who genuinely listen, who don't just hear your words but understand the emotions behind them, can be transformative. These are the close friends who stand with you, unwaveringly, as you navigate the twists and turns of healing. Their empathy and understanding create a cocoon of support that can truly make a world of difference in your recovery and your sense of empowerment.

Now, I won't deny that it can be really tough when some individuals you hope would be there for you end up unable to provide the support you need. It's discouraging, no doubt. But here's the thing: their inability to offer the support you deserve doesn't diminish your worth. You deserve to be heard, to have your experiences acknowledged, and to be treated with respect. Here's an important realization: your healing isn't contingent on your abuser's recognition of what they've done. You don't need their validation to heal. You're not waiting for them to acknowledge your pain before you can start your recovery journey. What you need, what can truly propel your healing, is the comfort and validation that come from others who understand, who empathize, and who see your pain for what it is.

It's like building a safety net of understanding and compassion. The people who provide that safety net, they're the ones who help you see the value of your voice, of your experiences. Their validation becomes the foundation on which you can rebuild, grow, and ultimately heal. Let's dive into these feelings more in the pages that follow.

Narcissistic Abuse Cycle

DISCARD

ABUSE BY PROXY & FLYING MONKEYS

WHEN PEOPLE ARE DISMISSIVE OF YOUR NEEDS AND FEELINGS, IT IS A REFLECTION OF THEIR INABILITY TO REGULATE THEIR EMOTIONS AND PROCESS THEIR OWN FEELINGS. YOU CAN'T HAVE A HEALTHY RELATIONSHIP WHILE PARTICAPTING IN UNHEALTHY RELATIONSHIP DYNAMICS. YOU EITHER DISAPPOINT OTHERS BY SAYING HOW YOU FEEL, OR DISAPPOINT YOURSELF BY NOT. A MAJOR CORNER STONE IN YOUR HEALING WILL BE REFLECTED IN THE WAYS YOU DISTANCE YOURSELF FROM RELATIONSHIPS THAT DON'T HELP YOU TO HEAL.

WHEN AND WITH WHOM DID YOU FIRST LEARN THAT YOU NEEDED TO BETRAY YOURSELF IN ORDER TO BE LOVED?

Narcissistic Abuse Cycle

DISCARD

ABUSE BY PROXY & FLYING MONKEYS

WHO DID THIS TO YOU AND NOBODY STOPPED THEM? WHO DID YOU SEE DO THIS IN YOUR FAMILY AND NOBODY STOPPED THEM?

_____

_____

_____

_____

_____

_____

_____

_____

_____

_____

_____

_____

_____

_____

_____

_____

_____

_____

_____

_____

_____

_____

Narcissistic Abuse Cycle

DISCARD

ABUSE BY PROXY & FLYING MONKEYS

LOOKING BACK ON PAST ENCOUNTERS WITH A HIGHLY TOXIC OR NARCISSISTIC INDIVIDUAL, HOW DID YOUR WOUNDED SELF REACT, AND HOW WOULD YOU LIKE YOUR HEALED, MORE EMPOWERED SELF TO RESPOND DIFFERENTLY NOW?

Narcissistic Abuse Cycle

DISCARD

Q&A

ISABELLA, **HOW DID YOU KNOW IT WAS TIME TO LEAVE?**
When you know, you know. However, it's important to note that the right decision won't always feel right in the moment. You only question the right decision when it's the harder option to make. Overtime, I became more fearful when I realized I stopped wanting to fight for our relationship because silence felt more peaceful than convincing him to see how his actions were hurting me. As I was leaving, I remember he said that I robbed him of his joy while he robbed me of my peace. What he failed to realize was his abusive and manipulative actions were not conducive to peace. Not only did he have to stop being abusive, he had to learn how to be kind. I realized more and more that this was a losing situation for me. Empathy without boundaries in this case, was a form of self abandonment.

WHAT ADVICE WOULD YOU GIVE TO PARENTS WHO STAY IN TOXIC RELATIONSHIPS FOR THE CHILDREN?
Some parents will stay for the children, while some parents will leave for the children. Either decision is difficult to make. The desire to stay for the children makes complete sense. However, I would ask my clients, "Would you want this relationship for your children?" Sometimes it's better to have an absent parent than an abusive one. Narcissists can be quite hurtful and manipulative during the separation process as they will hate you more than they love their kids. It's a decision that should be made with self compassion and self-patience in mind.

WAS I BROKEN WHEN I CHOOSE THIS RELATIONSHIP?
Overt and covert narcissist have the same goals: control and manipulation. However, the way they go about getting their needs manifests differently. One is a deviant dictator, while the other plays the victim. That said, sometimes you don't really know who a person is until it's too late. If you hurt someone enough times, any secure person is going to feel insecure. But you are not insecure. You were with someone who was unsafe and your nervous system was sending you signals via your intuition that you were ignoring.

WHAT FIRST STEPS WOULD YOU SUGGEST FOR SURVIVORS WHO ARE HEALING FROM NARCISSISTIC ABUSE?

-**Step 1:** Change your environment. You can't heal in the same environment that hurt you.

-**Step 2:** Go 'No-Contact'. This will be hard but is necessary for your healing. This will feel a lot like cutting off a limb to save the rest of the body, however, it is a crucial boundary in order for you to one day thrive.

-**Step 3:** Embrace a cocoon period. Your emotions and nervous system will be entirely out of whack and will take some time to heal. During the healing process, you will find yourself in hypersensitive states of both highs and lows. Prepare for this by grounding yourself to a safe community, mental health specalist or uplifting personal development content. This last one is very specific as it will help you to feel like you are pushing the needle on healing versus spinning your wheels ruminating.

-**Step 4:** Seek a safe community and counselor. We can't go at this alone. If you cannot afford mental healthcare, invest your energy in finding a support group to help you to heal. I had my family and best friends at my side. However, I know many of us are not always so lucky. If our wounds were created in unsafe relationships, they can only be healed in safe ones.

-**Step 5:** In order to slowly begin to feel like yourself, you must start doing all of the healthy things that your relationship prevented you from doing. Remember who you were before that relationship hurt you. Reconnect with old friends, rediscover new ones, reinvent yourself as many times as you need to until you begin to feel like you again.

-**Step 6:** Love yourself they way you wish they would have loved you.

Narcissistic Abuse Cycle

DISCARD

REACTIVE ABUSE & THE GREY ROCK METHOD

As we delve deeper into the discard phase of the narcissistic abuse cycle, we come across two insidious tactics employed by narcissists: smear campaigns and abuse by proxy. During this stage, the narcissist, feeling threatened by the loss of control and supply, may resort to damaging the victim's reputation through lies, rumors, and false accusations – that's the smear campaign. Additionally, they might recruit others, known as flying monkeys, to do their bidding and further victimize the target – that's abuse by proxy. Now, let's shift our focus to reactive abuse, a phenomenon that occurs as a response to the narcissist's manipulation and provocation. It's essential to understand how the narcissist can leverage this strategy to play the victim, pretending to be innocent of their actions and blaming the reactive abuse for their self-imposed circumstances. This twisted narrative can further isolate and disempower the victim, making it crucial to unravel these complexities and learn how to break free from the vicious cycle of narcissistic abuse.

Reactive abuse is like being caught in a twisted game of emotional tug-of-war with a narcissist. It happens when you've been subjected to ongoing mistreatment and manipulation, and you finally reach a breaking point and react in a confrontational or aggressive manner. It's a response that's triggered by the relentless abuse you've endured. Now, here's where the narcissist's manipulation tactics come into play. They're masters at pushing your buttons and baiting you into a reaction. They know just what to say or do to provoke a response from you. It could be relentless criticism, gaslighting, or even playing mind games to make you doubt yourself. The thing is, they want to see you lose control because that gives them power.

They want to use your reaction against you. They're looking for that moment when you finally snap, so they can turn the tables and play the victim. It's like they're saying, "See? Look how crazy you're acting! I'm the innocent one here." It's a messed-up manipulation tactic designed to keep you trapped and confused. They want to keep you doubting yourself and your sanity. It's all about control for them. But here's the thing: You don't have to fall for their game. You can reclaim your power and break free from this toxic cycle. It starts with awareness. Recognize the patterns of manipulation and provocation. Take a step back and reflect on your emotional triggers. Understand that their goal is to keep you off balance on purpose.

During the devaluing and discard phase of the Narcissistic Abuse Cycle, going Grey Rock will be your saving grace here. Remember, the Grey Rock Method is a strategy employed by individuals dealing with narcissistic abuse to protect themselves and minimize engagement with the narcissist. It involves becoming as emotionally unresponsive and uninteresting as a "grey rock," thereby decreasing the narcissist's interest and reducing their attempts to manipulate or provoke a reaction. When interacting with a narcissist, the Grey Rock Method encourages you to:

(1) Emotionally Detach: Maintain a calm and neutral demeanor, avoiding emotional reactions or engaging in arguments. By depriving the narcissist of the emotional response they seek, you reduce their satisfaction and incentive to continue the abusive behavior.

(2) During this time also limit personal information: Share minimal personal details or opinions, as narcissists may use this information against you or exploit vulnerabilities. Keep conversations superficial and avoid providing them with ammunition to manipulate or hurt you.

Remember, the Grey Rock Method is not a one-size-fits-all solution, and it may not be suitable or effective in every situation. If you are dealing with narcissistic abuse, seeking support can provide additional guidance and strategies for healing and protection. Especially as the weaponize empathy and isolation against their victims.

Narcissistic Abuse Cycle

DISCARD

NARCISSISTIC COLLAPSE

Transitioning from the Gray Rock method to the challenging phase of ending a relationship with a narcissistic or highly toxic partner can be a daunting and emotionally charged journey. As someone who had to navigate this difficult path, I can empathize with the profound fears and uncertainties that can arise during this process. The Gray Rock method, with its emphasis on becoming emotionally unresponsive and uninteresting to the narcissist, is often employed as a survival strategy to protect one's own mental and emotional well-being. However, it's important to recognize that when a narcissist senses that their source of validation and control is slipping away, they may experience a Narcissistic Collapse, which can be a highly tumultuous and potentially dangerous time. Ironically, in my own experience, the fear of what my former partner might do to himself if I left kept me trapped in a toxic relationship for far too long. Though he had a much larger social circle than I did, he had no where near the same level of emotional support. No one could help him because no body *knew* him. Not like I did. Despite leaving him because of his abusive behavior, the part of me that deeply loved him was still concerned for his general wellbeing. This underscores the importance of seeking support and guidance to navigate this delicate transition with care and safety in mind.

Narcissistic collapse is a term often used in psychology and mental health to describe a significant and often dramatic breakdown or deterioration in the psychological and emotional functioning of a person with narcissistic personality traits or narcissistic personality disorder (NPD). It occurs when the individual's grandiose and inflated self-image is severely challenged or threatened, leading to a crisis in their sense of self-worth and identity.
Key characteristics and components of narcissistic collapse include [88]:

- **Extreme Vulnerability:** During a narcissistic collapse, individuals who typically present themselves as confident and self-assured become intensely vulnerable and emotionally fragile. Their façade of invincibility crumbles, revealing deep insecurity and self-doubt.

- **Emotional Turmoil:** Those experiencing a narcissistic collapse may exhibit intense emotional distress, including anxiety, depression, rage, and desperation. They may struggle to regulate their emotions, leading to erratic and unpredictable behavior.

- **Loss of Self-Esteem:** The collapse often involves a profound loss of self-esteem. Narcissists rely heavily on external validation and admiration to maintain their self-worth, and when this is threatened or withdrawn, their self-esteem plummets.

- **Reality Distortion:** Some individuals facing a narcissistic collapse may engage in reality distortion, denial, or delusions as a way to protect their fragile self-image. They may blame others for their problems or refuse to accept responsibility for their actions.

- **Social Isolation:** As their relationships become strained due to their difficult behavior and emotional turmoil, narcissists may find themselves increasingly isolated from others, which can exacerbate their distress.

- **Suicidal Ideation:** In severe cases, a narcissistic collapse can lead to suicidal thoughts or self-destructive behavior, as the individual struggles to cope with the overwhelming sense of worthlessness.

When it comes to the complexities related to the human experience, we lie about things we are insecure about. We lie about truths that we cannot face. A Narcissist's character is a reflection of who they are consistently. Even in the face of a Narcissistic Collapse, many Narcissists and other highly toxic individuals will struggle with real change due to their inability to confront the very parts of themselves they actively conceal. If lying keeps a Narcissist sick, the only way for them to begin to heal is to tell the truth. It's important to note that not all individuals with narcissistic traits or NPD will experience a narcissistic collapse, and the severity and duration of such an episode can vary widely among individuals. Additionally, the term "narcissistic collapse" is not an official psychiatric diagnosis but rather a conceptual framework used by clinicians and researchers to describe a phenomenon observed in some individuals with narcissistic tendencies.

Narcissistic Abuse Cycle

HOOVER

REVERSE HOOVER

As we continue our exploration of the narcissistic abuse cycle, we now transition from the discard phase to the Hoovering phase. This is the last phase in the Narcissistic Abuse Cycle. Keep going, you're doing great! In the discard phase, the narcissist has devalued and discarded their victim, leaving them feeling hurt, confused, and abandoned. But the story doesn't end there. Narcissists will attempt to come back when their lives get worse over time. That's where the hoovering phase comes in. The Hoovering phase is where the narcissist attempts to reel their victim back in, like a vacuum cleaner sucking them back into the toxic relationship. This phase is named after the famous brand of vacuum cleaners, as it reflects the narcissist's desperate attempts to sweep their victim back under their control. During the Hoovering phase, the narcissist uses a variety of manipulative tactics to regain power and attention. [89] They may shower the victim with affection, promises of change, and apologies, seeking to exploit their vulnerability and desire for love and validation. The narcissist knows exactly which buttons to push to draw their victim back into their web of control. In this phase, it's crucial for the victim to recognize the narcissist's manipulative tactics and resist the urge to fall back into the same patterns.

The Hoovering phase can be incredibly confusing and emotionally charged, as the victim may still have feelings for the narcissist and yearn for the initial love-bombing and idealization they experienced. However, staying strong and maintaining No Contact is essential to breaking free from the cycle of abuse and reclaiming one's power and self-worth. By understanding the dynamics of the Hoovering phase and the insidious tactics employed by narcissists, survivors of narcissistic abuse can better protect themselves and work towards healing and recovery. Let's dive deeper into this phase and explore strategies for maintaining boundaries and building resilience against the narcissist's attempts to draw them back in.

Since narcissists are by nature pathologically self-centered and often stunningly cruel, they ultimately make those around them unhappy, if not miserable, and eventually drive many people away. If individuals pull away or try to go no contact, narcissists may attempt to hoover (as in vacuum suck) them back within their realm of control. They try to hoover through a variety of means, from promising to reform their behavior, to acting unusually solicitous, to dangling carrots such as gifts or money. Here, Narcissists will display a complex and calculated approach by weaponizing an emotional reserve of affectionate gestures. Their gestures are nothing more than a transaction, which they intend to exploit down the road. They rationalize their hurtful actions by keeping score through grandiose apologies and sporadic displays of affection, ultimately justifying their hurtful behavior. Here's how:

- **Initial Discard:** The narcissist has previously devalued or discarded the victim, leaving them feeling hurt, confused, and possibly ending the relationship or cutting off contact.
- **Reappearance:** After some time has passed, the narcissist resurfaces, often with a sudden burst of attention or affection. They may reach out through calls, messages, or even showing up in person, acting as if nothing happened or portraying themselves as changed or remorseful.
- **Love-Bombing:** During the hoovering phase, the narcissist may engage in love-bombing, which involves overwhelming the victim with excessive praise, flattery, promises, and attention. They try to reignite the initial feelings of idealization and make the victim question their decision to leave.
- **False Change:** The narcissist may present themselves as transformed or willing to address the issues that led to the previous problems. They may apologize profusely, promise to seek therapy, or make other grand gestures to convince the victim that things will be different this time. There's a difference between behavioral modification and behavioral change. Behavioral change can be seen with consistency and time. In a relationship with a narcissist, you are likely to experience an apology followed by a lack of accountability. You're allowed to be hurt by the things they did to harm you and expect that the person you love will do their part in helping you to heal. Watch out for the differences between a mistake and a pattern of behavior.
- **Manipulation and Control:** Once the victim is lured back into the relationship or dynamic, the narcissist often resumes their manipulative and controlling behaviors. They revert to their patterns of devaluation, gaslighting, and exploitation, gradually diminishing the victim's self-esteem and independence once again.

However, if they find replacement sources of supply they may simply walk away from old ones. Narcissistic hoovering can be incredibly challenging to resist, as it preys on the victim's emotional vulnerabilities, desires for validation, and hopes for change. Don't worry, I've been here too. The most confusing of them all for me to comprehend was the reverse hoover. Oh boy. Allow me to tell you more.

Narcissistic Abuse Cycle

HOOVER

REVERSE HOOVER

A reverse Hoover is a term used to describe a tactic employed by narcissists to discard or reject someone who has tried to break free from their control or end the relationship. Unlike a traditional Hoover, where the narcissist tries to draw the person back in, a reverse Hoover involves the narcissist rejecting or discarding the person instead. An example of a reverse Hoover could be when a person who has been in a relationship with a narcissist decides to leave or establish boundaries. In response, the narcissist may suddenly act disinterested, indifferent, or even hostile towards the individual. They might ignore their calls or messages, belittle their achievements, or devalue their worth. Or if they block you and unblock you without reaching out.

Their intention is to suck you back in by remaining at the forefront of your mind by enticing your curiosity. By baiting you into reaching out to them first, they set you up to be immediately discarded and/or discredited because of the past. This subtle form of retaliation allows them to still have access to you in order to hurt you - but only if you disrespect your own boundaries. This behavior is meant to confuse and hurt their targe, making them question their decision to leave or assert boundaries. Narcissists engage in reverse Hoovers for various reasons. Firstly, it allows them to maintain a sense of power and control over the situation.

By rejecting the person before they have a chance to fully detach, the narcissist can maintain a perceived upper hand. Additionally, reverse Hoovers serve as a way for narcissists to regain a sense of superiority and ego validation. By devaluing the person who has attempted to leave, they can try to reestablish their dominance and assert their importance. It's important to recognize reverse Hoovers for what they are: manipulative tactics aimed at maintaining control and causing emotional harm. Understanding this behavior can help individuals who have experienced narcissistic abuse to stay firm in their boundaries and protect their emotional well-being.

That said, some attachments will end before we are ready for them to. Many of us will stay in relationships for the illusion of "safety," not realizing that the relationship is the source of why we may feel unsafe in the first place. Strength is not about learning how to survive a toxic environment but rather, it's about feeling empowered enough to leave them. Though we can't prevent harmful behaviors from happening, we can remove ourselves when they do. Emotional or physical abuse in a relationship is about control. Control is a trauma response. Remember, their unhealed wounds are no reason for them to hurt you. The hard truth is that sometimes people you love will mistreat you because they do not love themselves. That is not a reason to stay or rescue them. It is an invitation to leave so they are empowered to rescue themselves. See the summary below on ways you can recognize and detach from harmful situations. Remember, you cannot achieve the relationship you desire by nurturing the type of relationship you don't. Below is a summary of the copious amounts of narcisstic emotional abuse and Hoovering tactics to keep at the forefront of your healing journey. I love you. Where ever you are in your healing journey, hang tight. Everything is going to be okay.

Emotional Abuse	Hoovering Tactics
-Contempt: Belittling, Name Calling, Criticism, Narcissistic Rage/Amnesia, Resentment	**-Acting Repentant:** False apology. "I'm sorry for all of the pain I caused you."
-Diverting: Blame Shifting, Countering, Guilt Tripping, Projecting, Shifting Goal Posts	**-Accidental:** Attempts to trigger you. "Sorry, that was for someone else."
-Emotional Invalidation: Silent Treatment, Stonewalling, Trivializing, Triangulation	**-Bait & Ghost:** Sends you a message, waits for your reply and ghosts you.
-Gaslighting: Lying, Manipulation, Denial, Self Esteem Reduction, Testing Behaviors	**-Crisis:** Attempts to court attention and sympathy. "I was in an accident."
-Isolation: Withholding Resources/Family, Friends/Affection/Information	**-Dismissing:** Pretending nothing happened. "How are you?"
-Ignoring Boundaries: Repeating The Same "Mistakes", Overlapping Relationships	**-Drive By:** Attempts to try to see you. "Do you have my mail?"
-Passive Aggressive: Ghosting, Breadcrumbing, Destructive Criticism, Negging	**-False Concern:** Pretending to sincerely care. "I heard your mom was sick."
-Victimization: Pity Play, Reactive Abuse, Narcissistic Injury, Eclipsing Emotions	**-Proclamation:** Epiphany & Change. "I realized it was just our communication!"
	-Round-About: Third party contacts you. Their mom saying your ex misses you.
	-Sentimental: Attempts to emotionally bond. "I saw this and thought of you!"

Narcissistic Abuse Cycle

HOOVER

FAKE RECONCILIATION

Even still, if a source of supply pulls away, they may attempt to hoover them back and/or look for other sources. These predators are excellent at disguising themselves as viable partners as they love bomb their next supply with sex, attention, gifts and praise to gain the admiration lost as a result of the end of a relationship. Narcissistic individuals are skilled manipulators, and one of their tactics for maintaining control and avoiding accountability is triangulation of their ex's. This cunning behavior involves creating false narratives and stirring up conflict between their ex-partner and their current partner. By doing so, they ensure that these two individuals never interact and compare notes, as that could expose the narcissist's past abusive behaviors.

Remember, triangulation serves multiple purposes for the narcissist. Firstly, it allows them to distance themselves from the consequences of their actions by keeping their past and present partners isolated from each other. By preventing any interaction, they can continue to manipulate and deceive without fear of loss or exposure. Additionally, triangulation provides the narcissist with a safety net. By leaving open lines of communication with their ex-partner, they can easily reach out if their current relationship fails or if they need an alternative source of supply. It also feeds their need for attention and control, as they can maintain a sense of power over both partners by keeping them at odds with each other. In this way, the narcissist perpetuates a web of manipulation and deceit, using triangulation as a tool to protect their false self-image and maintain dominance over their victims. If they feel regret, it is not because they hurt you. It is for losing something that they value. To them, you are a possession, not a real person. Recognizing these tactics is essential for those affected by narcissistic abuse, as it can help them break free from the cycle of manipulation and regain control over their own lives and emotions.

Below are two examples of how an individual can also put themselves into a situation of engaging in a reverse hoover with a narcissist during the discard phase.

1. After a painful breakup with a narcissistic partner, the individual starts to feel lonely and longs for the connection they once had. Feeling nostalgic, they decide to send the narcissist a heartfelt text, expressing how much they miss them and reminiscing about the good times they shared.
2. An individual who has ended a toxic relationship with a narcissist suddenly feels overwhelmed by guilt and self-doubt. They start to believe that they were the cause of the relationship's demise and feel responsible for the narcissist's unhappiness. In an attempt to seek validation and closure, they reach out to the narcissist, hoping for reassurance and to mend the broken bond.

The unfortunate truth is, a narcissist will exploit your willingness to forgive them as permission to continue their harmful behavior. If you forgave them once, they are conditioning you to forgive them again. Remember, forgiveness can be reassessed or revoked if a repeated pattern continues to resurface. Because an apology without changed behavior is just manipulation. Fake reconciliation is a tactic often used by narcissists that convey a lack remorse or efforts to genuinely repair for any reasonable duration of time. Here's the thing, pain is in the eye of the beholder. The person asking for forgiveness does not get to determine the impact of their actions, severity of the consequences or when/if forgiveness is given. Narcissists and highly toxic people will often try to apply pressure to dictate the pace with which the victim lets their guard down, and lets them in. Fake reconciliation and remorse can be tactics used to suck their victims back into a relationship with the intention of future faking until a more appealing supply comes along.

Damage control is not the same as remorse. They will do this to avoid their fear of abandonment vs acknowledge the pain they've caused you. The same mistake repeated over and over again is no longer a mistake - but rather, a decision. The nuance in a narcissist's effort to make amends lies in the fact that admitting their wrongdoing seldom aims to alleviate the victim's suffering and discomfort. Instead, it's an attempt to manipulate the victim into alleviating the narcissist's own guilt and seeking their validation for the harm they've inflicted. They somehow manage to use their crocodile tears to act more hurt about the pain *they* caused *you* as you rush to their rescue and are expected to save them from the consequences of *their* actions. They will attempt to rush your healing process so they don't have to sit in the discomfort of helping you to heal the parts of you they hurt. Then, cue the discard process once again. It is abusive behavior when someone cannot treat you right, while also refusing to let you go. To a Narcissist, treating you well half the time, cancels out treating you poorly the other half.

A good indicator of future behavior is past behavior. I get it, "*What if they change?*" However, *what if they don't?* Which position is more risky to be in? Which situation do you stand to suffer the most in?

Narcissistic Abuse Cycle

HOOVER

FAKE RECONCILIATION

Often times, a Narcissist will not provide you with closure on purpose. By withholding closure, they attempt to keep you connected. Often times, expecting civil closure from a narcissist is like expecting compassion from a carrot. It's silly and never going to happen. This tactic is used to intentionally trigger you, in order to control you. In otherwords, they do this on purpose. These examples of manipulative apologies from narcissists often shift the blame onto the victim or minimize the narcissist's actions. They lack genuine remorse and take no responsibility for their hurtful behavior, ultimately furthering the cycle of manipulation and control in the relationship. Below are a few statements a highly toxic or narcissitc person will use to deflect blame during the fake reconciliation process:

- I'm sorry you feel that way."
- "I didn't mean to hurt you, but you provoked me."
- "I'm sorry, but you know I have a short temper."
- "I apologize for what happened, but it was just a joke, you're too sensitive."
- "I'm sorry if my actions upset you, but you need to understand I have a lot of stress in my life right now."
- "I'm sorry, but you should know I'm not perfect, nobody is."
- "I apologize for what I did, but you need to admit your part in this situation too."
- "I'm sorry, but you know I can't help it when I get angry."
- "I'm sorry you took it the wrong way, that wasn't my intention."
- "I'm sorry, but you have to admit you have a lot of issues you need to work on too."

When you're not yet ready to accept an apology, it's essential to be honest and assertive in communicating your feelings. Here are ten phrases you can use:

1. "Thank you for apologizing, but I need some time to process everything."
2. "I appreciate your apology, but I'm still hurt and need space to heal."
3. "I'm not ready to accept your apology right now, as I'm still trying to understand my feelings."
4. "I acknowledge your apology, but I'm not sure if I can move forward just yet."
5. "I'm grateful for your apology, but I need time to consider if forgiveness is possible."
6. "Your apology is a step in the right direction, but I'm not ready to move past this yet."
7. "I'm still trying to make sense of what happened, and I'm not ready to accept your apology fully."
8. "I'm glad you apologized, but I need to work through my emotions before I can respond."
9. "Your apology means a lot to me, but I need to prioritize my healing before addressing this."
10. "I hear your apology, but I'm not ready to make a decision about it at the moment."

Some aggressors may use communication as a hoovering tactic to keep themselves at the forefront of their victims mind. For the aggressor, this type of validation seeking is a maladaptive form of self-soothing. It's harmful when used to manipulate their victim's emotions for egoic gain. An aggressor may weaponize love bombing by romanticizing a false sense of reconciliation and promises to change or do better. Once the chase ends and feelings dissipate, they discard and disappear - leaving their victims feeling empty and depleted. Where the discard ends and the hovering begins, remember that closure is only sought after for two reasons: Guilt or Resentment. Some aggressors will seek closure to alleviate their guilt, not their victim's pain. Remember, if the relationship were healthy, closure would not be necessary. For that reason, it is important to recognize when someone's attention lacks intention. It's equally as important to remember that forgiveness does not require reconnection or reconciliation. In other words, you can love someone, you can even forgive someone and still not want them back. Maintaining a healthy distance will help you avoid disrespect. Remember, it's okay to take your time when someone apologizes, especially if the hurt is significant. Be patient with yourself, and honor your feelings.

As I made the decision to finally walk away, his hoovering efforts conveyed just how much he was still wanted me to stay. But here's the thing, you can't hurt someone and expect their energy to still be the same. I didn't leave because I stopped loving him. I left because the longer I stayed with him, the more I stopped loving myself. So instead, I decided to raise my standards. In doing so, I allowed that to be an opportunity for him to rise and meet me there. All I knew was I was not going to allow myself to get close to someone who had the ability to trigger me back into a person I had just leveled up from. As his friend once told me, sometimes "the lucky one" isn't the one that stayed - but *the one that got away.*

Narcissistic Abuse Cycle

SUMMARY OF TERMS & DEFINITIONS

35 EMOTIONALLY ABUSIVE MANIPULATION TACTICS NARCISSISTS USE

EMOTIONAL ABUSE *IS* DOMESTIC VIOLENCE

- Gaslighting: Manipulating someone into questioning their own reality and sanity.
- Love bombing: Overwhelming someone with excessive affection and attention to gain control and manipulate their emotions.
- Triangulation: Creating conflicts or tensions between individuals to maintain control and boost their ego.
- Projection: Blaming others for their own faults, behaviors, or feelings. *Often times, their projection is a confession.*
- Silent treatment: Ignoring or withdrawing affection and communication as a means of control and punishment.
- Hoovering: Trying to draw someone back into a relationship or interaction after a period of abuse or abandonment.
- Verbal abuse: Using harsh language, insults, or put-downs to demean and control others.
- Smear campaign: Spreading false or negative information about someone to damage their reputation.
- Victim mentality: Playing the victim to elicit sympathy, manipulate others, and avoid accountability.
- Manipulative charm: Using charisma, flattery, and charm to win people over and gain control.
- False empathy: Feigning empathy to manipulate others' emotions and gain their trust.
- Financial manipulation: Controlling or exploiting someone financially to gain power and control.
- Boundary violations: Disregarding or violating personal boundaries to exert control and invade someone's space.
- Emotional blackmail: Using guilt, threats, or manipulation to make someone comply with their demands.
- Covert aggression: Employing subtle and indirect means of aggression, such as passive-aggressive behavior or backhanded compliments.
- Intellectual superiority: Belittling others' intelligence or knowledge to assert dominance and undermine their self-confidence.
- Stonewalling: Refusing to engage in communication or give any response to frustrate and manipulate the other person.
- Manipulative guilt: Making someone feel guilty for their actions or decisions, even when unwarranted, to gain control.
- False promises: Making empty promises or commitments to manipulate and keep others hooked.
- Negging: Using subtle insults or backhanded compliments to undermine someone's self-esteem and manipulate their emotions.
- Blame shifting: Shifting the blame onto others for their own mistakes or shortcomings.
- Scapegoating: Assigning blame and responsibility to someone else as a means of deflecting attention from themselves.
- Double standards: Holding others to different standards than they hold themselves to, creating a sense of unfairness.
- Emotional manipulation: Using emotions to control or manipulate others, such as guilt, fear, or pity.
- Intermittent reinforcement: Providing rewards or positive reinforcement inconsistently to keep someone hooked and seeking validation.
- False accusations: Making baseless accusations to discredit and control others.
- Smiling assassins: Presenting a charming and friendly facade while harboring malicious intentions.
- Control through affection: Using love, intimacy, and affection as a means of control and manipulation.
- Gaslighting by proxy: Convince others to doubt or question the target's sanity or credibility.
- Discarding and devaluing: Suddenly devaluing or discarding someone after idealizing them to exert control and cause emotional pain.
- Emotional isolation: Isolating someone from friends, family, or support networks to increase dependence and control.
- Cognitive dissonance: Creating confusion or contradictory beliefs in someone's mind to maintain control and power.
- Exploiting vulnerabilities: Identifying and exploiting someone's weaknesses or insecurities for personal gain.
- Guilt-tripping: Manipulating someone by making them feel guilty for asserting their needs or boundaries.
- Love withdrawal: Withholding affection or love as a form of punishment or control.

Emotional manipulation is an abusive tactic used to get a desired response from their target by covertly using words, tonality, behaviors or body language to silence, scare or shame their victims into submission. Abuse isn't always yelling, hitting or throwing things. Abusers can weaponize appearing calm to make their victims feel crazy. Those who are codependent on their partners approval will abandon themselves in order to receive love from someone else.

SUMMARY OF TOPIC 2

-The Narcissistic Abuse Cycle consisted of idealization, devaluation, discard and hoovering

-Emotional abuse is domestic violence

-Narcissists are hidden in plain sight and intentionally utilize manipulation tactics that confuse their victims into believing their reaction to their disrespectful actions were the victims fault

The Imani Mvmt

TRAUMA INFORMED RESILIENCY COACHING

Reflecting on your experience within the abuse cycle of a narcissistic relationship, how did the idealization, devaluation, and discard phases impact your self-esteem and sense of self-worth? How do you think these cycles of abuse influenced your perception of what a healthy relationship should look like? Write your answer in the space below.

_____

_____

_____

_____

_____

_____

REFLECTION QUESTIONS

Consider the tactics and manipulation techniques used by the narcissist during the abuse cycle. How did these strategies affect your emotions, thoughts, and behaviors? In what ways did they make you question your own reality and undermine your confidence? Write your answer in the space below.

_____

_____

_____

_____

_____

_____

_____

_____

_____

_____

_____

_____

_____

_____

_____

REFLECTION QUESTIONS

Now that you have gained awareness of the abuse cycle, how can you use this knowledge to empower yourself and break free from its grip? What steps can you take to prioritize your own healing and establish healthier boundaries in future relationships? How can you harness your newfound understanding to prevent being drawn back into similar dynamics? Write your answer in the space below.

NAVIGATING NARCISSISM

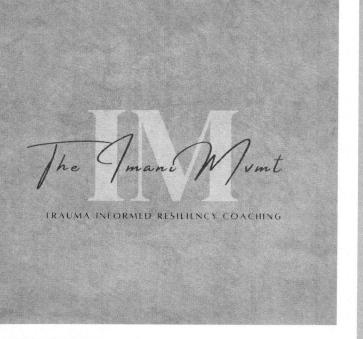

Healing The Collective One Individual At A Time

03

Resiliency & Recovery

140

PART 3 OF 3

3 Key Objectives

1)Psychology of Post Narcissist Stress Disorder (PNSD)

2)Physiology of Post Narcissist Stress Disorder (PNSD)

3)Resilency & Recovery

INTENTIONS

Reflecting on the patterns and red flags you noticed during the highly toxic relationship, what valuable lessons have you learned about setting boundaries and recognizing healthy versus unhealthy dynamics in relationships? How can these lessons guide you in cultivating healthier connections moving forward?

Write your answer in the space below.

_____

_____

_____

_____

_____

_____

_____

_____

_____

_____

_____

_____

_____

_____

_____

_____

_____

Remember, reflection is a powerful tool for gaining insight and promoting growth. Give yourself permission to explore your experiences with compassion and curiosity. By delving into these questions, you can deepen your understanding of the impact of the narcissistic relationship and pave the way for healing, growth, and the creation of healthier relationships in the future.

Navigating life after the discard phase of the narcissistic abuse cycle can be an incredibly challenging journey. This is due to a combination of psychological and physiological factors that can profoundly impact survivors. Firstly, victims often experience an overwhelming sense of loss and grief as they mourn the relationship they once had, leading to emotional turmoil. Additionally, the constant manipulation and gaslighting during the abuse cycle can leave individuals questioning their reality, fostering self-doubt and eroding self-esteem. Physiologically, the stress and trauma endured can result in heightened anxiety, depression, and even physical health issues, making the aftermath of narcissistic abuse particularly difficult to overcome. Trauma bonds, the emotional attachments formed in the midst of abuse, can be exceptionally hard to break. Remember, these bonds are established through intermittent reinforcement – periods of affection mixed with abuse – creating a sense of emotional dependence.

This dependency is reinforced by the narcissist's ability to alternately provide comfort and inflict pain, leaving survivors yearning for the "good times." The psychological trauma endured in the relationship further deepens these bonds, as survivors might internalize a distorted belief that they deserve the mistreatment or that the abuser is the only source of validation. For these reasons, trauma bonds are challenging to break both psychologically and physiologically due to various factors that contribute to their strength and resilience. The thing is, trauma bonds resemble the same psychological and physiological response as an addiction which is why you can't just "think" your way out of them.

The pain of breaking a trauma bond amplifies in intensity when we have not yet addressed our unhealed childhood wounds that enabled them in the first place. The pain experienced in the present is a reflection of the pain that was left unhealed from the past. When you are breaking out of a trauma bond, you're not just breaking up with your partner. You're breaking up with an un-acknowledged longing for an unresponsive parent and parts of yourself that you suppressed that came alive when you were with your partner. When you're breaking a trauma bond, you're not just letting go of toxicity - you're letting go of certain parts of yourself that also felt positive while you were with them. Here are some reasons why trauma bonds can be difficult to break:

1. **Survival Mechanism:** Trauma bonds often form as a survival mechanism in situations of prolonged abuse or captivity. The brain's instinctual response to danger is to establish a connection with the abuser as a means of self-preservation. This biological response can make it incredibly difficult to detach from the abuser, as the bond is deeply ingrained at a primal level.
2. **Cognitive Dissonance:** Trauma bonds create cognitive dissonance, which is the psychological discomfort that arises from holding contradictory beliefs or feelings. Victims may simultaneously experience love, attachment, and fear towards their abuser, leading to a confusing and conflicting emotional state. The mind tries to reconcile these conflicting emotions, often resulting in a strong psychological pull to maintain the bond.
3. **Trauma Bond Reinforcement:** Trauma bonds are reinforced through a cycle of abuse, intermittent reinforcement, and occasional acts of kindness or affection from the abuser. This cycle creates a pattern of hope, followed by disappointment, which further strengthens the bond. The sporadic reinforcement can be highly addictive, as victims continuously seek validation and positive attention from their abuser.
4. **Emotional Dependency:** Trauma bonds often result in an unhealthy emotional dependency on the abuser. Victims may have low self-esteem, feel incapable of surviving without the abuser, or fear the consequences of leaving. This emotional dependency makes it challenging to break free, as the thought of losing the relationship can trigger intense anxiety and feelings of emptiness.
5. **Isolation and Manipulation:** Abusers often isolate their victims from external support systems, making it harder for them to seek help or find the strength to leave. Additionally, abusers employ manipulative tactics such as gaslighting, which can distort the victim's perception of reality, making them doubt their own experiences and reinforcing the bond.

RESILIENCY & RECOVERY

HOPE & HEALING

As we delve into the intricate aftermath of trauma bonds with narcissists and the challenging process of breaking free from their grip, it's important to recognize the profound emotional withdrawals that follow the discard phase. Navigating this landscape requires a comprehensive understanding of the psychological intricacies involved, paving the way for a discussion on the subsequent cognitive challenges such as brain fog and dissociation that survivors often grapple with as they strive to regain control over their own identities. Narcissistic abuse can have a significant impact on the victim's mental health, including the development of brain fog. Brain fog is a feeling of mental confusion or difficulty concentrating. It can make it hard to think clearly, remember minor details, or make decisions. Victims of narcissistic abuse may experience brain fog as a result of the constant gaslighting, manipulation, and emotional abuse they have endured. [90]

Therefore, it's important to approach this topic with compassion and understanding, as healing from narcissistic abuse is a challenging process whose impacts include:

- **Emotional Dysregulation:** Narcissistic abuse can lead to emotional dysregulation, where individuals may experience intense mood swings, anxiety, depression, or a sense of emotional numbness. The constant manipulation, gaslighting, and emotional rollercoaster of the abusive relationship can disrupt the brain's ability to regulate emotions effectively.
- Hypervigilance and Anxiety: Survivors of narcissistic abuse often develop hypervigilance, a state of heightened alertness and anxiety. This heightened state is a result of the constant need to anticipate the narcissistic abuser's unpredictable behavior and protect oneself from potential harm. The brain becomes wired to be on constant guard, leading to ongoing anxiety and a sense of being unsafe.
- **Cognitive Dissonance:** Narcissistic abuse often involves gaslighting and manipulation, which can create cognitive dissonance. The survivor's beliefs, values, and reality are constantly challenged, causing confusion and internal conflict. This cognitive dissonance can lead to self-doubt, mistrust of one's own perceptions, and difficulty in making decisions.
- Trauma Responses: Narcissistic abuse can cause complex trauma, which can manifest in various ways. Survivors may experience intrusive thoughts, nightmares, flashbacks, or emotional and physical distress triggered by reminders of the abusive experiences. The brain's response to trauma can disrupt memory processing, leading to fragmented or dissociated memories of the abuse.
- **Rebuilding Self-Esteem and Trust:** Narcissistic abuse often erodes a person's self-esteem and trust in themselves and others. It takes time and effort to rebuild these aspects of one's identity. Engaging in self-care, therapy, and supportive relationships can help restore a sense of self-worth and develop healthier boundaries.

Some ways to begin healing from narcissistic abuse and brain fog include:

Not all wounds are visible

Seeking professional help: Working with a trauma informed therapist or coach can help you process your experiences and develop coping strategies to manage symptoms

Practicing self-care: Engaging in activities that bring you joy and relaxation, such as exercise, yoga, or spending time in nature, can help reduce stress and improve mental clarity. Bring it back to basics. The simple things often provide the most safety.

Setting boundaries: Establishing clear boundaries with the narcissistic abuser and limiting contact with them can help reduce the emotional toll of the abuse and improve mental clarity. Engage in cognitive-behavioral therapy (CBT): CBT can help you identify and change negative thought patterns and behaviors that contribute to brain fog.

Connecting with a supportive community: Surround yourself with people who support and validate your experiences. This can include friends, family members, or support groups for survivors of narcissistic abuse. It's important to remember that healing from narcissistic abuse and brain fog takes time and patience. With the right support and self-care, it is possible to recover and rebuild a fulfilling life.

RESILIENCY & RECOVERY

HOPE & HEALING

It's important to recognize that survivors of narcissistic abuse often experience a phenomenon known as "brain fog" in the aftermath of the abuse. This cognitive cloudiness can make it challenging to think clearly or make decisions. What's even more difficult is when survivors find themselves dealing with post-separation abuse from the narcissistic individual, as this can intensify the already painful effects of the abuse they endured. Post-separation abuse in the context of a relationship with a narcissist is a deeply challenging and painful experience that many individuals go through. It occurs after a person has left or ended a relationship with a narcissistic partner but continues to face emotional, psychological, or even physical abuse from the narcissist.

Imagine you've had the courage to leave a relationship with someone who exhibited narcissistic traits or had a narcissistic personality. You might have hoped that once you're out of the relationship, things would get better, but unfortunately, that's not always the case.

Post-separation abuse by a narcissist can take various forms:

1. **Harassment**: The narcissistic ex-partner may bombard you with incessant calls, texts, or emails, often with the intent to control or manipulate you.
2. **Stalking**: Some narcissists resort to stalking, which can be deeply distressing and intrusive, making you feel like your privacy and safety are constantly threatened.
3. **Smear Campaigns**: They might spread false or damaging information about you to friends, family, or on social media, attempting to ruin your reputation and isolate you further.
4. **Legal Manipulation**: Narcissists can use the legal system to their advantage, filing unnecessary lawsuits or custody battles to exert control and drain your resources.
5. **Financial Manipulation**: They may withhold financial support or manipulate assets to keep you dependent or in financial distress.
6. **Emotional Manipulation**: The narcissist can continue to play mind games, manipulating your emotions and causing self-doubt.

The impact of post-separation abuse is profound and can include:

- **Emotional Distress**: You might feel anxious, depressed, or constantly on edge due to the ongoing harassment and manipulation.
- **Isolation**: The narcissist's efforts to damage your relationships with friends and family can leave you feeling alone and unsupported.
- **Financial Strain**: Dealing with legal battles or financial manipulation can be financially devastating.
- **Safety Concerns**: In severe cases, the abuse can escalate to physical violence or threats, putting your safety at risk.

To anyone who has experienced or is currently enduring the challenging aftermath of post-separation narcissistic abuse, please know that your strength is remarkable, and your feelings are valid. The journey to healing from such a traumatic experience can be incredibly tough, and it's okay to acknowledge the pain and confusion you may be feeling. You are not alone and your resilience in navigating through these difficult times is a testament to your inner strength. Remember that healing is a gradual process, and each step you take towards reclaiming your life is a courageous one. It's important to remember that post-separation abuse is not your fault, and you don't have to endure it alone. When supporting my clients through such challenging times, I highly recommend documenting instances of abuse, maintaining boundaries, and to consider obtaining a restraining order if necessary as means of protection.

That's because, as we know, Narcissists are experts at using manipulation techniques to maintain control and avoid taking responsibility for their actions. Especially during the end of a relationship. One tactic they may employ is the use of double negatives, which can confuse and shift the blame onto their partner while simultaneously presenting themselves as the innocent party. For example, imagine a scenario where a narcissistic partner has been emotionally abusive and dishonest throughout the relationship. When the relationship is on the brink of ending, they might say something like, "I never meant to hurt you, and I don't think I didn't try my best." In this statement, the double negatives serve to create ambiguity and distance them from their harmful behavior. By saying "I never meant to hurt you," they try to avoid taking accountability for their actions. The second part of the sentence, "I don't think I didn't try my best," suggests that they did make an effort, but it implies doubt, making it seem like they are unsure about their actions. Talk about some pretty tricky nuances, huh?

These manipulative double negatives create confusion, leaving their partner second-guessing themselves and wondering if the narcissist is genuine in their remorse. The narcissist aims to play the victim by portraying themselves as someone who tried their best but somehow failed, instead of acknowledging the intentional harm they caused and failed to take adequate responsibility for.

When dealing with a narcissistic partner during a breakup, it's essential to be aware of these manipulative tactics. Look out for:
1. **Ambiguous Statements:** Pay attention to statements that lack clarity and directness, especially when it comes to their responsibility in the relationship's breakdown.
2. **Shifting Blame:** Observe if they consistently redirect the blame onto others or external circumstances, rather than taking ownership of their actions.
3. **Contradictions in Communication:** Be cautious of conflicting messages or mixed signals that can lead to confusion and self-doubt.

Now, I want you to imagine this scenario: After a breakup with a narcissist, they approach their friends or family and recount the events with an air of innocence. They might say something like, "I tried so hard to make it work, but they just couldn't appreciate me. I did everything I could, but they were always so distant and cold. They just couldn't understand my busy work ethic and allowed their own past trauma to interfere in our relationship." The difference between the side of the story a Narcissist tells versus the version the victim tells, is that one is a distortion of the truth and the other is a recountal of it. In this carefully crafted narrative, they cunningly leave out their own abusive behaviors and manipulative tactics. The emotional and psychological abuse they subjected their partner to goes unmentioned, allowing them to cast themselves as the victimized nice guy. This half-truth story aims to win sympathy, making it look like the breakup was solely the victim's fault. This is also how triangulation occurs.

It's as insincere as the job interviewee who mentions a seemingly positive trait like being a perfectionist as their biggest weakness. It's a way of trying to answer a common question about weaknesses while avoiding the risk of revealing a genuine vulnerability.

To protect yourself from falling into the trap of their narrative, it's crucial to be aware of a couple of red flags:

1. **Seeking Validation from Multiple Sources:** Narcissists may go to great lengths to garner validation and sympathy from various people. If they seem overly concerned about how others perceive the breakup and continuously seek reassurance for their victimhood, be cautious.
2. **Pattern of Blame and Denial:** Observe if the narcissist consistently blames others for their problems and denies any wrongdoing on their part. If they avoid taking responsibility for their actions and portray themselves as the perpetual victim, it's a sign of their manipulative tendencies.

When dealing with a narcissistic ex-partner, it's essential to trust your instincts. Especially as they intentionally try to interfere with your healing journey. Understanding the patterns of emotional abuse and manipulation can help you maintain your boundaries and protect your emotional well-being. Often times, even if you have proof, their shame will enable them to reactively shift blame and deny the truth. As invalidating as this feels, you do not need their validation to legitimatize the pain they put you through. You just need the validation of a safe and supportive community. Remember, you are not responsible for their behavior, and you have the right to break free from toxic relationships. In time, you'll find yourself in a place of empowerment, free from the grip of manipulation, and ready to embrace healthier, loving connections.

RESILIENCY & RECOVERY

HOPE & HEALING

RELATIONSHIP BETRAYALS

I vividly remember a time just before I left my former partner when he made a startling statement. He openly admitted that he would fabricate a story about why our relationship ended. He planned to shift the blame entirely onto himself and point to my past traumas as the cause of our breakup. In his eyes, he would paint himself as a savior, someone trying to protect me from being labeled as "broken." He did so while conveniently ignoring his own history of dishonesty in our relationship, his abusive communication style, and his lack of remorse and accountability. Looking back, I recall how I initially questioned him about his past relationships when we first got together. His responses were often vague and left me feeling confused. He claimed that all his previous relationships had ended because he knew he could "never see himself marrying them." What he didn't reveal, and what I later discovered when I went through his phone, was that he had shattered their trust by repeating the same harmful patterns with them, as he had done with me. They had started to see through his actions and were on the verge of holding him accountable when he chose to end things first. I share this to emphasize that your feelings and experiences are valid, and you are not alone in facing such complexities in a relationship. I promise you, not everyone will hurt you the way that they did.

Connecting the cunning manipulation tactics like pity plays and double negatives, let's slightly compound this focus by comprehending the deeper layers of relationship betrayals as we explore a concept known as "Dupers Delight." This exploration leads us to the unsettling realization of the sadistic tendencies within narcissistic individuals, as they derive a disturbing sense of pleasure from inflicting harm and psychological turmoil upon their unsuspecting victims. In other words, some narcissists or other highly toxic individuals genuinely gain satisfaction from reminiscing on the pain they caused you. This is often times why sending that "last text message explaining to them how they hurt you" goes invalidated. The intentional invalidation of your emotional experiences gives them satisfaction as they watch you submit and surrender. Especially during the post-separation abuse phase. These actions can cause significant emotional harm and erode trust between partners. Pretty crazy, right? Here are some of the many ways they engage in Dupers Delight:

- Gaslighting: Manipulating the victim's perception of reality, making them doubt their own memory, judgment, or sanity.
- Constant lying: Deceiving the partner with a web of lies and half-truths to maintain control and power.
- Ignoring your needs and taking you for granted
- Not standing up for you or prioritizing the needs of others over your own
- Betraying the relationship for external validation
- Sharing your secrets with others without your approval
- Emotional manipulation: Exploiting emotions, fears, and vulnerabilities to gain an upper hand in the relationship.
- Verbal abuse: Consistently belittling, criticizing, and demeaning the partner to diminish their self-worth.
- Silent treatment: Ignoring and refusing to communicate as a form of punishment and control.
- Financial control: Controlling and restricting access to finances, creating dependency and limiting the partner's independence.
- Social isolation: Isolating the partner from friends and family to maintain control and prevent outside support.
- Guilt-tripping: Using guilt and emotional manipulation to make the partner comply with their demands.
- Blame-shifting: Avoiding responsibility for their actions by constantly shifting blame onto the partner.
- Withholding affection and love: Using love and affection as a reward for compliance and punishment for disobedience.
- Exploiting vulnerabilities: Manipulating and using the partner's weaknesses against them to maintain power.
- Invasion of privacy: Snooping, monitoring, or invading the partner's personal space without consent.
- Manipulating children: Using the children as pawns to control or harm the partner emotionally.
- Threats and intimidation: Making threats to instill fear and ensure compliance with their wishes.
- Triangulation: Introducing a third person into the relationship to create jealousy and insecurity.
- Undermining achievements: Belittling the partner's accomplishments and diminishing their self-confidence.
- Excessive control: Dictating and disrespecting every aspect of the partner's life, such as their appearance, hobbies, and interests.
- Love-bombing and devaluation cycles: Oscillating between extreme affection and harsh devaluation to keep the partner off balance emotionally.
- Stalking or cyberstalking: Invading the partner's online presence or physically tracking their movements without consent.
- Emotional blackmail: Threatening to harm oneself or others if the partner doesn't comply with their demands.
- Projection: Projecting their negative traits onto their partner, making them feel responsible for the narcissist's feelings and actions.

- Withholding Affection and Approval: Narcissists use intermittent reinforcement by withholding affection, attention, or approval. This inconsistency keeps the partner on edge, trying to earn their narcissistic partner's love and approval.
- Manipulative Praise and Criticism: Narcissists use manipulative praise to control their partner's behavior, followed by harsh criticism to keep them in line.

In an abusive narcissistic relationship, betrayal can take various forms beyond infidelity. Often times when we are so used to putting the needs of others ahead of our own, we may feel guilty for setting a boundary. That's because we have been conditioned to focus on the needs and emotional experiences of others at the expense of neglecting our own. This concept is known as pathological accommodation. This refers to ways of being that function unconsciously to preserve a needed attachment when that bond has been traumatically threatened. [91] Loving someone harder in order to make them love you is a trauma response. Loving someone harder at the expense of abandoning yourself, is also a trauma response. Narcissists are skilled at weaponizing and withholding love against their victims which allows them to mask their betrayals while they rejoice in cowardice satisfaction we now know as Dupers Delight.

Woof. Navigating a relationship with a narcissistic individual can be like walking through a minefield of emotional manipulation and betrayal. These individuals often take a twisted pleasure in causing you pain, even after the relationship has ended. In the aftermath, as you embark on your healing journey, they may cunningly disguise covert acts of cruelty behind acts of kindness. For instance, they might reach out under the pretense of concern, only to use this connection as a means to undermine your progress and disrupt your healing journey.

I remember a situation shortly after parting ways with my former partner when a mutual friend of ours was organizing a baby shower. Even after our relationship had ended, I had managed to maintain a loving friendship with her, as she had been incredibly supportive of me following our separation. In the lead-up to her baby shower, my former partner contacted me via email, asking if I wanted some of the items from our shared home, given that I had left with only three boxes. However, I couldn't help but feel untrusting of his intentions. I was fearful he might be trying to draw me back into our old life and manipulate me into returning to the relationship. I didn't know what to do. I was torn and absolutely flooded with emotions. I called his mother to ask for her advice. To which she encouraged me to stay strong and reminded me of the reasons I left him in the first place.

As we exchanged a few emails, I explained that I would consider coming by to collect the remaining items after the baby shower. He responded by saying he had "kindly" decided not to attend the baby shower, citing his desire to "respect" the meaningful relationship I had with our mutual friend. He claimed he didn't want to interfere with a relationship that meant so much to me. Essentially, he was implying, "I'm taking the high road by not going to the event so that you can feel safe and maintain your important friendship without me." However, when I asked my friend about the validity of his statement, she clarified the truth: "He's not attending because he wasn't invited." This revelation shed light on his attempt to manipulate the situation and gave me a clearer understanding of his actions. Until now, I'm sure he blamed my hesitation to take him back on life circumstances. Not knowing that it was once again his actions that prevented me from reconnecting with him and us being together ever again.

Narcissists and other highly toxic individuals may use "Duper's Delight" for several reasons:

1. **Control and Power:** Narcissists have a strong desire for control and power over others. When they successfully manipulate or deceive someone, it reinforces their sense of superiority and dominance.
2. **Sense of Superiority:** Narcissists often have an inflated sense of self-importance and view themselves as smarter or more cunning than others. Successfully deceiving someone feeds into this belief and boosts their ego.
3. **Validation of Their False Self:** Narcissists often construct a false self-image to hide their insecurities and vulnerabilities. The success of their manipulation can validate this false self, making them feel more secure and powerful.
4. **Attention and Admiration:** Narcissists thrive on attention and admiration from others. When they manipulate someone successfully, they may receive praise or admiration, which further boosts their ego.

That's why often times when you tell a toxic person they've hurt you with their countless betrayals, they may minimize or dismiss your pain. Seeing you in more pain as they invalidate your emotions and experience reminds them of the power and control they have over you. Secretly provoking your pain while withholding relief from it forces your nervous system into dysregulation. Here, they can trigger you relentlessly as they further condition you to believe that they are helping you while secretly hurting you.

RESILIENCY & RECOVERY

HOPE & HEALING

NO CONTACT

Shifting gears from the unsettling presence of someone toxic who finds satisfaction in their dupers delight, we now venture into the realm of establishing a crucial boundary: going completely no contact with a narcissist. This transformative step involves reclaiming your power and prioritizing your well-being by severing ties with a manipulative individual. By exploring the journey from recognizing the twisted pleasure of dupers delight to the empowering decision of cutting off all contact, we gain insights into the healing process and the path towards emotional liberation.

Going no contact is a term that carries significant weight and importance in the context of narcissistic relationships and can have psychological benefits for the victim. Imagine this scenario: You've been entangled in a toxic dynamic with a narcissist, where your emotions have been manipulated, your boundaries crossed, and your self-worth diminished. It's an emotionally draining and tumultuous experience, to say the least. It's similar to cutting off a limb to save the rest of the body, especially when it comes to breaking trauma bonds. As we know, trauma bonds go beyond psychological connections; they also have a biological component, which makes them particularly challenging to sever. When we're caught in these bonds, it becomes difficult to think beyond our current emotions, especially when our survival instincts are simultaneously in flight or fight mode. Consequently, we often find ourselves frozen in the relationship, experiencing heightened anxiety, hypervigilance, and even dissociation. One of the bravest things you'll ever do in your life is prioritizing your own healing. This is because those you allowed into your life while you were hurting cannot accompany you on the next stage of your healing journey. Even if they are the ones you deeply love. Going no contact involves cutting off all communication and contact with the narcissist or highly toxic individual. It's about establishing a protective boundary to safeguard your well-being and reclaim your personal power. But why is it psychologically beneficial?

Let's explore that. First and foremost, going no contact allows you to create space for healing. When you're constantly exposed to the toxic presence of a narcissist, it's challenging to gain clarity, process your emotions, and rebuild your sense of self. By cutting off contact, you remove yourself from the ongoing cycle of abuse, manipulation, and emotional turmoil. Secondly, going no contact provides a chance for you to reclaim your autonomy. Narcissists thrive on control and dominance, and by going no contact, you're asserting your independence and taking back control over your own life. It's an empowering step towards regaining your freedom and breaking free from the chains of their toxic influence. Moreover, going no contact protects you from further psychological harm. When you remain in contact with a narcissist, they can continue their manipulative tactics, gaslighting, and emotional abuse. By severing ties, you create a barrier that shields you from their toxic behaviors, allowing you to focus on your own healing and well-being.

Fun Fact: Narcissists often exploit religion and spirituality as a tool to camouflage their abusive behavior, perpetuating a facade of righteousness while concealing their true intentions. This manipulation is particularly insidious when individuals who proclaim to follow certain moral values and beliefs use them as a smokescreen to justify or bypass their hurtful actions. In my personal experience, I was involved with someone who identified as being deeply Christian. Yet his actions contradicted the very principles he professed to uphold. To truly repent, involves recognition, remorse, responsibility, resolution and restitution. The nuance here as it relates to narcissists or other highly toxic individuals is the depth of their "repentance" only goes as far as recognition. In other words, they lack the ability or awareness to follow through on the other key components.

An apology is not the same as accepting accountability. While claiming to embrace love, compassion, and empathy, my former partner's behavior towards myself and others were characterized by emotional manipulation, control, and disregard for anyone's well-being. This dissonance between their proclaimed faith and their actions left me feeling confused and deeply hurt. Some narcissists adeptly employ spiritual language, quotes, and teachings to maintain control over their victims. They may twist religious doctrines to manipulate emotions and induce guilt, often convincing their targets that enduring the abuse is a test of their faith or that they should forgive unconditionally. This exploitation of spirituality can trap victims in a web of confusion, as they struggle to reconcile the kind and compassionate image of their partner with the harsh reality of their behavior. This is why going No Contact is so important as you detach from someone who is highly skilled in using any means necessary to continue to abuse their partner's by manipulating their heart strings for secondary gain.

RESILIENCY & RECOVERY

HOPE & HEALING

NO CONTACT

For the record, one cannot claim to be a follower of God and spirituality while acting in ways misaligned with those values. Actions not matching words is manipulation at it's finest. Going no contact also gives you the opportunity to rediscover yourself. I remember during my toxic relationship, losing sight of my own identity, desires, and passions. By stepping away and disconnecting from a narcissist or other highly toxic individual, you can reconnect with your true self, explore your interests, and rediscover your own worth outside of their influence.

In my case, recognizing how narcissists or other highly toxic individuals weaponize religion and spirituality is essential for breaking free from their manipulative hold. By understanding the tactics they employ to maintain control, victims can regain their agency, seek support from trusted sources, and find healing outside the confines of a relationship that exploits their beliefs. Lastly, going no contact helps to break the addictive cycle that often exists in narcissistic relationships. The highs and lows, the intermittent reinforcement—it can create an addictive bond that keeps you trapped. By going no contact, you're breaking that cycle and allowing yourself the chance to find healthier relationships and regain your emotional stability.

This takes strength, support, and self-care to enforce and maintain. But ultimately, it can be a transformative step towards reclaiming your life, healing from the wounds inflicted by the narcissist, and paving the way for a brighter, healthier future. Those of us who have been abused by a narcissist may choose to cut ties altogether with that person. Typically people who end up going no contact have had their boundaries violated in traumatic ways that eventually push them to shut down all communication with the narcissist - choosing distance over disrespect. For adult children of narcissists, going no contact is typically a deeply ambivalent and painful choice that feels like a matter of survival in order to break the cycle of hurt and to attempt to heal.

Remember, going no contact with a highly toxic or narcissistic individual is not a decision made lightly. It is a testament to your mental strength and emotional resilience. When you embark on this journey, you're not just grieving the person you thought they were, but also mourning the possibilities and dreams you had invested in the relationship. The pain can be so soul crushing that it may make you want to shield yourself from love altogether. I've been there too. However, true healing doesn't mean cutting yourself off from love. Instead, it empowers you to cut ties with anyone who proves to be unloving.

As Dolly Parton once said, "We dont walk away to teach people a lesson. We walk away because we finally learned ours."

A lonely truth is that everyone talks about cutting people off or letting toxic people go. However, nobody really talks about the grief that comes with having to stand faithful on that decision knowing it's not what you wanted but is what's necessary for your personal growth and psychological well-being.

Speaking from personal experience, you're not only healing from the wounds inflicted by the toxic person not loving you, but you're also addressing the parts of yourself that may still be deeply in love *them*. It's a complex and often painful journey because, at times, these feelings might seem conflicting and confusing. Taking space is all about healing the parts of yourself that were initially drawn to toxic individuals, understanding the underlying factors that led to those connections, and learning how to recalibrate your internal compass toward healthier relationships. Healing means that you no longer identify as a victim or feel the need to become a villain.

Moreover, healing also involves a shift in your perception of what constitutes a healthy relationship. It's about unlearning destructive patterns and retraining yourself to recognize and appreciate the qualities of healthy individuals around you. This transformation isn't just about moving on; it's about evolving into someone who can form loving, respectful, and nurturing connections while maintaining the strength and boundaries to protect your own well-being. It's a journey that requires immense courage, self-reflection, and the belief that you deserve the love and respect you're now determined to find in healthier relationships.

My deepest wish for you is that you take the time to genuinely heal and not just find ways to become stronger or more self-sufficient. That's because you deserve to be in loving and safe environments that bring out the softness in you; not the survival. In doing so, you will find that there's no need to be guarded as those around you have no desire to see you hurt or feel attacked.

RESILIENCY & RECOVERY

HOPE & HEALING

POST-NARCISSISTIC STRESS DISORDER (PNSD)

Taking the courageous step of going no contact with a narcissist or highly toxic individual is a powerful act of self-care and a crucial part of healing. It's not just about breaking free from a toxic relationship; it's a profound declaration of self-worth and an investment in your mental and emotional well-being. This journey can be challenging, but it's also incredibly empowering, as it allows you to reclaim your inner peace and rebuild your sense of self. Especially for those recovering from post-narcissistic stress disorder (PNSD). Post-Narcissistic Stress Disorder (PNSD), also known as Narcissistic Abuse Syndrome, is a term used to describe the psychological and emotional aftermath experienced by individuals who have been in relationships with narcissistic individuals.

It is not officially recognized as a formal diagnosis in the Diagnostic and Statistical Manual of Mental Disorders (DSM-5), which is the standard classification of mental health disorders. However, it's a concept that has gained attention within the field of psychology due to the significant and often long-lasting impact of narcissistic abuse on a person's mental and emotional well-being.

PNSD is characterized by a range of symptoms and emotional responses that can persist even after the individual has ended the relationship with the narcissist. These symptoms may include:

1. Anxiety and Hypervigilance: Individuals may experience persistent anxiety, fear, and hypervigilance as a result of the emotional manipulation and instability they endured during the relationship.
2. Depression: Feelings of sadness, hopelessness, and worthlessness can linger, often stemming from the emotional abuse and manipulation inflicted by the narcissist.
3. Flashbacks and Intrusive Thoughts: Memories of the abuse, as well as intrusive thoughts about the narcissist, may cause distress and difficulty in moving forward.
4. Low Self-Esteem: The constant criticism and devaluation from the narcissist can lead to a diminished sense of self-worth and self-esteem.
5. Difficulty Trusting Others: After being betrayed and manipulated by the narcissist, individuals may struggle to trust others, even in healthy relationships.
6. Social Isolation: Narcissistic abuse can lead to a withdrawal from social interactions and a fear of forming new relationships.
7. Emotional Numbness: Some individuals may experience a sense of emotional numbness or detachment as a coping mechanism.
8. Fear of Repercussions: The fear of retaliation or further manipulation from the narcissist may prevent individuals from fully disengaging from the relationship.
9. Boundaries and Self-Care Challenges: Survivors may struggle with setting healthy boundaries and practicing self-care, as they were conditioned to prioritize the narcissist's needs over their own.
10. Guilt and Shame: Manipulation and gaslighting from the narcissist can lead to feelings of guilt and shame, even after the relationship ends.

CPTSD stands for Complex Post Traumatic Stress Disorder, a condition common in narcissistic abuse victims, as well as in people with pathological narcissism. CPTSD includes a wide range of disabling symptoms, including some or all of the following disturbances: hypervigilance; generalized fear, anxiety, and agitation; over-reactivity; insomnia; nightmares and/or night terrors; self-isolation; difficulty trusting; self-destructive behavior; and intrusive thoughts. Narcissistic abuse runs deeper than most people realize, often leaving profound emotional scars that can be just as debilitating as physical abuse. The chronic emotional manipulation, gaslighting, and psychological warfare inflicted by narcissists can erode a person's self-esteem, sense of self-worth, and overall mental well-being. Yet, society frequently fails to fully comprehend the depth of this trauma, downplaying the severity of a victim's experience. This lack of recognition can intensify the feelings of isolation and self-doubt that survivors already contend with, making it all the more challenging to heal and recover. It's crucial for us as a society to acknowledge the profound and lasting impact of narcissistic abuse, particularly as it relates to conditions like post-narcissistic stress disorder, and to offer the compassion, support, and understanding that survivors need to rebuild their lives.

As the saying goes, "An unhealthy partner will find a way to turn your independence into co-dependency, confidence into insecurity, extroversion into introversion, happiness into hopelessness, hope into helplessness without anyone noticing - not even the victim." (Unknown)

RESILIENCY & RECOVERY

HOPE & HEALING

Transitioning from the complex aftermath of post-narcissistic stress disorder, we embark on a journey of empowerment by exploring the transformative potential of utilizing The Jade Technique. This technique offers a path to reclaiming one's sense of self, fostering resilience, and cultivating a foundation for healing after the emotional turmoil of narcissistic abuse.

JADE stands for Justify, Argue, Defend, and Explain. When interacting with a narcissist, they often thrive on provoking emotional reactions and engaging in power struggles. [92] But here's the thing: the JADE technique encourages you to break free from that cycle and regain your power.

1. Justify: Instead of feeling the need to justify your actions, choices, or boundaries to a narcissist, remind yourself that you have the right to make decisions that are best for you. Trust your own judgment and embrace the confidence to set your boundaries without justifying them.
2. Argue: Engaging in arguments with a narcissist can be exhausting and futile. Recognize that they often manipulate conversations to control and dominate. Instead of getting entangled in their web of manipulation, choose to disengage from unnecessary arguments and preserve your energy for more positive interactions.
3. Defend: Narcissists love to push your buttons and make you feel defensive. However, defending yourself can often lead to a never-ending cycle of attacks and attempts to undermine your self-worth. Remember that you don't owe anyone an explanation for who you are or the choices you make. Embrace your self-worth and prioritize your emotional well-being.
4. Explain: It's tempting to explain yourself to a narcissist in the hopes that they will finally understand and validate your perspective. But the truth is, they may never truly understand or empathize. Instead of investing energy in explaining yourself repeatedly, redirect that energy toward self-care and surrounding yourself with supportive individuals who appreciate and respect you.

When dealing with a highly toxic person who intentionally invalidates your emotions, the best defense is a strong offense. Using phrases like:

-I'm sorry you feel that way
-Your anger is not my responsibility
-I think we remember details differently
-I will not tolerate being spoken to / treated like this
-If you would like to communicate, I am only available to do so respectfully

By practicing the JADE technique, you reclaim your power and protect your emotional well-being. Don't allow a bad situation to turn you into someone bitter, but rather, emerge as someone who is better. That is how you take your power back. Your healing is your offering to the world. You cannot contribute to peace if you are at war with others. That does not mean that you must engage in toxic forgiveness in order to move on. It simply means that you do not allow your bad experiences to turn you into a bitter person. After everything you've gone through, protecting the purity of your heart and moving with integrity is how you prioritize your inner peace and contribute to world peace. A quote that helped me to heal was: "You are not unstable, you were mistreated. You did not make anything up, it really happened. You are not paranoid, your trust was violated. You didn't ask for it, it was out of your control. You're not lying, you're speaking your truth. You didn't ruin their life, they did that to themselves. You are not hostile, you are cautious. You are not living in the past, you are reflecting and recovering." (-*Unknown*) This quote highlights the ways in which a highly toxic individual can be invalidating of their victim's experience — so much so that the victim begins to invalidate *their own* experience. That's why utilizing the JADE Technique is a powerful tool in resiliency and recovery.

RESILIENCY & RECOVERY

HOPE & HEALING

TRAUMA DENIAL & ABUSE AMNESIA

Here's the thing, leaving an abusive narcissistic relationship is a complex and emotionally challenging journey, often accompanied by psychological distortions that result from the trauma endured during the toxic partnership. One such distortion is "pathological accommodation," where the victim adapts to the abuser's demands, losing their sense of self in the process. As survivors escape, they may experience "euphoria recall," selectively remembering positive moments with the narcissist, further complicating their decision to leave. [93] Additionally, the "fading affect bias" could lead to diminished recollection of negative emotions, making it harder to fully grasp the severity of the abuse suffered. [94] Coping mechanisms like "dissociation" and "amnesia" may also emerge, allowing the individual to detach from painful memories as a protective measure. Moreover, "reverse projection" might occur, with the survivor internalizing false guilt or responsibility for the narcissist's toxic behavior. [95]

Trauma denial, also known as traumatic amnesia or dissociative amnesia, is a psychological defense mechanism in which individuals unconsciously suppress or forget traumatic events or experiences as a way to cope with the overwhelming emotions and distress associated with those events. [96] This can lead to a lack of awareness or memory of the trauma, creating a disconnect between the individual's conscious understanding and the reality of their past experiences. In the context of victims of narcissistic abuse, trauma denial often manifests as a way to navigate the intense emotional turmoil during the discard phase of the narcissistic cycle of abuse. This phase involves the narcissist withdrawing attention, love, and validation, leaving the victim feeling discarded, devalued, and confused.

Here's how victims of narcissistic abuse may unknowingly engage in trauma denial during the discard process:

1. **Dissociation and Emotional Numbness:** Victims of narcissistic abuse may dissociate from the traumatic experiences as a way to protect themselves from overwhelming emotions. This can lead to emotional numbness, detachment, and a sense of "spacing out."
2. **Abuse Amnesia:** As the discard phase unfolds, victims might experience periods of "abuse amnesia," where they forget or downplay the hurtful behaviors and mistreatment they endured. This can contribute to the cycle of hope and despair, as they momentarily forget the pain they've experienced.
3. **Idealization of the Narcissist:** During the discard phase, victims might inadvertently focus on the idealized version of the narcissist from the initial stages of the relationship. This idealization can overshadow the negative experiences, contributing to denial of the abuse.
4. **Minimizing or Rationalizing:** Victims may rationalize or minimize the abuse, convincing themselves that the narcissist's actions were not as hurtful as they actually were. This rationalization can be a defense mechanism to protect their self-esteem and sense of control.
5. **Focusing on the Good Times:** Victims may dwell on the positive moments they shared with the narcissist, blurring the lines between the joyful experiences and the traumatic ones. This focus on the "good times" can overshadow the reality of the abuse.
6. **Self-Blame and Guilt:** Victims might internalize the narcissist's manipulation and blame themselves for the relationship's deterioration. This self-blame can prevent them from fully acknowledging the extent of the abuse.

Abuse amnesia, in the context of narcissistic relationships, refers to a psychological phenomenon where the victim tends to forget or minimize the abusive behavior they experienced in the relationship. It's a form of cognitive dissonance, where the person's mind struggles to reconcile the contradictory experiences of being mistreated and the positive aspects of the relationship. In narcissistic relationships, the abuser often utilizes a cycle of idealization, devaluation, and occasional "hoovering" (attempts to draw the victim back) to maintain control and keep the victim emotionally attached. During the idealization phase, the victim may experience love bombing and affection, which creates a bond and emotional dependence on the abuser.

RESILIENCY & RECOVERY

HOPE & HEALING

TRAUMA DENIAL & ABUSE AMNESIA

As we know, this can lead to a form of trauma bonding, where the victim may feel a sense of loyalty and attachment even when treated poorly. As a result, when the devaluation phase occurs, and the victim experiences emotional, verbal, or psychological abuse, their mind may try to protect them from the painful truth by repressing or forgetting the negative experiences. The victim might downplay the abuse, make excuses for the abuser, or rationalize their behavior. This can create a cycle of ongoing abuse, as the victim keeps returning to the relationship despite the harmful dynamics. Abuse amnesia can make it challenging for the victim to recognize the toxic nature of the relationship and take steps to protect themselves. It's crucial for survivors of narcissistic abuse to engage in healing and self-compassion to break free from the effects of abuse amnesia and reclaim their autonomy and emotional well-being. Healing can be painful because most of the scars that we wear on our hearts weren't created by our enemies. They were created by the people who were closest to us who claimed to love us. Loving and leaving a Narcissist can be an extremely painful experience. In both cases, you are damned if you do, damned if you don't as both outcomes will result in pain and loss.

I get it — Sometimes we see the best in people and stay longer in relationships than we should is because our fearful inner child is trying so hard to not be abandoned by another. In such cases, we are more willing to ignore red flags and abandon ourselves. Ironically, when we start to heal, we often are met with overwhelming feelings of sadness. That's because we are no longer numb to the reality of how much we were treated badly, and are now faced with the responsibility of repairing the pain imposed onto us. I fell into this cycle too.

Understanding the occurrence of abuse amnesia involves considering the intricate workings of our brain and body. Various factors come into play, and one of them is brain chemistry. Let's take a moment to explore the different brain chemicals involved and their effects, keeping in mind that this is a simplified explanation [98]:

- **Oxytocin**, often called the "bonding hormone," plays a role in forming emotional connections. It can create a deep bond between individuals, even in abusive relationships, making it challenging to break free.
- **Dopamine**, sometimes referred to as the "reward neurotransmitter," is responsible for feelings of craving, pursuit, longing, and motivation. In abusive relationships, it can create a longing for the intermittent moments of affection or kindness, reinforcing the cycle.
- **Endogenous Opioids,** our body's natural painkillers, can contribute to the complex dynamics. Withdrawal from the relationship can be excruciatingly painful, while the fleeting moments of affection or positive reinforcement can feel intensely pleasurable.
- **Cortisol**, a stress hormone, can be elevated in abusive situations due to the constant emotional turmoil. This heightened stress can cloud judgment and make it even more challenging to see the situation clearly.

That said, did you know that it takes an average of 7 attempts for a survivor to leave their abuser and stay separated for good? Leaving is one of the most dangerous times in an abusive relationship. [99]

Detoxing from an abusive narcissistic relationship is no walk in the park, that's for sure. As you detox their presence from you life, it can take months or even years to recondition your mind and body to believe that it is finally safe. It's like trying to cleanse your mind and heart from a toxic substance that's seeped deep within. You're not just healing from the scars you can see; it's the invisible wounds too. It's grappling with a rollercoaster of emotions, from anger to sadness to confusion, all while trying to rediscover who you are outside of that toxic dynamic.

Remember, loving others should never come at the expense of neglecting yourself. One of the most empowering choices you can make when leaving a narcissistic partner is when you stop trying to change them and you begin to choose yourself. However, these decisions can feel heavy at times. That's because in both love and life, one of the most challenging lessons you will ever learn is how to discern between when to try harder and when to step away. Answer the reflection questions in the pages that follow to understand more about your potential experience with trauma denial and abuse amnesia. You're doing a great job. I am so proud of you!

RESILIENCY & RECOVERY

HOPE & HEALING

TRAUMA DENIAL & ABUSE AMNESIA

HOW HAS THE FEAR AND UNCERTAINTY SURROUNDING LEAVING AN ABUSIVE OR TOXIC NARCISSISTIC RELATIONSHIP IMPACTED YOUR SENSE OF SELF-WORTH AND YOUR ABILITY TO ENVISION A DIFFERENT FUTURE?

RESILIENCY & RECOVERY

HOPE & HEALING

TRAUMA DENIAL & ABUSE AMNESIA

CAN YOU DESCRIBE THE SPECIFIC WAYS IN WHICH THE MANIPULATIVE TACTICS OF THE NARCISSIST HAVE CONTRIBUTED TO YOUR HESITATIONS AND CHALLENGES IN BREAKING FREE FROM THE RELATIONSHIP?

RESILIENCY & RECOVERY

HOPE & HEALING

TRAUMA DENIAL & ABUSE AMNESIA

IN WHAT WAYS HAVE THE ISOLATION AND CONTROL TACTICS EMPLOYED BY THE NARCISSIST OR HIGHLY TOXIC INDIVIDUAL IN YOUR LIFE INFLUENCED YOUR PERCEPTION OF YOUR SUPPORT SYSTEM AND YOUR ABILITY TO SEEK HELP?

RESILIENCY & RECOVERY

HOPE & HEALING

TRAUMA DENIAL & ABUSE AMNESIA

HOW DO/DID YOU ENVISION YOUR LIFE CHANGING ONCE YOU ARE NO LONGER IN THE ABUSIVE RELATIONSHIP, AND WHAT ARE SOME OF THE FEARS OR OBSTACLES THAT ARISE WHEN CONTEMPLATING THIS NEW CHAPTER?

RESILIENCY & RECOVERY

HOPE & HEALING

You're doing a really incredible job processing through some very difficult emotions and experiences. I'm so proud of you for making it this far as we heal and grow together. Don't give up just yet! We are close to the finish line! Moving on —

So, there's this old proverb that goes: Imagine being bitten by a snake. And instead of helping yourself and recovering from the poison, you try to catch the snake and find out the reason it bit you and to prove to the snake that you didn't deserve the pain it caused you. This poison eventually leads to your death.

This is what it's like loving or even leaving a narcissist. It's not the bite that kills you, it's the small doses of venom that we fail to release ourselves from. It's the difference between loving someone to pieces who is tearing you to pieces on purpose. Part of what kept me in my abusive relationship longer than necessary, especially at the hands of an ill-equipped couples therapist, was well-intended bad advice I received when I tried to voice what was happening in my relationship.

Well-intended bad advice, often offered with good intentions, can inadvertently contribute to keeping people trapped in toxic relationships, particularly when dealing with narcissistic abuse. Here are 20 examples of such advice and why they can be harmful:

- **"Just be patient and things will get better."** Harmful because: It downplays the severity of the abuse and perpetuates the false hope that the narcissist will change.
- **"Try harder to make it work."** Harmful because: It places the responsibility on the victim to fix the relationship, despite the fact that narcissists rarely change.
- **"Keep the peace at all costs."** Harmful because: It encourages the victim to tolerate abuse to avoid conflict, enabling the narcissist's behavior.
- **"Focus on their good qualities."** Harmful because: It dismisses the extent of the abuse and reinforces the cycle of idealization and devaluation.
- **"Just ignore their behavior."** Harmful because: It minimizes the impact of the abuse and implies that the victim should tolerate mistreatment.
- **"Think positively and things will improve."** Harmful because: It places the blame on the victim's mindset rather than addressing the abusive behavior.
- **"You're too sensitive, toughen up."** Harmful because: It invalidates the victim's feelings and experiences, making them doubt their own perceptions.
- **"It's just a phase they're going through."** Harmful because: It normalizes the abusive behavior and delays the victim's realization of the toxic nature of the relationship.
- **"You need to save them from their issues."** Harmful because: It perpetuates the victim's role as a rescuer, enabling the narcissist's manipulative behavior.
- **"They must love you deep down, despite everything."** Harmful because: It romanticizes the idea that abuse is a twisted form of love, which is not accurate or healthy.
- **"You're lucky to have them."** Harmful because: It makes the victim feel indebted to the narcissist, ignoring the harmful effects of the relationship.
- **"Try couples therapy."** Harmful because: It assumes both parties are willing to change, when narcissists often manipulate therapy sessions.
- **"Keep your family problems private."** Harmful because: It isolates the victim from support networks, making it easier for the narcissist to maintain control.
- **"You're the only one who can help them."** Harmful because: It reinforces the victim's guilt and prevents them from prioritizing their own well-being.

RESILIENCY & RECOVERY

HOPE & HEALING

SPEAKING YOUR TRUTH

- **"They'll change when they see how hurt you are."** Harmful because: It wrongly assumes that the narcissist will feel empathy and change their behavior.
- **"You're overreacting."** Harmful because: It gaslights the victim, making them doubt their own feelings and experiences.
- **"Stick it out for the sake of the children."** Harmful because: It disregards the damaging impact of exposing children to an abusive environment.
- **"Just focus on yourself and the relationship will improve."** Harmful because: It shifts the responsibility entirely onto the victim, ignoring the narcissist's abusive behavior.
- **"No one will ever love you like they do."** Harmful because: It instills fear of being alone and dependent on the narcissist.
- **"Forgive and forget."** Harmful because: It pressures the victim to ignore the impact of the abuse and continue enabling the narcissist's behavior.

These examples of well-intended bad advice can inadvertently trap victims in toxic relationships by perpetuating a cycle of abuse, minimizing the victim's experiences, and reinforcing the narcissist's control over their victim. While we can have compassion for others, the thing that often times makes a highly toxic person's behavior so unforgiving is that they are conscious enough to know what they are doing. They just don't care. This was such a painful truth that took years for me to understand.

I remember experiencing so much cognitive dissonance because I deeply wanted to believe that he was a good person, while all evidence I had was contrary to that belief. I struggled to believe that the person I saw so much good in at the beginning failed to exist in the end. My heart struggled to accept the reality my mind already knew. Over time I realized that there's a difference between someone who *can't* change, and someone who *won't* change. Sadly, you can't change someone who doesn't see a problem with their behavior - especially when they are the sole beneficiary.

When you are in a relationship with someone who is shame-avoidant, they may use strategies to deflect, dismiss or deny your reality. In such cases, it is healthier to lose someone who hurts you than to lose yourself trying to keep someone who is unwilling to change. The part of you that needs them to change, *is the part in you that needs to change*. However, for many of us who grew up in broken homes as children, we are likely more determined to keep our relationships together as adults. This unresolved trauma can leave us feeling terrified of losing the person we are most afraid of. Thereby enabling us to stay silent about the treatment we experience in our relationships as we are further shamed into submission.

As you heal, you are no longer required to protect them at the expense of your inner peace. As you grow, you will begin to let go of the idea that you must stay silent in order to remain safe. Telling my story while intentionally preserving his privacy was my attempt at bringing myself peace - Not to start a war. Though, I understand that he may not see it that way.

Overtime I learned that revealing the truth only feels like retaliation to those who struggle with accepting the reality and responsibility of their actions. Sharing the lessons I've learned was my greatest effort to help you to heal from the same hurt I've also been through. As I healed, I realized the distinction between a person who has undergone healing and one who remains unhealed lies in their reactions to their triggers: healed individuals may be provoked by lies, whereas unhealed individuals react negatively to the truth. The latter may become incensed the moment you speak up about accurate accounts of what they did to you for fear of how that may impact their reputation. Unfortunately, narcissistic or other highly toxic individuals are more concerned with hiding their malicious intentions versus healing from them.

This can enable the illusion of smoke and mirrors. "Smoke and mirrors" is a phrase used to describe deceptive or misleading tactics that create an illusion or hide the truth. It often refers to actions or situations that are designed to distract, confuse, or manipulate others, making something appear different from what it really is. In the context of narcissistic relationships, "smoke and mirrors" aptly captures the dynamic created by narcissists to manipulate and control their victims. Narcissists excel at presenting a facade that hides their true intentions, personalities, and behavior. When it comes to narcissistic relationships, sometimes we are so focused on preventing the house from burning down that we overlook the smoke that is preventing us from breathing.

Narcissists use a manipulative tactic known as "fracturing" to control and manipulate their victims, playing on their vulnerabilities and unhealed wounds. Fracturing involves breaking down a person's sense of self, self-esteem, and confidence to make them dependent on the narcissist for validation and approval. Your healing will begin at the end of your appeasing and people pleasing behaviors. Instead of trying to fix a relationship that requires self sacrifice, find a relationship that honors your self respect.

The sad truth is that friends, family, coaches or even therapist who don't fully understand narcissistic abuse will say shameful things like, "The symptom is loving a narcissist. The root cause is not loving yourself more." Shame is a complex emotion that can linger in the shadows, shaping our perceptions and responses. Often, it's unconsciously projected onto those who have been in or are recovering from narcissistic relationships. We hear the whispered judgments, the subtle insinuations that if only they loved themselves enough, they wouldn't have fallen victim to an abusive partner.

But the truth is far more intricate. Narcissists are adept at wearing masks, weaving webs of deceit that can entangle even the most cautious hearts. They manipulate, gaslight, and warp reality until their victims find themselves trapped in a distorted version of love. By the time they realize the depth of the deception, the damage has already been done. Trauma bonds, those insidious connections forged amidst the chaos, go beyond psychological; they embed themselves in the very fibers of our being, making it excruciatingly difficult to sever ties. In the narcissist's realm, the avoidance of growth and change is a cruel dance. They construct a facade, an elaborate performance that allows them to sidestep the discomfort of personal evolution. These patterns aren't just psychological but deeply rooted in their physiological makeup. And as for those ensnared in their web, leaving becomes a battle against the bonds that are as strong as they are toxic.
.

Consider the world we live in, where patriarchal norms persistently rear their head. Women are often blamed for staying in abusive relationships, but the societal structures that perpetuate these cycles often evade our scrutiny. Especially when society focuses on protecting women without punishing men. These structures emphasize female self-sacrifice and servitude, rewarding them for endurance instead of championing their self-worth and empowerment. Reflect on this example: Women are trained to believe that their worth lies in their ability to fix and nurture, to absorb pain without breaking. These ideals make it incredibly challenging to extricate oneself from a toxic relationship. And that's where the tragedy lies: the fault isn't in their inability to leave, but in the very culture that shames and entraps them. Women are often burdened with staying in an abusive relationship or going at life alone. In my own experience, living in hell wasn't a place; it was a person. It's a paradox of emotions, as I grapple with loving someone who caused so much pain. As our pastor once shared, "There's a difference between a one-time sin and a lifestyle of sin." This distinction is profound. Just as a single mistake can differ from a pattern of destructive behavior, leaving an abusive relationship isn't always as straightforward as it seems. The intricacies of trauma, manipulation, and societal pressure converge to create a web that's incredibly hard to break free from. The post-separation injustice after leaving a toxic relationship is real.

RESILIENCY & RECOVERY

HOPE & HEALING

FRACTURING & SMOKE IN MIRRORS

IF YOU FIND YOURSELF BEGGING TO BE TREATED WITH LOVE, RESPECT, COMMITMENT, THE BARE MINIMUM OF HUMAN DECENCY, I'M NOT SAYING THEY ARE A NARCISSIST. BUT I AM SAYING THEY MIGHT NOT THE ONE. THERE COMES A POINT IN YOUR LIFE WHEN YOU HAVE TO STOP ASKING "WHY ARE THEY TREATING ME THIS WAY" AND START ASKING "WHAT UNHEALED PART OF ME TOLERATES THIS KIND OF BEHAVIOR?"

HOW DO THEY MAKE YOU FEEL VS HOW DO YOU FEEL ABOUT THEM?
INFERIOR, REPLACEABLE, ANXIOUS, UNWORTHY, HUMILIATED, LIKE AN AFTER THOUGHT, A LOSS OF DIGNITY, LIKE YOU HAVE TO SELF ABANDON IN ORDER TO MAINTAIN A RELATIONSHIP WITH THEM, LIKE YOU HAVE TO BEG THEM TO GIVE SHOW YOU HUMAN DECENCY, LIKE THEY WANT PARTICIPATION POINTS FOR HONORING THE BASIC TERMS OF A HEALTHY RELATIONAL AGREEMENT,

RESILIENCY & RECOVERY

HOPE & HEALING

FRACTURING & SMOKE IN MIRRORS

WHAT ASPECTS OF YOURSELF HAVE YOU NOTICED SLIPPING AWAY OR BECOMING LESS PROMINENT SINCE ENTERING THIS RELATIONSHIP?

_____

_____

_____

_____

_____

_____

_____

_____

_____

_____

_____

_____

_____

_____

_____

_____

_____

_____

_____

RESILIENCY & RECOVERY

HOPE & HEALING

THE REALM OF RELATIONSHIPS, ONE OF THE MOST POWERFUL ACTS OF LOVE IS LEARNING TO LOVE YOURSELF. WHEN YOU EMBRACE SELF-LOVE, YOU SET THE FOUNDATION FOR A HEALTHY AND FULFILLING CONNECTION WITH YOUR PARTNER.LOVING YOURSELF IN YOUR RELATIONSHIP MEANS HONORING YOUR WORTH, EMBRACING YOUR UNIQUE QUALITIES, AND EMBRACING SELF-COMPASSION. IT'S ABOUT SETTING BOUNDARIES THAT PROTECT YOUR EMOTIONAL WELL-BEING AND COMMUNICATING YOUR NEEDS AND DESIRES AUTHENTICALLY. BY NURTURING YOUR OWN HAPPINESS AND PERSONAL GROWTH, YOU BRING A RADIANT ENERGY TO THE RELATIONSHIP.

HOW WOULD YOU DESCRIBE YOUR OWN NEEDS, DESIRES, AND GOALS BEFORE AND AFTER ENTERING THIS RELATIONSHIP?

RESILIENCY & RECOVERY

HOPE & HEALING

FRACTURING & SMOKE IN MIRRORS

IN WHAT WAYS DO YOU FEEL YOUR IDENTITY HAS BEEN INFLUENCED OR SHAPED BY YOUR PARTNER? HOW DO YOU FEEL ABOUT THESE CHANGES?

RESILIENCY & RECOVERY

HOPE & HEALING

CAN YOU IDENTIFY ANY PATTERNS OR BEHAVIORS IN THE RELATIONSHIP THAT MAKE YOU FEEL LIKE YOU'RE LOSING TOUCH WITH WHO YOU ARE? HOW DO THESE SITUATIONS MAKE YOU FEEL?

RESILIENCY & RECOVERY

HOPE & HEALING

SELF ABANDONMENT

Fracturing can be one of the most painful experiences for those who have experienced Narcissistic abuse. I remember loving my former partner so much that I so badly wanted to save him from his trauma — not realizing how I was becoming traumatized in the process. Remember, not every relationship is meant to last forever. Some serve as stepping stones toward a brighter, more self-affirming future. Through the pain, the growth, and the healing, you pave the way for a love that honors who you truly are—a love that flourishes in authenticity and empowers you to stand strong. Grieving the parts of you that still held love for the one who neglected you is a tender process. It's about honoring the pain, allowing it to wash over you instead of pushing it away. By embracing this grief, you're empowering yourself to embark on a new path forward. It's a journey that might be arduous, but it leads to liberation and empowerment. Taking the time to heal from a toxic relationship is an investment in your own well-being. It's a process that brings about peace, clarity, and resilience. By doing the inner work, you break the pattern and lay the foundation for a healthier, more fulfilling partnership in the future. Below are a few ways we self abandon in relationships as a result of fracturing:

1. Constantly prioritizing the needs and wants of your partner over your own.
2. Ignoring or suppressing your own emotions and feelings to avoid conflict.
3. Apologizing excessively, even when it's not warranted.
4. Going along with decisions or actions that you are uncomfortable with to keep the peace.
5. Avoiding expressing your true thoughts and opinions out of fear of rejection or disapproval.
6. Neglecting your own self-care and well-being to focus solely on your partner's needs.
7. Sacrificing your own goals and dreams to accommodate your partner's ambitions.
8. Tolerating disrespectful or abusive behavior in the name of maintaining the relationship.
9. Constantly seeking validation and approval from your partner, relying on their opinions to shape your self-worth.
10. Suppressing your own boundaries and allowing your partner to consistently overstep them.
11. Overcompensating and over-giving to prove your worth and value.
12. Avoiding conflict at all costs, even if it means suppressing your own needs and desires.
13. Neglecting your own personal interests and hobbies to focus solely on your partner's interests.
14. Putting your partner's happiness and satisfaction above your own.
15. Taking responsibility for your partner's emotions and trying to fix or rescue them.
16. Feeling guilty or selfish when you prioritize your own needs and desires.
17. Constantly seeking external validation and reassurance from your partner.
18. Ignoring warning signs or red flags in the relationship because you fear being alone.
19. Losing touch with your own identity and values as you adapt to your partner's preferences.
20. Allowing your partner to consistently undermine your self-confidence and self-esteem.

Self-abandonment in narcissistic relationships is an understandable survival mechanism, but it often comes at a high emotional cost. In these toxic dynamics, individuals may compromise their own needs, feelings, and boundaries to appease the narcissistic partner. This painful process can lead to a profound sense of loss and disconnection from one's authentic self. However, it's essential to remember that healing and resilience are possible. With support, self-reflection, and self-compassion, individuals can gradually reclaim their sense of identity and self-worth. By breaking free from narcissistic relationships and prioritizing their own well-being, survivors can discover their strength and capacity for growth, forging a path towards a brighter, healthier future filled with self-love and genuine connections.

RESILIENCY & RECOVERY

HOPE & HEALING

But be aware, for those of us that stay in highly toxic relationships for too long, we may have the unconscious desire to overcorrect on our self abandoning tendencies as we develop a mild case of what we call, "Narcissistic fleas".

"Narcissistic fleas" is a colloquial term that's often used in discussions about narcissistic behavior or traits. It refers to the idea that someone who has been in a relationship with a narcissist, particularly for an extended period, may inadvertently adopt some narcissistic traits or behaviors themselves, similar to how someone might pick up fleas from a pet. Remaining in fight or flight for too long can alter your personality in detrimental ways.
Here's how narcissistic fleas work:

- **Imitating Narcissistic Behavior**: After prolonged exposure to a narcissist's manipulative and self-centered behaviors, the person on the receiving end may start to mimic some of these behaviors. This could include being more self-centered, manipulative, or lacking empathy in certain situations.

- **Survival Mechanism**: In many cases, people develop these traits as a survival mechanism. They may have learned from experience that adopting some narcissistic traits can help them cope with the narcissist's behavior or protect themselves from emotional harm.

- **Unintentional and Temporary**: It's important to note that these narcissistic traits are usually unintentional and temporary. They are not indicative of a full-blown narcissistic personality disorder. Instead, they represent a response to an unhealthy and toxic environment.

- **Recovery and Healing**: With awareness and a commitment to healing and self-improvement, individuals can work to shed these narcissistic fleas over time. Therapy, self-reflection, and support from loved ones can be valuable resources in this process.

Surviving in a relationship with a narcissist can be emotionally draining and psychologically damaging. People who develop these temporary traits often do so as a means of self-preservation. Often these "villains" were once victims who grew tired of playing small and being shut down. In our journey to unlearn abuse, it's important to approach it with kindness and compassion for ourselves. We need to gently let go of the survival strategies we developed while enduring abusive relationships. These coping mechanisms, while once crucial for our survival in an unsafe environment, may not serve us well when we're seeking healing in safer spaces. A quote that helped me through my healing journey was:

"Hero's and villains always have the same back story. Pain. The difference is, what they choose to do about it. The villain says "The world hurt me, I will hurt it back." Hero's say, "The world hurt me, I'm not going to let it hurt anyone else." Hero's use pain. Villains are used by it."- Unknown

Heroes: Those who have been in narcissistic relationships can choose to become "heroes" by using their experiences and pain as a catalyst for personal growth and healing. They may seek therapy, support, and self-care to address the emotional wounds and prevent further harm, not only to themselves but to others who may encounter narcissistic individuals in the future. Healing becomes a means of breaking the cycle of abuse. Villains: While it's essential not to label individuals as villains, some people who have been deeply affected by narcissistic abuse may unintentionally perpetuate harmful behavior patterns. If they respond to their pain with anger, bitterness, or a desire for revenge, they risk continuing a cycle of negativity and potentially harming others. Recognizing the need for healing and choosing a different path is crucial in avoiding this outcome. Remember, it's natural for pain to build walls around us as a protective mechanism, but as we embark on our healing journey, we're actually creating new pathways forward. These pathways are filled with hope, growth, and the opportunity to build healthier connections and a brighter future. Be gentle with yourself, and know that you are capable of embracing healing and positive change.

RESILIENCY & RECOVERY

HOPE & HEALING

NARCISSISTS THRIVE OFF YOUR ABILITY TO SELF-SACRIFICE, PLAY SMALL, BETRAY YOUR BOUNDARIES, PEDESTAL THEM, HAVE LOW SELF-WORTH, LACK SELF-ADVOCACY, BE CONFLICT-AVOIDANT, AND REMAIN CODEPENDENT. THEY ALSO DEPEND ON YOUR DENIAL OF TRAUMA, HOPEFULNESS, AND TENDENCY TO PEOPLE-PLEASE. IN MANY WAYS, THEIR CODEPENDENCY ON YOU STEMS FROM EXPLOITING THESE WEAKNESSES, ALLOWING THEM TO AVOID SELF-REFLECTION AND PERSONAL GROWTH. AS SOON AS YOU START STANDING UP FOR YOURSELF WITH APPROPRIATE BOUNDARIES, YOU'LL NOTICE THAT MANY TOXIC RELATIONSHIPS NATURALLY BEGIN TO FALL AWAY. THESE RESPONSES WERE YOUR COPING MECHANISMS, HELPING YOU STAY SAFE WHILE YOU WERE IN SURVIVAL MODE, MY LOVE. HOWEVER, AS YOU PROGRESS INTO THE NEXT STAGE OF YOUR LIFE, THEY ARE NO LONGER NECESSARY. HEALING WILL REQUIRE YOU TO DO THE OPPOSITE OF WHAT KEPT YOU SAFE IN THE PAST. REMEMBER, I LOVE YOU, AND EVERYTHING IS GOING TO BE OKAY..

WHO DID YOU HAVE TO BECOME IN ORDER TO MAKE YOUR RELATIONSHIP WITH A NARCISSIST WORK?

RESILIENCY & RECOVERY

HOPE & HEALING

SELF ABANDONMENT + NARCISSISTIC FLEAS

HOW HAS SELF-ABANDONMENT MANIFESTED IN YOUR LIFE DURING THE NARCISSISTIC RELATIONSHIP? REFLECT ON SPECIFIC INSTANCES WHERE YOU PUT THE NARCISSIST'S NEEDS BEFORE YOUR OWN, DISREGARDING YOUR WELL-BEING.

_____

_____

_____

_____

_____

_____

_____

_____

_____

_____

_____

_____

_____

_____

_____

_____

_____

_____

_____

_____

_____

RESILIENCY & RECOVERY

HOPE & HEALING

SELF ABANDONMENT + NARCISSISTIC FLEAS

HOW HAS THE NARCISSISTIC PARTNER'S MANIPULATIVE BEHAVIOR INFLUENCED YOUR SENSE OF SELF-WORTH AND SELF-ESTEEM, CONTRIBUTING TO FEELINGS OF SELF-ABANDONMENT?

RESILIENCY & RECOVERY

HOPE & HEALING

SELF ABANDONMENT + NARCISSISTIC FLEAS

WHAT COPING MECHANISMS DID YOU DEVELOP TO SURVIVE IN THE NARCISSISTIC RELATIONSHIP, AND HOW MIGHT THESE PATTERNS OF SELF-ABANDONMENT STILL BE AFFECTING YOUR CURRENT LIFE AND RELATIONSHIPS?

RESILIENCY & RECOVERY

HOPE & HEALING

IN WHAT WAYS DID THE NARCISSISTIC PARTNER EXPLOIT YOUR VULNERABILITIES AND EMOTIONAL NEEDS, LEADING TO FURTHER SELF-ABANDONMENT IN THE RELATIONSHIP?

_____

_____

_____

_____

_____

_____

_____

_____

_____

_____

_____

_____

_____

_____

_____

_____

RESILIENCY & RECOVERY

HOPE & HEALING

HOW CAN YOU BEGIN THE PROCESS OF RECLAIMING YOUR SENSE OF SELF AND PRACTICING SELF-COMPASSION TO HEAL FROM THE SELF-ABANDONMENT THAT OCCURRED IN THE NARCISSISTIC RELATIONSHIP? CONSIDER WHAT STEPS YOU CAN TAKE TO PRIORITIZE YOUR WELL-BEING AND BUILD HEALTHIER BOUNDARIES MOVING FORWARD.

RESILIENCY & RECOVERY

HOPE & HEALING

Woof! I know these reflection questions can be tough at times. It's difficult to comprehend the experiences we have endured and find compassion for ourselves in the process. It's even more difficult when we begin to open up about the abuse we have endured only to be met with a lack of compassion paired with victim blaming. Victim-blaming in narcissistic relationships can be especially traumatizing to the survivor after they leave due to several reasons:

1. Invalidation of Experience: Victim-blaming denies the survivor's experiences and emotions, making them feel unheard and invalidated. This further damages their self-esteem and confidence.
2. Reinforcement of Self-Doubt: Survivors often struggle with self-doubt after leaving a narcissistic relationship. Victim-blaming reinforces this self-doubt and can lead the survivor to question their judgment and decisions.
3. Re-Traumatization: Victim-blaming re-traumatizes the survivor, reminding them of the emotional abuse they endured in the relationship. It can trigger feelings of shame, guilt, and anxiety.
4. Emotional Isolation: Blaming the victim can cause the survivor to withdraw from seeking help or support, fearing they won't be believed or understood. This emotional isolation can hinder their healing process.
5. Cycle of Abuse: Perpetuating victim-blaming attitudes can enable the abuser and perpetuate the cycle of abuse, making it more challenging for survivors to break free.

To stop victim-blaming and support survivors of narcissistic relationships, individuals and society can take the following steps:

1. Educate and Raise Awareness: Raise awareness about narcissistic abuse and its effects. Educate people about victim-blaming and its harmful consequences.
2. Practice Empathy: Listen to survivors with empathy and compassion. Avoid judgment and offer support without blame or shame.
3. Challenge Stereotypes: Refrain from perpetuating stereotypes that blame the victim. Understand that abuse can happen to anyone, regardless of their background or personality.
4. Believe Survivors: Trust the survivor's account of their experiences. Avoid questioning or doubting their truth.
5. Hold Abusers Accountable: Confront abusive behavior and hold the abuser accountable for their actions. Encourage them to seek professional help and take responsibility for their behavior.
6. Create Safe Spaces: Foster environments where survivors feel safe to share their stories and seek help without fear of judgment.
7. Supportive Resources: Advocate for and support resources such as counseling, therapy, support groups, and helplines dedicated to survivors of narcissistic abuse.
8. Promote Empowerment: Encourage survivors to rebuild their self-esteem, regain control of their lives, and focus on their healing journey.

Victim-blaming in the context of narcissistic abuse is profoundly detrimental because it compounds the suffering of survivors who have already endured immense emotional, psychological, and sometimes even physical harm. Such blame reinforces the toxic narrative that survivors are somehow responsible for the abuse they've endured, perpetuating feelings of guilt and self-doubt that were often instilled by the narcissistic abuser themselves. It invalidates the pain and trauma experienced by survivors, making it harder for them to seek support, healing, or escape from the cycle of abuse. Compassion and understanding are essential when addressing narcissistic abuse, as they allow survivors to begin the crucial journey of reclaiming their self-worth and rebuilding their lives free from blame and judgment. Neutrality in this instance can feel extremely invalidating to narcissistic abuse survivors and can create a sense of indifference to their experience. By taking these steps, we can create a more supportive and understanding society that empowers survivors of narcissistic abuse and helps them heal from the trauma they experienced.

As this relates to my story; loving someone who puts you in survival mode will shame you into thinking you're too sensitive. This illusion will enable you to overlook all the ways it made you strong. The crazy part is, I not only felt shame for staying, but also shame for leaving. "You're going to leave your beautiful life over text messages and a few fights?" I felt helpless trying to over-explain to those around me the severity of what happened. Maybe others would have overlooked his abuse. I realized I was becoming stronger as I was no longer willing to tolerate it. Though he never physically hit me, but he did everything in his power to break my soul. What most people don't know is that not all abuse is physical and not all scars are visible. This is why victim blaming can be so damaging to survivors.

The lies, manipulation, text messages, photos, flying monkeys, coersion, wasn't enough for many people to validate my experience. Not even our couples therapist. But it was enough for me. Overexplaining as a result of a trauma response to being in a narcissistic relationship can stem from several psychological mechanisms that develop as coping strategies to deal with the abusive dynamics. Here are some reasons why individuals may tend to overexplain in this context:

1. Seeking validation: In a narcissistic relationship, the victim's thoughts and feelings are often dismissed or invalidated. Overexplaining becomes a way to seek validation and justification for their experiences and emotions.

2. Gaslighting and self-doubt: Narcissists often use gaslighting tactics to manipulate their victims into questioning their reality and perceptions. As a result, survivors may feel compelled to overexplain to convince themselves and others that their experiences are valid.

3. Fear of backlash: In a narcissistic relationship, expressing oneself authentically can lead to emotional or verbal abuse. Overexplaining may become a protective mechanism to avoid confrontation and the associated negative consequences.

4. Trauma bonding: Victims of narcissistic abuse may develop trauma bonds with their abusers. Overexplaining can be an attempt to preserve the connection and attachment to the narcissist, even though it is unhealthy.

5. Emotional numbing and dissociation: After prolonged exposure to emotional abuse, survivors may become disconnected from their emotions. Overexplaining can be a way to reconnect with and make sense of their feelings.

6. Self-preservation: In some cases, overexplaining might be an unconscious attempt to avoid further abuse by preemptively providing reasons or excuses that may placate the narcissistic partner.

7. Low self-esteem: Narcissistic relationships often erode the victim's self-esteem, leading them to doubt their worth and constantly seek approval. Overexplaining can be a way to try to regain the narcissist's approval, even though it's rarely attainable.

8. Lack of closure: Narcissists are notorious for abruptly ending relationships or leaving victims confused and hurt. Overexplaining might be an attempt to find closure and make sense of the abrupt disconnection.

Overexplaining in response to trauma can be a way for survivors to cope with the psychological wounds inflicted by a narcissistic relationship. Recognizing these patterns and seeking support from trauma-informed professionals can be crucial in healing and breaking free from the lingering effects of narcissistic abuse. When it comes to those healing from narcissistic abuse, remember that emotional abuse is just as psychologically harmful as physical abuse. And that many survivors of abuse are not just healing from the abuse they encountered, but the invalidation they received when they weren't believed or supported when they asked for help. When engaging with abuse survivors, it's important to be mindful of our language and approach.

Here are 10 commonly insensitive phrases and suggestions for reframing them with more compassion from a trauma-informed perspective:

- Insensitive Phrase: "If it were so bad, why didn't you leave?"
  - Reframe: "I'm here to support you, and I understand that leaving an abusive situation can be extremely complex and difficult. How can I help you now?"
- Insensitive Phrase: "It's time to move on."
  - Reframe: "Healing takes time, and everyone's journey is unique. I'm here to support you as you navigate your healing process, at your own pace."
- Insensitive Phrase: "Just forget about it."
  - Reframe: "Your experiences are significant, and I'm here to listen whenever you feel comfortable sharing. Your feelings and memories are valid."
- Insensitive Phrase: "I know how you feel."
  - Reframe: "While I can't fully understand your experience, I'm here to listen and support you. Your emotions are important, and I'll do my best to empathize."
- Insensitive Phrase: "But you seemed fine."
  - Reframe: "I'm sorry for any misunderstanding. Many survivors develop coping mechanisms that mask their pain. I'm here to support you whenever you're ready to talk."
- Insensitive Phrase: "Aren't you over it by now?"
  - Reframe: "Healing from trauma takes time and is a personal journey. I'm here to support you as you continue to grow and recover."
- Insensitive Phrase: "It happened so long ago, why are you still upset?"
  - Reframe: "Trauma can have long-lasting effects, and it's normal to be affected by past experiences. Your feelings matter, and I'm here to support you in your healing process."
- Insensitive Phrase: "You should just confront your abuser."
  - Reframe: "Confrontation can be a challenging step in the healing process. Only you can decide if and when it's the right choice for you. I'm here to support you regardless."
- Insensitive Phrase: "It wasn't that bad."
  - Reframe: "Your experiences and emotions are valid, regardless of others' perceptions. I'm here to listen and support you without judgment."
- Insensitive Phrase: "You're lucky it wasn't worse."
  - Reframe: "Your experience was deeply impactful, and I'm here to provide support and understanding. Your feelings and pain are valid."

Listen, navigating a narcissistic relationship can feel like an emotional tightrope, where your only choices seem to be giving up or trying harder. Letting go or being dragged along. The relentless cycle of manipulation, self-centeredness, and emotional turmoil can leave you feeling trapped and drained. But remember, there's always a way out—a path to healing and liberation. Sadly, not every relationship is destined for a happy ending. Some are there to illuminate our path, showing us the intricacies of how not to love, so we can better learn to cherish and honor ourselves. They teach us how to avoid settling, how to rise up and assert our worth, and how to cultivate a love that nourishes us rather than drains us.

These relationships are like crucibles of growth, forging us into stronger versions of ourselves. They reveal the importance of not shrinking to fit someone else's expectations, and not over-giving without reciprocity. Through the trials and tribulations, we learn the power of loving fiercely and unconditionally, as well as the strength to gracefully walk away when that love is no longer nourishing. The journey of leaving a toxic relationship requires immense courage. It's a brave step to let go of someone you deeply cared for, especially when your heart ached for nothing more than the relationship to flourish. But in doing so, you're asserting your own value and saying yes to your well-being. Remember, active listening, empathy, and validation are crucial when engaging with abuse survivors. It's essential to respect their boundaries, be patient, and offer support without judgment. Encouraging professional help from therapists or support groups can also be beneficial. I found healing in THE IMANI MVMT Connection Circles I created to connect with others just like me.

RESILIENCY & RECOVERY

HOPE & HEALING

COMMON MISCONCEPTIONS & EMOTIONAL WOUNDS TO HEAL FROM

The thing about abusive relationships is that is does not stem from a lack of control. It's built off of an inherent belief system and set of values. Lacking integrity and empathy is a reflection of someone's character, not just their mental health.

1. **Misconception**: Abuse is only physical violence.
   a. **Reality**: Abuse can take various forms, including emotional, verbal, psychological, financial, and sexual abuse. Physical violence is just one aspect of abuse, and other forms can be equally damaging.
2. **Misconception**: Abuse is always obvious and easily recognizable.
   a. **Reality**: Abuse can be subtle and insidious, making it challenging to identify, especially when it's emotional or psychological in nature. Abusers may manipulate their victims and gaslight them, causing confusion and self-doubt.
3. **Misconception**: Abuse only happens in romantic relationships.
   a. **Reality**: Abuse can occur in any type of relationship, including friendships, family dynamics, and workplace interactions. Power imbalances and controlling behaviors can manifest in various settings.
4. **Misconception**: People who experience abuse are weak or passive.
   a. **Reality**: Abuse can happen to anyone, regardless of their strength or personality. Abusers often target vulnerabilities, and victims may stay in abusive situations due to fear, manipulation, or a lack of support.
5. **Misconception**: Leaving an abusive relationship is easy.
   a. **Reality**: Leaving an abusive relationship can be incredibly difficult and dangerous. Victims may face threats, retaliation, or financial dependency, making it challenging to break free. Additionally, emotional attachments and trauma bonds can complicate the decision to leave.

It is essential to recognize the complexity of abuse and the various forms it can take. Increasing awareness and understanding about abuse can help individuals identify unhealthy patterns in relationships and offer support to those experiencing abuse. If you or someone you know is in an abusive situation, seeking help from support networks, hotlines, or professionals is crucial for safety and healing.

Here are five examples of each type of emotional wound:

- Abandonment Wound: a) Feeling deeply anxious and insecure in relationships, fearing that others will leave or reject you. b) Struggling with a fear of intimacy and avoiding emotional closeness to prevent potential abandonment. c) Experiencing intense feelings of loneliness and isolation, even when surrounded by people. d) Overcompensating for the fear of abandonment by becoming overly dependent on others. e) Feeling unworthy of love and believing that you are inherently unlovable, leading to self-sabotaging behaviors in relationships.

- Shame Wound: a) Constantly feeling inadequate and having a persistent belief that you are not good enough. b) Experiencing intense feelings of embarrassment and humiliation even in minor situations. c) Engaging in self-criticism and negative self-talk, being overly self-conscious about perceived flaws. d) Avoiding social interactions and isolating oneself due to a fear of judgment and rejection. e) Feeling undeserving of success and happiness, often leading to self-sabotage and missed opportunities.

- Neglect Wound: a) Struggling with low self-esteem and self-worth due to a lack of emotional nurturing during childhood. b) Difficulty in forming secure attachments and maintaining healthy relationships. c) Feeling emotionally numb or disconnected from others, finding it challenging to express or identify emotions. d) Seeking constant external validation and approval, as internal validation is lacking. e) Becoming overly self-reliant and independent, finding it difficult to ask for help or support.

- Trust Wound: a) Having significant difficulty trusting others, assuming that people will deceive or betray you. b) Being overly guarded and closed off in relationships, making it challenging to be vulnerable. c) Repeatedly experiencing betrayal or disappointment in relationships, reinforcing trust issues. d) Struggling to establish and maintain healthy boundaries with others, leading to feelings of being taken advantage of. e) Having an intense fear of being hurt emotionally, making it challenging to fully invest in relationships.

Remember that emotional wounds are complex and interconnected, and individuals may experience a combination of these wounds to varying degrees. Healing from these wounds often involves self-awareness, therapy, and supportive relationships that foster emotional growth and resilience.

RESILIENCY & RECOVERY

HOPE & HEALING

EMOTIONAL RELEASE EXERCISE

WHAT ASPECTS OF YOURSELF MIGHT YOU NEED TO CONFRONT IF YOU WEREN'T
PREOCCUPIED WITH TRYING TO CHANGE THE OTHER PERSON? ARE THERE CERTAIN
PARTS OF YOU THAT REMAIN UNCHANGED, ALLOWING YOU TO KEEP AN UNHEALTHY
RELATIONSHIP IN YOUR LIFE?

RESILIENCY & RECOVERY

HOPE & HEALING

EMOTIONAL RELEASE EXERCISE

IN THE SPACE BELOW, COMPLETE THIS SENTENCE, "I RESENT THE WAY YOU…" WRITE DOWN ALL THE THINGS YOU RESENT ABOUT THE THINGS THE TOXIC PERSON IN YOUR LIFE DID TO YOU AND HOW THEY MADE YOU FEEL. IF THERE'S ANYTHING YOU WISH YOU COULD TELL THEM IF YOU THOUGHT THEY COULD LISTEN, WHAT WOULD YOU SAY? GIVE YOURSELF PERMISSION TO VENT FREELY. THIS IS YOUR SAFE PLACE.

RESILIENCY & RECOVERY

HOPE & HEALING

COGNITIVE DISSONANCE & THE PATH TO HEALING

I remember the time when I decided to end my relationship with my former partner. It was a tough period for me. I found myself feeling quite down about myself because I thought I had ann anxious attachment style. I kept beating myself up, thinking I was weak, overly dependent, and always trying to please others. I doubted whether I truly loved myself enough to make the difficult decision to leave. I also struggled to move past the countless text messages I discovered and the lies he told about his connections with other women. I kept telling myself that maybe if I could just accept these situations, forgive his constant "forgetfulness", and turn a blind eye to his hidden lies, everything would magically get better. I convinced myself that I had it all together, that I could heal and become a healthier person while still holding onto something that was ultimately unhealthy for me. Looking back, I now realize it's a clear sign of an unhealthy situation when you find yourself constantly trying to come up with new ways to cope with and cover for, their hurtful behavior. It was a challenging time, but I'm learning to be more compassionate towards myself as I reflect on it.

Overtime, I realized that I don't have an anxious attachment style and I wasn't insecure, I was just reacting appropriately to being in an abusive relationship. I was being gaslighted into thinking I was having an inappropriate response to abuse behavior. In every other area of my life, in all of my rich, life long friendships, I had never questioned my worth, safety or felt anxiety. This was an indicator to me that maybe it wasn't me, but the environment I was in. A toxic relationship is more likely to change you, than you are likely at changing it. That's why trauma informed care is so important when it comes to challenges related to mental health. How is your current reality a reflection of an unhealed wound from the past? My attachment to him was based on a projection of who I wanted him to be, not a reflection of who he actually was. Below is a sentiment I wrote as I reflected on my fears and my freedom:

I woke up this morning realizing that I was free. Yet there was nothing I wanted more than to be held back in captivity : Cognitive Dissonance & The Path To Healing

When our mind and body are so used to living in captivity, freedom won't always feel freeing. Just like healthy love won't always feel safe. When you're so used to living in survival mode, the biggest shock to the nervous system is realizing that you are finally safe. Picture this: you've been confined for so long, your mind starts to find a strange comfort in that familiar space. It becomes a sort of twisted safety net amidst all the chaos and suffering.

You learn to survive and make sense of the world within those walls. It's not an ideal situation by any means, but it's what you know, and your mind tries to find stability in that. Now, fast forward to the moment when freedom comes knocking on your door. It should be a joyous occasion, right? The very thing you've been yearning for all that time. But here's the catch: your mind and soul have grown accustomed to living in that captivity. The idea of stepping beyond those walls, even though it means freedom, can be downright unsettling. It's like your mind and soul have become uncomfortable with the very notion of being free.

"I'm free, I think. I shut my eyes and think hard and deep about how free I am. But I can't really understand what it means. All I know is I'm totally alone. All alone in an unfamiliar place, like some solitary explorer who has lost their compass and their map. Is this what it means to be free?" -Karuki Murakami

It's important to approach this whole situation with compassion and understanding. When someone has endured abuse and captivity, the road to healing and reintegration is far from easy. The conflicting emotions, the guilt, the sense of loss—it's all part of that cognitive dissonance. And it takes time to sort through those mixed-up thoughts and feelings. That's why change can feel scary, even if it's good for us. So, even when we finally find ourselves in a healthy, loving relationship, it can be a bit of a shock to the system. We're not used to the kindness, the support, and the sense of emotional safety. It's almost like we're waiting for the other shoe to drop, for the familiar chaos to creep back in. We may even become the very chaos we try to avoid. As if we create a self sabotaging self fulfilling prophecy to prove ourselves right - that love and life can't always be this easy. That everything we desire has to be hard.

But here's the thing: a healthy love and life are supposed to feel different. It's not supposed to be a rollercoaster ride of ups and downs. It's about respect, communication, and mutual growth. It's about feeling safe, valued, and cherished. And that can take some getting used to when we've been conditioned to expect anything but that. That said, don't push away the very things you've prayed for all because you're fearful you are unworthy of it or because it feels unfamiliar. Life can be easy and love doesn't always have to be so hard. ***I love you. You're doing a great job.***

Healing from narcissistic abuse is a complex process, and the signs of progress may vary from person to person. However, here are ten common signs that indicate you are on the path to healing from narcissistic abuse:

1. **Increased self-awareness:** You begin to recognize the effects of the abuse on your emotional and mental well-being. This self-awareness allows you to identify negative thought patterns and behaviors that were instilled during the abusive relationship.
2. **Acceptance of the past:** Instead of dwelling on the past or feeling stuck in victimhood, you acknowledge the abuse and its impact on your life. This acceptance is essential to move forward and build a healthier future.
3. **Setting boundaries:** You develop the ability to set and enforce healthy boundaries in your relationships. You prioritize your needs and protect yourself from potential emotional harm.
4. **Reduced self-blame:** You stop blaming yourself for the abuse and recognize that it was not your fault. The responsibility lies with the abuser, not the victim. You're okay sitting with the discomfort of your temporary feelings.
5. **Reconnecting with your values and interests:** As healing progresses, you start rediscovering your passions and interests that might have been suppressed during the abusive relationship.
6. **Improved emotional regulation:** You find it easier to manage your emotions and reactions. The extreme emotional rollercoaster that often comes with narcissistic abuse begins to stabilize.
7. **Healthy relationships:** You begin to cultivate healthier relationships with others based on mutual respect, empathy, and support. Toxic relationships are gradually replaced with positive connections. You no longer feel the need to over-explain for fear of losing the acceptance of those who were never your allies. You no longer need to over-function in your relationships and know that you are inherently worthy not because of what you can do for others or how you can make them feel, but rather, because you exist.
8. **Lessened feelings of isolation:** You realize that you are not alone in your experiences. Connecting with support groups, therapy, or like-minded individuals can provide validation and comfort.
9. **Increased self-compassion:** You develop a kinder and more forgiving attitude toward yourself. You recognize that healing takes time and allow yourself the space to recover at your own pace.
10. **Sense of empowerment:** You regain a sense of control over your life and make decisions that align with your well-being and personal growth. This newfound empowerment helps you move forward with confidence. You're fine with being mis understood.

Also, Here Are Some Reminders That Helped Me To Heal, That May Help You Too:

- The way people treat you is a refelction of their paradigms and how they feel about themselves. The treatment that you allow is a reflection of your current paradigms and how you feel about yourself.
- God saw your future and they didn't fit it in. No amount of inner work will make the wrong partner right for you
- You picked them while they were still healing, before you learned boundaries and self love
- God answered your prayer "If this relationship isn't right for me, remove it")
- You prayed for a healthy partner, and they weren't it
- You were meant for more
- Grief says "I miss them-it hurts" , Relief says "Take a deep breath, Confusion asks, "Why did it end?" , Acceptance says "Not every relationship is meant to last" -The Millennial Therapist
- Leaving someone because they continue to live in dysfunction is not abandonment, its self care.
- Normalize being in alignment over obligation. Sometimes we must let go of the life we planned to make space for the life aligned with our purpose.
- You can't force someone to respect you but you can refuse to be disrespected
- You disrespect yourself every time you re-engage with someone who disrespected you
- At your very best, you still won't be good enough for the wrong person. At your very worst, you will still be worth it to the right one
- In the end, the happy memories hurt the most
- You weren't discarded - The Universe set you free
- Domestic violence is a progressive behavior. It gets worse and worse over time. It starts out with mental and emotional abuse and can lead to physical abuse
- "You're very hard to manipulate when you're clear, You're very hardto influence when you're sovereign."-Unknown

RESILIENCY & RECOVERY

HOPE & HEALING

Q&A

WHAT IS THE BEST WAY TO HURT A NARCISSIST OR GET REVENGE?

This is going to sound so cliche, but the best revenge is truly no revenge at all. It's to heal and to grow into the best version of yourself that they no longer have access to. Narcissist hate boundaries and their biggest fear is being exposed and abandoned. This is why they surround themselves with an endless amount narcissistic supply. When you truly heal into a version of yourself that finds them irrelevant and you begin to feel indifferent about their existence, this will trigger their attachment wounds and send them into a spiral. Even if they were the one to discard you first. Only to a toxic person, will your healing hurt them and your empowerment will be the thing that disempowers them. Use the pain to propel you instead of allowing it to hold you back. When you channel your energy from fighting the old, to building the new, you win.

DESPITE KNOWING OUR RELATIONSHIP WAS UNHEALTHY, BUT WHY AM I STRUGGLING TO GET OVER THE NARCISSIST?

Lets take it back to childhood. If we grew up in homes where we were physically or emotionally neglected, we may have engaged in a concept known as "trauma denial". Trauma denial is when we refuse to acknowledge or accept that we've experienced a traumatic event or have been deeply hurt in some way. It's like wearing rose-colored glasses and pretending everything is fine when, deep down, we know it really isn't.

We do this because as children who were codependent on our primary caregivers for survival, we didn't have the ability to simply walk away from unhealthy situations. Therefore, we were in a freeze response. Because our mind and body is always trying to protect us, we developed this cognitive distortion (trauma denial) to enable a fantasy bond to preserve our sense of survival when we experienced a ruptured connection. Now, when it comes to breaking fantasy bonds in relationships after a breakup, trauma denial can be a real roadblock. You see, fantasy bonds are these illusions we create in our minds about our relationships. We start idealizing the person and the relationship itself, often overlooking the red flags or ignoring the pain we've experienced. Trauma denial plays a sneaky role in this process because it keeps us trapped in this fantasy world. We might refuse to accept that our ex-partner hurt us deeply or that the relationship wasn't healthy. Instead, we cling to this idealized version of the person and the connection we once had, even if it's no longer serving us.

It's like we're living in a rom-com movie, hoping for that magical reunion or believing that they'll change overnight. We might tell ourselves stories like, "Maybe we just need a break," or "They didn't mean to hurt me that badly." These narratives can be comforting, but they prevent us from moving on and healing. Trauma denial stops us from confronting the pain head-on and working through it. As a child, we didn't have a choice but to stay in unhealthy dynamics and tolerate their neglect. As an adult, you have a choice to remove yourself from harmful situations where your needs are not being met and finding emotionally available people who can meet them. Walking away from a partner as an adult is hard because our inner child perceives this decision as walking away from a parent.

It's important to acknowledge and process the hurt we've experienced in order to grow and move forward. By denying the trauma, we're essentially denying ourselves the opportunity to heal and create healthier relationships in the future.So, if you find yourself in this situation, it's crucial to take off those rose-colored glasses and face the reality. Remember, it's okay to acknowledge your pain and prioritize your well-being. Breakups are tough, but with time and self-care, you'll find your way to brighter days ahead.

ISABELLA, DO YOU FORGIVE HIM?

I understand him. And in many ways, understanding surpasses forgiveness. Nowadays there are few and fleeting moments when I think about the pain he caused and experience small bursts of retroactive anger. But then I remember that his character is his karma and that he is just as much his own dose of poison as he is anyone else's. While he suffers in secrecy, I healed by allowing myself to be seen. Narcissistic or other highly toxic individuals can't hide who they are. Due to their low levels of self awareness, what they don't know is how obviously their toxicity is hidden in plain sight. It's in the way they're surrounded by a million people and still feel alone. Or in the way that they can have it all and yet it's never enough. Or in the way that they can only obtain happiness by hurting others. While they might be good at lying to others, it is these very character flaws that prevent them from fully being able to lie to themselves. And yet, they still try. I knew our relationship was over when I had to choose between loving him and protecting myself. In many ways, I'm grateful he wasn't the man I needed him to be. Because if he were, I wouldn't be the most empowered version of myself that I am today.

RESILIENCY & RECOVERY

HOPE & HEALING

Hello My Love,

We made it to the very end and I am so proud of you. Healing from wounds created in unsafe relationships often involves a deep understanding of the dynamics at play. Imagine emotional wounds as delicate, fragile areas within your inner self that require care and protection. When these wounds were formed in relationships characterized by harm, toxicity, or insecurity, they become like raw vulnerabilities in need of proper nurturing to mend.

Safe relationships, on the other hand, provide the essential environment for healing. Just as a wound in your body heals best when it's kept clean and protected from further harm, emotional wounds are similarly tended to in safe, nurturing relationships.Imagine emotional wounds as scars that have developed within us due to experiences of pain, betrayal, or neglect in the past. Much like physical scars, these emotional wounds can hinder our ability to experience emotional well-being and form healthy connections. If these wounds were created in relationships that lacked safety and nurturance, they've left us with a sense of vulnerability and mistrust.

Healing these wounds becomes a journey of transformation, and safe relationships are the healing medicine we need. Just as a wound on our skin requires a clean and protective environment to heal without infection, emotional wounds thrive in environments that provide understanding, empathy, and safety. When we surround ourselves with individuals who genuinely care about our well-being, listen without judgment, and offer support, we create the conditions necessary for our wounds to heal. Safe relationships provide a space where we can share our pain, fears, and vulnerabilities without the fear of exploitation or judgment. The empathy and validation we receive from these relationships act as the antidote to the toxic emotions that have festered within us. Over time, the scars of past wounds begin to fade as we experience acceptance, love, and healing interactions.

Choosing to engage with safe relationships for our healing journey is a courageous step. It means we're prioritizing our well-being and recognizing that the wounds we carry deserve the care and compassion necessary for complete healing. While the scars of our past experiences may never completely disappear, they can become a part of our story that no longer defines our present and future. Healing in safe relationships empowers us to reclaim our emotional well-being and create a foundation for healthier connections in the future.

As we heal, we embark on a journey of personal transformation. We embrace healthier coping strategies, cultivate emotional regulation skills, and construct positive relational patterns. In doing so, we not only heal ourselves but also contribute to a more compassionate and resilient society. The ripples of our healing journey extend beyond our own lives, influencing future generations and shaping a healthier, more connected world. On day, you will awaken to the profound realization that your greatest display of strength extends beyond the resilience cultivated through healing from toxic relationships. It resides, even more significantly, in your capacity to embrace vulnerability and allow your tender, authentic self to flourish in the safety of genuine love.

The healing journey from unhealed trauma to healthy relationships is a formidable one, but its impact is immeasurable. By shedding light on our patterns, by healing ourselves, we contribute to world peace by engaging in safe relationships that give us a sense of inner peace. The power to break the cycle lies within us, and through healing, we create a legacy of resilience, compassion, and hope for generations to come.

I love you and I wish you happiness - not just healing.

With love,

Isabella Imani

SUMMARY OF TOPIC 3

-Trauma Bonds are difficult to break due to a combination of psychological and physiological factors that can profoundly impact survivors.

-Victim-blaming in the context of narcissistic abuse is profoundly detrimental because it compounds the suffering of survivors who have already endured immense emotional, psychological, and sometimes even physical harm.

-Fracturing involves breaking down a person's sense of self, self-esteem, and confidence to make them dependent on the narcissist for validation and approval.

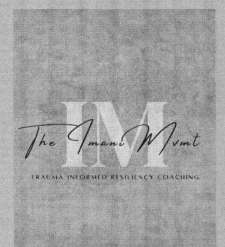

What emotions and thoughts emerge when you reflect on moments of self-abandonment during or after the narcissistic relationship? How can you now nurture and prioritize self-compassion and self-connection in your journey towards recovery? Write your answer in the space below.

_____

_____

_____

_____

_____

_____

YOU'RE

RESILIENT

THE IMANI MVMT

JOIN THE MVMT

If you're seeking a brighter future beyond the clutches of a narcissistic bond, I invite you to join us in our transformative masterclass: "Breakup to Breakthrough: From Hurting to Healing." At www.imanimvmt.com. Here, we provide a safe and supportive space to guide you on a journey from heartbreak to empowerment. Our comprehensive approach will help you unravel the complexities of healing from toxic relationships, rediscover your worth, and reclaim your sense of self.

With trauma informed insights and practical strategies you'll gain the tools needed to break free from the pain and pave the way for a healthier, more fulfilling future. Remember, you're not alone—there's strength in embracing the path to healing. Visit us today and take the first step toward your breakthrough. Your journey from hurting to healing starts here, and we're here to walk it with you, every step of the way.

SEE YOU THERE!

WWW.IMANIMVMT.COM

PROGRAMS & SERVICES

COACHING AT YOUR CONVENIENCE	ACCOUNTABILITY & COMMITMENT	COMMUNICATION ON YOUR TERMS

COACHING AT YOUR CONVENIENCE

- Unlimited Messaging
- 1 Hour Video Session Each Week
- Effective & Convenient
- Support, Accountability & Resources

ACCOUNTABILITY & COMMITMENT

HOW IT WORKS

-Alignment
-Identify Goals
-Remove Obstacles
-Heal Emotional Wounds
-Overcome Mental Blockages

TERMS & CONDITIONS

-No Long Term Contracts
-Month to Month Commitments
-24/7 Private Messaging Platform
-Additional Hourly Sessions Available

COMMUNICATION ON YOUR TERMS

 Hi! I'm here for you!

UNLIMITED MESSAGING

 VIDEO

 AUDIO

 IN PERSON

1:1 / GROUP COACHING

-Daily Healing Work
-Weekly Sessions Via Zoom or In Person
-Unlimited Text & Voice Note Via Telegram

CORPORATE COACHING

-Daily 1:1 & Team Coaching
-Weekly Lunch & Learns
-Monthly Offsites & Team Assessment

PROGRAMS & PRODUCTS

-THE IMANI MVMT Resilience Planners
-Exclusive Membership Portal
-Trauma Informed Certification Program

START A
CONNECTION CIRCLE

JOIN THE THOUSANDS OF INDIVIDUALS PARTICIPATING IN A MEANINGFUL COMMUNITY COMMITTED TO EMOTIONAL WELLNESS. FOR FREE RESOURCES AND ADDITIONAL DETAILS VISIT:

WWW.IMANIMVMT.COM

THE IMANI MVMT

- **Abuse Amnesia:** Forgetting or minimizing past instances of abuse, often as a psychological defense mechanism.
- **Abuse By Proxy:** When a narcissist uses others to carry out their abusive behavior on their behalf.
- **Actor Observer Bias:** The tendency to attribute one's abusive actions to external factors while attributing the same actions by others to their inherent character.
- **Age Gap Relationships:** Relationships with significant age differences that can be exploited by narcissists for power and control.
- **Antagonistic Narcissism:** A subtype of narcissism characterized by hostility, manipulation, and a desire to provoke negative reactions in others.
- **Brain Fog:** Cognitive confusion and impairment often experienced by victims of narcissistic abuse due to chronic stress.
- **Cognitive Empathy:** Understanding another person's emotions and thoughts, often used by narcissists for manipulation.
- **Compassionate Empathy:** Feeling and understanding another person's emotions with genuine care and concern, in contrast to cognitive empathy.
- **Covert Contracts:** Unspoken, often unrealistic expectations that one person has in a relationship, typically used by narcissists to create obligations.
- **Covert Narcissism:** Narcissistic behavior that is hidden, subtle, and not immediately apparent.
- **Crazy Making:** Manipulative tactics used by narcissists to confuse and disorient their victims.
- **Cortisol:** A stress hormone often elevated in victims of narcissistic abuse due to chronic stress.
- **Cortisol Addiction:** A dependency on the adrenaline and cortisol rush that can occur during abusive episodes.
- **DARVO:** An acronym for Deny, Attack, and Reverse Victim and Offender, a common tactic used by abusers to deflect responsibility.
- **Dark Empathy:** The ability to understand another person's pain and emotions but without genuine compassion, often used manipulatively.
- **Discard:** The phase in a narcissistic relationship when the narcissist abandons or devalues their victim.
- **Dopamine:** A neurotransmitter associated with pleasure and reward, often manipulated by narcissists to create addiction in their victims.
- **Emotional Awareness:** The capacity to recognize and understand one's own emotions and those of others.
- **Emotional Empathy:** The ability to genuinely share and understand the emotions of others.
- **Empathy:** The capacity to understand and share the feelings of others, which narcissists often lack.
- **Empaths:** Individuals who are highly attuned to the emotions of others and may be targeted by narcissists for their sensitivity.
- **Eroticized Rage:** The fusion of sexual desire and anger, sometimes seen in abusive relationships.
- **Euphoria Recall:** Remembering positive moments in a relationship to rationalize or minimize abuse.
- **Fading Affect Bias:** A cognitive bias where negative emotions fade faster from memory than positive ones, impacting how abuse is remembered.
- **Flying Monkeys:** Individuals manipulated by narcissists to support and enable their abusive behavior.
- **Gaslighting:** Manipulative tactics to make the victim doubt their own reality, often leading to confusion and self-doubt.
- **Gray Rock:** A strategy where victims of narcissistic abuse become unresponsive and emotionally uninteresting to the narcissist to protect themselves.

- **Hoover:** Attempts by a narcissist to suck their victim back into the abusive relationship after a discard phase.
- **Idealization:** The phase in a narcissistic relationship where the narcissist puts their victim on a pedestal.
- **Interpartner Violence:** Abuse within a romantic relationship, which can involve physical, emotional, or psychological harm.
- **Jade Technique:** A method used by victims to disengage from abusive interactions by not defending or justifying themselves.
- **Love Bombing:** Intense and overwhelming affection and attention used by narcissists to manipulate and seduce their victims.
- **Machiavellianism:** A personality trait characterized by manipulation, deceit, and a disregard for morality.
- **Madonna-Whore Complex:** A psychological complex where a person sees women as either pure and virtuous (Madonna) or seductive and immoral (Whore).
- **Malignant Narcissism:** A severe form of narcissism characterized by a combination of narcissism, antisocial behavior, and aggression.
- **Narcissistic Abuse Cycle:** The repeating pattern of idealization, devaluation, and discard in narcissistic relationships.
- **Narcissistic Collapse:** A breakdown or loss of the narcissist's self-image or facade.
- **Narcissistic Injury:** A threat to the narcissist's self-esteem or self-worth, often resulting in rage or emotional turmoil.
- **Narcissistic Parent:** A parent with narcissistic traits who can be emotionally abusive and manipulative toward their children.
- **Narcissistic Prayer:** A repetitive request for forgiveness, often insincere, used by narcissists to maintain control.
- **Narcissistic Rage:** An intense and disproportionate anger or emotional outburst in response to perceived criticism or injury to the narcissist's ego.
- **Overt Narcissism:** Obvious and grandiose narcissistic behavior.
- **Pain Bodies:** Emotional pain and trauma accumulated over time, often exploited by narcissists.
- **Parentification:** When a child is forced to take on the role of a parent, often in narcissistic families.
- **Pathological Accommodation:** Going to extreme lengths to accommodate a narcissist's demands.
- **Pathological Lover:** A person who becomes obsessed with the narcissist despite abusive treatment.
- **Pathological Lying:** Habitual and compulsive lying, often used by narcissists to manipulate.
- **Peter Pan Syndrome:** A pattern of immaturity and avoidance of adult responsibilities.
- **Psychological Splitting:** Viewing people and situations in black-and-white terms, common in narcissistic relationships.
- **Rage Eyes:** A term describing the intense and angry gaze of a narcissist.
- **Reverse Hoover:** When the victim of narcissistic abuse attempts to re-engage the narcissist after a discard phase.
- **Reverse Projection:** Accusing others of the very behavior the narcissist is engaging in.
- **Scapegoat:** A family member or individual targeted by a narcissist for blame and abuse.
- **Shame:** A deep and painful emotion often manipulated by narcissists to control their victims.
- **Still Face Experiment:** A psychological experiment demonstrating how infants react to maternal withdrawal.
- **Smear Campaign:** A coordinated effort by a narcissist to damage the reputation of their victim.
- **Stockholm Syndrome:** When victims of abuse develop feelings of attachment and even loyalty to their abuser.
- **Stone Walling:** A behavior where a person becomes unresponsive and emotionally unavailable in a relationship.
- **Surrogate Mother Experiment:** A psychological experiment examining attachment and maternal bonds.
- **The Dark Triad:** A term describing three personality traits - narcissism, Machiavellianism, and psychopathy - often present in abusive individuals.
- **The Lost Child:** In a narcissistic family, a child who becomes invisible and withdrawn to avoid

THE IMANI MVMT

REFERENCES

WORKS CITED

- Harley Therapy. (n.d.). Emotional awareness. https://www.harleytherapy.co.uk/counselling/emotional-awareness.htm
- BrainFacts. (2018). The anatomy of emotions. https://www.brainfacts.org/thinking-sensing-and-behaving/emotions-stress-and-anxiety/2018/the-anatomy-of-emotions-090618
- Lavenda, O., & Khomich, I. I. (2021). Emotional intelligence as a predictor of burnout syndrome among psychology students. Scientific Reports, 11(1), 1-9. https://www.nature.com/articles/s41598-021-94920-z
- Cherry, K. (2021). How childhood abuse changes the brain. Verywell Mind. https://www.verywellmind.com/childhood-abuse-changes-the-brain-2330401
- News-Medical.net. (n.d.). Heritability of narcissism. https://www.news-medical.net/health/Heritability-of-Narcissism.aspx
- Morrison, M. (2021). Dopamine: The narcissist's greatest weapon against you. Medium. https://medium.com/hello-love/dopamine-the-narcissists-greatest-weapon-against-you-7a97aa77dea5#:~:text=The%20narcissist%20begins%20using%20what,A%20major%20source%20of%20dopamine.
- WebMD. (2021). What is dopamine? https://www.webmd.com/mental-health/what-is-dopamine
- Thomas, C. (2023). A psychologist explains narcissist boredom [Video]. Men's Health. https://www.menshealth.com/trending-news/a37068443/psychologist-explains-narcissist-boredom-video/#
- Whitbourne, S. K. (2021). The 13 traits of a narcissist. Psychology Today. https://www.psychologytoday.com/us/blog/lifetime-connections/202110/the-13-traits-narcissist
- Lewis, J. (2022). Will a frog actually allow itself to be boiled alive if you raise the temperature slowly? Today I Found Out. https://www.todayifoundout.com/index.php/2022/12/will-a-frog-actually-allow-itself-to-be-boiled-alive-if-you-raise-the-temperature-slowly/#:~:text="…if%20a%20frog%20had%20a,It%20will%20die.
- Randi Fine. (n.d.). Roles of children in narcissistic families. https://www.randifine.com/post/roles-of-children-in-narcissistic-families#:~:text=The%20three%20roles%20given%20in,"lost%2Finvisible%20child."&text=Initially%20one%20child%20is%20given,extension%20of%20the%20narcissist%20parent.
- Choosing Therapy. (n.d.). Narcissistic family structure. https://www.choosingtherapy.com/narcissistic-family-structure/
- Lavenda, O., & Khomich, I. I. (2016). Parental impact on children's socialization. Journal of Psychology & Psychotherapy, 6(1), 1-3. https://pubmed.ncbi.nlm.nih.gov/26830110/
- California State University, Sacramento. (2017). Parentification. https://scholarworks.calstate.edu/downloads/2514np20z
- Ross, C. (n.d.). Narcissistic men and their mothers. Psychology Today. https://www.psychologytoday.com/us/blog/the-mysteries-love/201611/narcissistic-men-and-their-mothers
- Choosing Therapy. (n.d.). The narcissistic father. https://www.choosingtherapy.com/narcissistic-father/#:~:text=Narcissistic%20fathers%20also%20emotionally%20damage,achievement%20is%20so%20over%2Dinflated.
- Stines, S. (2019). What happens to sons of narcissistic fathers. Psychology Today. https://www.psychologytoday.com/us/blog/toxic-relationships/201908/what-happens-sons-narcissistic-fathers
- Campbell, W. K., & Foster, C. A. (2002). Narcissism and commitment in romantic relationships: An investment model analysis. Personality and Social Psychology Bulletin, 28(4), 484-495. https://pubmed.ncbi.nlm.nih.gov/17435931/
- Project Energise. (n.d.). Peter Pan syndrome. https://projectenergise.com/peter-pan-syndrome/
- The Center for Growth. (n.d.). Trauma bonding. https://www.healthline.com/health/mental-health/trauma-bonding
- Hendrick, S. S., & Hendrick, C. (2018). Age differences in long-term relationships. Psychology Today. https://psychcentral.com/relationships/age-difference-in-relationships
- Knutzen, J. (2022). Wendy's syndrome and codependency. Medium. https://medium.com/@jeanknutzenzy/wendys-syndrome-and-codependency-da980d1cfda4
- Rabin, L. (n.d.). Narcissistic mothers: The long-term effects on their daughters. Verywell Mind. https://www.verywellmind.com/narcissistic-abuse-cycle-stages-impact-and-coping-6363187#:~:text=The%20narcissistic%20abuse%20cycle%20refers,are%20of%20no%20further%20use.
- The White Rabbit. (n.d.). Alice in Wonderland character descriptions. Alice-in-Wonderland.net. https://www.alice-in-wonderland.net/resources/analysis/character-descriptions/alice/
- Anitha, N. (n.d.). Fatherless daughter syndrome: Psychological effects of an absent father on a girl. Be At Anxiety. https://beatanxiety.me/fatherless-daughter-syndrome-psychological-effects-of-an-absent-father-on-a-girl/#:~:text=The%20absence%20of%20a%20father's%20consistent%20presence%20can%20lead%20to,healing%20and%20growth%20are%20possible.

THE IMANI MVMT

REFERENCES

WORKS CITED

- The Atlantic. (2013). The real-world consequences of the manic pixie dream girl cliche. https://www.theatlantic.com/sexes/archive/2013/07/the-real-world-consequences-of-the-manic-pixie-dream-girl-clich-233/277645/
- Haritaki, M., & Toghiyani, Z. (2020). The dark triad: Predicting the preference for ethical conduct in the workplace. Personality and Individual Differences, 166, 110204. https://www.tandfonline.com/doi/abs/10.1080/19419899.2020.1785534
- Simply Psychology. (n.d.). Understanding the covert narcissist. https://www.simplypsychology.org/malignant-narcissism.html#:~:text=Malignant%20narcissists%20are%20aggressive%2C%20arrogant,deserve%20special%20treatment%20or%20privileges.
- Clearview Treatment Programs. (n.d.). Narcissistic abuse recovery: The five types of narcissist. https://www.carlacorelli.com/narcissistic-abuse-recovery/the-five-types-of-narcissist-which-one-are-you-dealing-with/#:~:text=An%20antagonistic%20narcissist%20displays%20the,enjoy%20making%20other%20people%20suffer.
- Clary, E., & Scott, B. (n.d.). Understanding the communal narcissist. Mantra Care. https://mantracare.org/therapy/narcissistic/communal-narcissist/#:~:text=A%20communal%20narcissist%20is%20someone,good%20deeds%20for%20other%20people.
- Psych Central. (n.d.). Borderline vs. narcissistic personality disorder: What are the differences? https://www.psychcentral.com/blog/repetition-compulsion-why-do-we-repeat-the-past#:~:text=Repetition%20compulsion%20involves%20repeating%20painful,involves%20unconsciously%20recreating%20early%20trauma.
- Joyful Heart Foundation. (n.d.). 1in6 Thursday: The emotional pain body part 1. https://www.joyfulheartfoundation.org/blog/1in6-thursday-emotional-pain-body-part-1#:~:text=It%20is%20an%20accumulation%20of,entity%20consisting%20of%20old%20emotion."
- Ineffable Living. (n.d.). Hopium addiction: How big a part has it played in your life? https://recoverfromemotionalabuse.com/2018/11/how-big-a-part-has-hopium-addiction-played-in-your-life/
- SBS Voices. (n.d.). Why trauma bonding makes it hard to leave abusive relationships. https://www.sbs.com.au/voices/article/why-trauma-bonding-makes-it-hard-to-leave-abusive-relationships/92rku4yxa#
- Healthdirect Australia. (n.d.). The role of cortisol in the body. https://www.healthdirect.gov.au/the-role-of-cortisol-in-the-body#:~:text=Cortisol%20is%20a%20hormone%20produced,cortisol%20is%20essential%20for%20health.
- Cleveland Clinic. (2021). Cortisol: The stress hormone. https://my.clevelandclinic.org/health/articles/22187-cortisol
- Tracy, N. (2018). Crazy-making behavior in abusive relationships. Psychology Today. https://www.psychologytoday.com/us/blog/traversing-the-inner-terrain/201910/crazy-making#:~:text=What%20is%20a%20"crazy"%2D,"crazy"%2Dmaking%20behaviors.
- Cherry, K. (2020). What is the actor-observer bias in psychology? Verywell Mind. https://www.verywellmind.com/what-is-the-actor-observer-bias-2794813
- Venosa, A. (n.d.). Narcissistic mirroring: The toxic tactic used by narcissists. Happy Project. https://happyproject.in/narcissistic-mirroring/#:~:text=Narcissistic%20mirroring%20is%20to%20make,for%20your%20approval%20and%20validation.
- Narcissistic Abuse Warrior. (n.d.). Narcissistic word salad: What it is and how to deal with it. https://abusewarrior.com/abuse/narcissistic-word-salad/
- Dabney, J. (2019). How to handle a crazymaker. Psychology Today. https://www.psychologytoday.com/us/blog/counseling-keys/201403/how-handle-crazymaker
- B. S. (2022). Pathological liar: 10 signs to watch out for. The Recovery Village. https://www.newportinstitute.com/resources/co-occurring-disorders/pathological-liar-signs/#:~:text=the%20lying%20behavior.-,Pathological%20lying%20is%20defined%20by%20some%20experts%20as%20lying%20five,white%20lying%2C%20and%20compulsive%20lying.
- Harari, Y. N. (2015). Sapiens: A Brief History of Humankind. Harper.
- Poumpouras, E. (2020). Becoming Bulletproof: Protect Yourself, Read People, Influence Situations, and Live Fearlessly. Simon & Schuster.
- Newport Institute. (n.d.). What is gaslighting abuse? https://www.newportinstitute.com/resources/mental-health/what_is_gaslighting_abuse/#:~:text=Gaslighting%20is%20a%20form%20of,their%20own%20judgment%20and%20intuition.
- Domestic Violence. (n.d.). The cycle of violence. https://domesticviolence.org/cycle-of-violence/
- Choosing Therapy. (n.d.). Narcissistic silent treatment: When a narcissist gives you the cold shoulder. https://www.choosingtherapy.com/narcissist-silent-treatment/#:~:text=Narcissistic%20silent%20treatment%20is%20when,the%20victim%20psychologically%20and%20emotionally.
- Gottman, J. M., & Tronick, E. (1977). The "still face" experiment. The Human Infant as a Dynamic Processor: A Study of Visual Co-Regulation, 37-64. https://www.gottman.com/blog/research-still-face-experiment/
- Greenough, W. T., & Black, J. E. (1992). Induction of brain structure by experience: Substrates for cognitive development. In M. R. Gunnar & C. A. Nelson (Eds.), Minnesota Symposia on Child Psychology (Vol. 24, pp. 155-200). Erlbaum.
- Strong, T. (n.d.). The role of the Madonna-whore complex in relationships. Modern Intimacy. https://www.modernintimacy.com/the-psychology-of-the-madonna-whore-complex/
- The Recovery Village. (n.d.). Eroticized rage: What is it and why is it harmful? https://www.relationalrecovery.com/its-not-about-the-sex-part-2/#:~:text=Eroticized%20Rage,-One%20of%20my&text=However%2C%20addiction%20is%20also%20an,sexually%20abused%20by%20his%20mother.
- Psych Central. (n.d.). Triangulation and narcissism. https://psychcentral.com/blog/psychology-self/2019/10/triangulation-and-narcissism
- Urban Dictionary. (n.d.). Monkey barring. https://www.urbandictionary.com/define.php?term=monkey%20barring
- National Domestic Violence Hotline. (n.d.). Help for friends and family members. https://www.thehotline.org
- yful Heart Foundation. (n.d.). Pain Bodies. [URL] https://www.joyfulheartfoundation.org/blog/1in6-thursday-emotional-pain-body-part-1#:~:text=It%20is%20an%20accumulation%20of,entity%20consisting%20of%20old%20emotion.
- Psych Central. (n.d.). Repetition Compulsion: Why Do We Repeat the Past? [URL] https://psychcentral.com/blog/repetition-compulsion-why-do-we-repeat-the-past#:~:text=Repetition%20compulsion%20involves%20repeating%20painful,involves%20unconsciously%20recreating%20early%20trauma.
- Ineffable Living. (n.d.). How Big a Part Has Hopium Addiction Played in Your Life? [URL] https://recoverfromemotionalabuse.com/2018/11/how-big-a-part-has-hopium-addiction-played-in-your-life/

THE IMANI MVMT

REFERENCES

WORKS CITED

- SBS Voices. (n.d.). Why Trauma Bonding Makes It Hard to Leave Abusive Relationships. [URL] https://www.sbs.com.au/voices/article/why-trauma-bonding-makes-it-hard-to-leave-abusive-relationships/92rku4yxa#
- Healthdirect Australia. (n.d.). The Role of Cortisol in the Body. [URL] https://www.healthdirect.gov.au/the-role-of-cortisol-in-the-body#:~:text=Cortisol%20is%20a%20hormone%20produced,cortisol%20is%20essential%20for%20health.
- Cleveland Clinic. (2021). Cortisol: The Stress Hormone. [URL] https://my.clevelandclinic.org/health/articles/22187-cortisol
- Tracy, N. (2018). Crazy-Making Behavior in Abusive Relationships. Psychology Today. [URL] https://www.psychologytoday.com/us/blog/traversing-the-inner-terrain/201910/crazy-making#:~:text=What%20is%20a%20"crazy"%2D,"crazy"%2Dmaking%20behaviors.
- Cherry, K. (2020). What Is the Actor-Observer Bias in Psychology? Verywell Mind. [URL] https://www.verywellmind.com/what-is-the-actor-observer-bias-2794813
- Venosa, A. (n.d.). Narcissistic Mirroring: The Toxic Tactic Used by Narcissists. Happy Project. [URL] https://happyproject.in/narcissistic-mirroring/#:~:text=Narcissistic%20mirroring%20is%20to%20make,for%20your%20approval%20and%20validation.
- Narcissistic Abuse Warrior. (n.d.). Narcissistic Word Salad: What It Is and How to Deal With It. [URL] https://abusewarrior.com/abuse/narcissistic-word-salad/
- Dabney, J. (2019). How to Handle a Crazymaker. Psychology Today. [URL] https://www.psychologytoday.com/us/blog/counseling-keys/201403/how-handle-crazymaker
- B. S. (2022). Pathological Liar: 10 Signs to Watch Out For. The Recovery Village. [URL] https://www.newportinstitute.com/resources/co-occurring-disorders/pathological-liar-signs/#:~:text=the%20lying%20behavior.-,Pathological%20lying%20is%20defined%20by%20some%20experts%20as%20lying%20five,white%20lying%2C%20and%20compulsive%20lying.
- Poumpouras, E. (2020). Becoming Bulletproof: Protect Yourself, Read People, Influence Situations, and Live Fearlessly. Simon & Schuster. [URL] https://www.barnesandnoble.com/w/becoming-bulletproof-evy-poumpouras/1132189160
- Newport Institute. (n.d.). What Is Gaslighting Abuse? [URL] https://www.newportinstitute.com/resources/mental-health/what_is_gaslighting_abuse/#:~:text=Gaslighting%20is%20a%20form%20of,their%20own%20judgment%20and%20intuition.
- Choosing Therapy. (n.d.). Narcissistic Silent Treatment: When a Narcissist Gives You the Cold Shoulder. [URL] https://www.choosingtherapy.com/narcissist-silent-treatment/#:~:text=Narcissistic%20silent%20treatment%20is%20when,the%20victim%20psychologically%20and%20emotionally.
- Gottman, J. M., & Tronick, E. (1977). The "Still Face" Experiment. The Human Infant as a Dynamic Processor: A Study of Visual Co-Regulation, 37-64. [URL] https://www.gottman.com/blog/research-still-face-experiment/
- Strong, T. (n.d.). The Role of the Madonna-Whore Complex in Relationships. Modern Intimacy. [URL] https://www.modernintimacy.com/the-psychology-of-the-madonna-whore-complex/
- The Recovery Village. (n.d.). Eroticized Rage: What Is It and Why Is It Harmful? [URL] https://www.relationalrecovery.com/its-not-about-the-sex-part-2/#:~:text=Eroticized%20Rage,-One%20of%20my&text=However%2C%20addiction%20is%20also%20an,sexually%20abused%20by%20his%20mother.
- Psych Central. (n.d.). Triangulation and Narcissism. [URL] https://psychcentral.com/blog/psychology-self/2019/10/triangulation-and-narcissism
- Urban Dictionary. (n.d.). Monkey Barring. [URL] https://www.urbandictionary.com/define.php?term=monkey%20barring
- National Domestic Violence Hotline. (n.d.). Help for Friends and Family Members. [URL] https://www.thehotline.org
-
- Psych Central. (n.d.). The 4 Attachment Styles in Relationships. [URL] https://psychcentral.com/health/4-attachment-styles-in-relationships
- Stamoulis, C. (2020). Understanding Narcissistic Injury. Psychology Today. [URL] https://www.psychologytoday.com/us/blog/the-legacy-distorted-love/202010/understanding-narcissistic-injury
- Vann, M. R. (2021). Narcissistic Rage: What You Need to Know. Healthline. [URL] https://www.healthline.com/health/mental-health/narcissistic-rage
- Joiner, T. E., Jr., & Rudd, M. D. (1996). Disentangling the Associations of Atypical Biases with Suicidal Ideation, Psychiatric Symptoms, and Impulsivity. Journal of Personality Assessment, 66(1), 153-166. [URL] https://www.tandfonline.com/doi/abs/10.1207/s15327752jpa6101_4
- Cherry, K. (2021). What Is Triangulation in Psychology? Verywell Mind. [URL] https://www.verywellmind.com/what-is-triangulation-in-psychology-5120617#:~:text=In%20psychology%2C%20triangulation%20is%20a,communication%2C%20often%20behind%20someone%27s%20back.
- Strong, T. (n.d.). The Psychology of the Madonna-Whore Complex. Modern Intimacy. [URL] https://www.modernintimacy.com/the-psychology-of-the-madonna-whore-complex/
- Dabney, J. (n.d.). It's Not About the Sex (Part 2): Eroticized Rage. Relational Recovery. [URL] https://www.relationalrecovery.com/its-not-about-the-sex-part-2/#:~:text=Eroticized%20Rage,-One%20of%20my&text=However%2C%20addiction%20is%20also%20an,sexually%20abused%20by%20his%20mother.
- Cherry, K. (2019). Triangulation and Narcissism: What You Need to Know. Psych Central. [URL] https://psychcentral.com/blog/psychology-self/2019/10/triangulation-and-narcissism
- Urban Dictionary. (n.d.). Monkey Barring. [URL] https://www.urbandictionary.com/define.php?term=monkey%20barring
- Simon, G. (2022). 5 Steps to Surviving a Narcissist's Smear Campaign. Psychology Today. [URL] https://www.psychologytoday.com/us/blog/invisible-bruises/202201/5-steps-surviving-narcissists-smear-campaign
- Ineffable Living. (n.d.). The Narcissist's Prayer: What It Reveals About Manipulative People. [URL] https://ineffableliving.com/the-narcissists-prayer/
- Cherry, K. (2021). Protecting Yourself From DARVO and Abusive Behavior. Verywell Mind. [URL] https://www.verywellmind.com/protecting-yourself-from-darvo-abusive-behavior-7562730#:~:text=DARVO%20is%20an%20acronym%20that,Area%20CBT%20Center%20and%20CBT online.
- National Domestic Violence Hotline. (n.d.). Get Help Today. [URL] https://www.thehotline.org
- Narcissistic Abuse Rehab. (n.d.). Types of Flying Monkeys and Their Roles in Narcissistic Abuse. [URL] https://www.narcissisticabuserehab.com/types-of-flying-monkeys/
- Mantra Care. (n.d.). The Collapsed Narcissist: Symptoms, Causes, and Recovery. [URL] https://mantracare.org/therapy/what-is-collapsed-narcissist/#
- Medium. (n.d.). The Narcissist's Twist: Reverse Hoovering. [URL] https://medium.com/illumination/the-narcissists-twist-reverse-hoovering-dfbe8787e91d
- Moving Forward After Abuse. (n.d.). Brain Fog and Narcissism: What You Need to Know. [URL] https://www.movingforwardafterabuse.com/brain-fog-narcissism/
- Harvey, L., Kashy, D. A., & Pettit, G. S. (2001). Pathological Accommodation in Couples. Family Process, 40(2), 163-181. [URL] https://www.tandfonline.com/doi/abs/10.1080/15551024.2017.1251184
- Jade. (2020). The Jade Technique: When Dealing With a Toxic Person. Medium. [URL] https://info-16578.medium.com/the-jade-technique-when-dealing-with-a-toxic-person-667ecd396ad0
- The Recovery Village. (n.d.). Euphoric Recall in Addiction Recovery: The Good and the Bad. [URL] https://www.therecoveryvillage.com/recovery/relapse/euphoric-recall/
- Kuss, D. J., Griffiths, M. D., & Binder, J. F. (2013). Internet Addiction in Students: Prevalence and Risk Factors. Computers in Human Behavior, 29(3), 959-966. [URL] https://www.ncbi.nlm.nih.gov/pmc/articles/PMC8508288/
- Venosa, A. (n.d.). Reverse Projection Psychology: When Narcissists Accuse You of What They're Guilty Of. Happy Project. [URL] https://happyproject.in/reverse-projection-psychology/#:~:text=In%20contrast%20to%20regular%20projection,claiming%20them%20as%20one%27s%20own.
- Cherry, K. (2019). Denial of Trauma: Signs and How to Overcome It. Psych Central. [URL] https://psychcentral.com/blog/denial-of-trauma-sign

Printed in the United States
by Baker & Taylor Publisher Services